FOUNDATIONS OF EDUCATION

FOUNDATIONS OF EDUCATION

Dr. Intakhab A. Khan

ANMOL PUBLICATIONS PVT. LTD.
NEW DELHI - 110 002 (INDIA)

ANMOL PUBLICATIONS PVT. LTD.
H.O.: 4374/4B, Ansari Road, Daryaganj
New Delhi - 110 002
Ph.: 23261597, 23278000
B.O.: No. 1015, Ist Main Road, BSK III Stage
III Phase, III Block
Bangalore - 560 085 (India)
Visit us at: www.anmolpublications.com

Foundations of Education

First Published, 2006

ISBN 81-261-2620-5

PRINTED IN INDIA

Published by J.L. Kumar for Anmol Publications Pvt. Ltd., New Delhi - 110 002 and Printed at Mehra Offset Press, Delhi.

Dedicated
to
My Grand Parents
for
Their Selfless Love
and
Affectionate Care

Contents

Acknowledgement

Though it is taken for granted that without Almighty's blessings no one would be able to do even a modest work. Yet, I would like to thank my lord who very kindly blessed me to be able to attempt in the area of writing.

Next, my parents deserve acknowledgement for what they suffered throughout their life, waiting to see the small plant growing in their yard by and by until it was able to give fruit.

It is now my humble duty to remember my learned teachers from primary schools to the university who exerted hard work to polish a raw stone like me.

I would like to particularly place on the record the names of AWB Qadri, Prof. Mohd. Miyan (my teacher, Guide and Head), Prof. (Miss.) Najma Amin, Prof. Ahrar Hussain, Prof. Ilyas Hussain, Dr. Ejaz Masih (all from Faculty of Education, JMI, New Delhi) for their help, cooperation and encouragement.

I feel pride in remembering the brotherly concern always shown by Dr. Ravindra Kumar, former Vice Chancellor, CCSU, Meerut, U.P., India.

I am glad to mention the name of my present boss, Dr. Ali Bin Mohsin Al-Hazmi, Dean, College of Health Sciences, Jazan, for his constant support and motivation.

It would be unjust if I don't record the suffering of my wife due to the fact that I paid attention more on academic activities than the family. I sincerely acknowledge the selfless love and affection of my sweet daughters (Hiba and Midha).

(Dr. INTAKHAB. A. KHAN)

Preface

The book 'Foundations on Education' is being published with a purpose to provide a purely Philosophical basis for the objectives of Education. Apart from it, there is ample material related to sociology, psychology and pedagogy. Thus, there are four major parts. The first part deals with the philosophy in general and peace philosophy in particular. The second part is related to Sociology of Education. This chapter deals with some related sub-aspects like, School, Society, Culture, etc., however, it has not been presented in detail. The third part is associated with psychological perspective which contains three sub-aspects: Scope and relevance of psychology in the field of Education, learning theories and motivation. The fourth and the last part deals with Education and Pedagogy. Infact, it has two sub-parts like Education and its relation to those philosophical aspects that have direct relation to theory and practice of Education. And, the second part deals with teaching-learning aspects which are practical side of the social, philosophical and psychological dimensions. In this part, there are chapters like, the teacher, motivation, the importance of teaching etc.

The present book is expected to meet the requirement of basically a reference material to be aptly used for the students of the courses like diplomas and degrees of Education in teachers' training institutions or Faculties of Education in all parts of India. Besides, this book will also benefit the post graduate students who are pursuing courses in different specialisations of Education. This book is expected to lay a special emphasis on the introduction and expansion of Peace Education in Educational Institutions which is perhaps the most promising discipline in near future.

In sum, the book would prove to be quite interesting for especially those who would like to get benefit of all the four perspectives of Education – Philosophy, Sociology, Psychology and Pedagogy.

Dr. INTAKHAB, A. KHAN

1

Philosophy

PHILOSOPHY: THE ESSENCE OF LIFE

In this modern world, an important concept like Philosophy has generally been misunderstood. People, in general, have developed an indifferent attitude towards the noblest idea. India is such a country where around 40 per cent population is still illiterate. However, attempts have been made to minimize and remove a curse like illiteracy. Simultaneously, the country is also trying to eliminate lack of education in the form of ensuring universal free, primary and compulsory education. But the country bothers little about 'quality education.'

Philosophy has even now been considered by most so-called educated people as something which has nothing to do with realities of life. It is believed that those who are philosophers are the people of different worlds. In fact, in this society, there are a few persons now left who could really be called as philosophers. And, most probably noble ideas like Philosophy can now only be expected to be professed and practised by the educationists.

Philosophy and education are two sides of the same coin. There is no controversy as to which side belongs to what. But, 'coin' is nothing but the 'life' of human beings.

Philosophy is the theoretical side and education is the practical and dynamic side of human life. Therefore, what we profess in philosophy for betterment of our life, should try to practise the same in our practical life.

The entire world is passing through a change. It is not sure whether the change is positive for the betterment of the society or it is leading towards the point where it started at the time of its emergence and evolution. People have started following materialistic ideals, therefore, spiritual and aesthetic values have started declining. This is the reason that philosophy in real sense of the term has no proper place in the life of people even in the beginning of the 21st century.

Life at present is nothing but a mechanical process. Human beings are working as computers. We have become materialist in attitude. Vocationalisation of Education is found to be a hurdle in the process of value oriented education.

Philosophy, education and life are interrelated. Education is nothing without philosophy. Most of the time education also helps in developing a good kind of philosophy for one's life. The concept 'life' is education and education is life' can obviously be interpreted that throughout life an individual continues to receive education, and education is as important as one's life.

The questions pertaining to branches of philosophy remains untouched if we don't define the very concept. However, different branches like 'Realism', 'Idealism', 'Naturalism' and 'Pragmatism' cannot be discussed here for want of space.

"Philosophy" in the words of Radhakrishnan "is the logical inquiry into the nature of reality". While Mahatma Gandhi said, "My life is my philosophy". Dr. R. Krishnan's approach has been based on abstract thinking with the genuine questions relating to 'Reality'. On the other hand, Gandhi's ideas were based on his practical experiences of life which he gained throughout.

If one analyzes these, one would get the essence of philosophy in every aspect of human life. Aristotle says that man is a social, political and gregarious animal. Karl Marx opines that man is a productive animal. On a different occasion, Aristotle remarked that the difference between educated and uneducated is the difference between the persons alive and dead. In one of the stanzas in Sanskrit, it has been expressed that one who does not possess either education (knowledge), workmanship, character etc. is like a 'deer' which wanders here and there in search of the fragrance. Islam focuses "Educated and uneducated can't be alike". Prophet Mohammed (PBUH) once said that one must receive education even if one has to go to China. Thus education can be rightly considered to be the most important of all human achievements. Education is a process of polishing by which a raw is converted into a precious stone. Man owes some responsibilities on his shoulders – the responsibility as a member of family, head of the family, a husband, member of society, association, organization and above all as a citizen of India. Most importantly, from the Islamic point of view, one is born to pray to God simultaneously with other socio-political responsibilities. The ultimate questions 'What is life' 'what are the purpose of life', now can't be answered for various reasons but the question in whatever shape it is raised falls in the realm of philosophy.

Intellectuals – philosophers are, nowadays, found to be highly concerned with the issues and problems that are currently prevailing in this society. They are afraid to call it a society due to the fact that the present society does not possess the characteristics of the same. It is now difficult to differentiate it from the ordinary crowd which is nothing but a group of a few people.

Education has been defined as "the betterment of society". The society has been passing through a very important phase of development. The present age is known as the curious age, the age of computers. We are obviously progressing towards scientific advancement but the uplift of society is still a question. We have to redefine the concept 'development'. We have to fix up the ultimate aims of human life and conceive the objectives of education. We have to explain the word like 'philosophy'. Then only it may be possible to decides which way we have to go and how to achieve the targets.

An indepth study of human achievements can show the real picture of the present day life and society. At the time of emergence of society people were said to be uncivilised. They did not know how to live, how to eat and how to dress. The dress-sense was completely missing. Now Fashion technology is on the top. People are wearing ultra-modern dresses. There is a sharp contrast. Previously, the clothes were used to hide the body and to look as good as possible. Now, the philosophy has changed. They wear clothes to expose the body with a hope that the women would be appreciated more in that particular style. They are, to some extent, right as the whole society has become like this. Greek Philosophy visualises the beauty as wealth which must be preserved but, the modern age which only bothers about temporal things and show-offs has forgotten the essence of human life.

The family structure is next to be looked at. Previously, there had been selfless love, attachment, togetherness, affection, a positive attitude among the members. They maintained real relations but now people have only functional relations as Moral values are falling day by day.

Corruption is prevailing all over the world. Illicit and extra-marital relations are very much found in the modern society. There are no ideals which can guide the human beings. People seem prone to commit suicide in this society just if they fail to achieve their wishes. This is an indicator that the present modern society is on the verge of declining on moral grounds.

Education has been said to be a crucial instrument of social change. Quantitatively, there have been a substantial achievements regarding the expansion of education but it has totally failed to inculcate the desired values. Besides, the present education system also fails to equip the modern learners to latest technologies or other urgent needs of life.

Philosophy has become useless for the people since education has become merely a means of employment and life has become nothing but a chance to be born and to live it any way with all kind of comforts and luxuries. People and society, now do not bother to have peace, contentment and a meaningful life. Money and wealth is something very important but ironically cannot provide peace of mind and spiritual rest. It is only one's philosophy and proper education that can define objectives and lead to a fruitful life.

The present situation demands renaissance and for this, the society needs philosophers-intellectuals like Maulana Azad, Gandhi, Tagore, Zakir Hussain, Radhakrishnan etc. who by virtue of their philosophies can reform the society and lead to the people towards the ultimate destiny the destiny which has to be finally achieved.

* * * * *

MAULANA AZAD, PHILOSOPHY AND EDUCATION

Maulana Azad belonged to a family of scholars. His father, Maulana Khairuddin, migrated to Arabia after 1857. Azad was born there. The family returned to India in 1868 and settled down in Calcutta.

Azad had, in more than one sense an orthodox Sufi background which later had been expressed in his work under the influence of Sufi Mystic 'Sarmad Shaheed'.

The environment in which Azad was born and brought up made a significant effect on his mind. Luckily, he happened to study the works of modern Arabic and Urdu writers. This introduced him to the modern and progressive thoughts.

The process of self-education made up for what he had missed during formal education under the supervision of his father and orthodox teachers. Self-education led him to constant discovery of the 'self in Azad. Meanwhile he found, in him, an intelligent man, an able writer and a promising journalist. His observations of the contemporary political situation in the Middle East compelled him to develop a broad outlook into politics. Thus, in him, there dwelt a dynamic politician who had often been admired even by Jawahar Lal Nehru.

Vision of Education in Azad's Writings and Speeches

Al-Hilal was initiated in 1913. Although Azad wanted Al-Hilal to be preparatory to his larger movement which he failed in doing so, yet there remains great accomplishment of the journal.

An evaluative and critical analysis of some of the emphasis in his writing has proved his effectiveness in changing muslim attitudes. This can be presented as under:

- Enjoining the Good and Forbidding the Evil,
- Democracy and leadership,
- Attainment of freedom,
- Muslims as rulers,
- Cooperation with Hindus,
- Western Education,

- Islam as the perfect guide for life.

Apart from the above points, Azad used Al-Hilal as a weapon for Khilafat movement (non-cooperation movement). Consideration of Azad's attempts to support Hindi-Muslim unity and the Khilafat movement on the basis of Quraan and Sunnat supports the verdict that Azad never succeeded in evolving from within Islam a political doctrine which could justify composite nationalism.

Azad's other activities in this period included educational and journalistic enterprise. At the time of his projected 'Hizbullah movement,' Azad had established the 'Darul Irshad' in Calcutta with a purpose to train young activists according to the teaching of Al-Hilal. And after his release, he began the Madarsa-e-Islamia in the largest mosque in Calcutta in December 1920. This school was part of the over all non-cooperation programme.

The following abstract is the part of the article written for 'Paigham' (1921) shows Maulana's religious outlook and political philosophy.

> "...I am a muslim, and by virtue of being a muslim this has become my religious duty. Islam never accepts as valid a sovereignty which is personal or is constituted by a bureaucracy of a handful of paid executives. Islam constitutes a perfected system of freedom and democracy. It has been sent down to get back for the human race the liberty which has been snatched away from it."

Azad's non-violence was like that Gandhi's. He however, could not follow 'Jehaad' as prescribed by Islam that one even can kill others to save one's life.

In his presidential address of Indian National Congress in September, 1923, he said, "suffer everything, but never turn our face away from what you consider to be right. This has been for ages the common advice of religion, morality, and nationalism in this world. It can truly be said that in the weak and helpless beginning of every religion, these principles are its only support and strength. We see it engraved upon the cross of Jerusalem. The streets of Mecca have heard its grand appeal... . A Christian martyr teaches us that it is better to be killed than to kill... This probably supports the concepts of non-violence advocated by Gandhiji and Russian Count Leo Tolstoy.

Al-Hilal also contributed a lot to Gandhiji's call for Swaraj. But, Maulana preferred Hindu-Muslim unity to Swaraj.

Azad and Quranic Commentary

Tarjuman-e-Quran was first published in 1931. Azad has been a devoted congress worker till 1938, but due to contest for Muslim leadership, Maulana deliberately kept himself aloof from the politics, thus decided and completed the commentary 'Tarjuman'. However, he had announced the project in the first issue of Al-Balagh in November 1915.

While giving a commentary, he believes that Quran speaks directly to the heart of man without any argumentation or dialectics. The desire to be open-hearted, broad-minded, and concerned with what all religions recognize as significant, which is expressed in Surat-al-Fatiha. He states, "In all that a Muslim does, it should be a rule of action that he helps whoever may be doing good, even if a non-muslim or an opponent and avoid helping whoever may be doing evil, even if a Muslim and a companion...if even an idolator honour and worship God in his own way, he should not be shown disrespect for the honour and worship of God is, in any event, the honour and worship of God".

Maulana speaks against partition on the basis of his political philosophy, "I have examined its likely effect upon the fortunes of Muslims in India.... I have come to conclusions that it is harmful not only for Muslims alone but for Muslims in particular.

Next to Al-Hilal, Maulana's outlook can be observed through Ghubar-e-Khatir (The Dust of Memories). It was however, the collection of private letters written to Azad's friends. Here follows a passage that reveals Azad's positive and aesthetic perception of life: "How strange that religion, philosophy, and ethics, all three, want to solve the problem of life, and yet all three have developed a bias against life".

Azad had an extra-ordinary perception of world around him. He conveys his ecstasy through this moving vision.

"You may believe it or not, but the fact is I have many times talked with towers, and whenever the dome of the Taj lifts its gaze to the silence, I have found its lips moving".

A real portrait of Azad emerges from Ghubar-e-Khatir of a man not troubled to fit is love of music, joys in life, and admiration for such theologians as Ibn Taimiya.

Azad as Minister of Education

Early in his career as a minister, Maulana contemplated shaping the future of India through Educational Policy, he envisaged the possibilities in the following way:

"Today India is free... She can have any kind of mental mould she pleases, will it be exclusive or will it be all inclusive, which has been the characteristics of Indian culture through out the ages?... In the advancement of nations there is no greater hindrance than narrow-mindedness. It is our duty to keep ourselves free from this disease in the new era of independence."

Part of Azad's mystique was his reputation as a man of great learning. This is valid, but we need to investigate the nature of that learning if we want to understand his mind and his contribution to thought. His leaning was the result of his phenomenal memory, his high intelligence, and his love of reading. His formal education was limited to the training in the modified Dars-e-Nizami he had received under his father's supervision. He may have had a good knowledge of western philosophy, he had read some western history and some English Literature, and he was able to comprehend certain principles of popular science. But, there is no solid proof to support such assumptions.

Azad could not have the opportunity of receiving western education. Yet, one can not claim that he did not have the knowledge or perception that could have been achieved by being in the west. Maulana was never against modern or scientific education. While delivering presidential address of 14th session of CABE in 1948. Maulana Saheb sates, "Our present difficulties, unlike those of Europe, are not creation of materialistic zealots, but of religious fanatics. If we want to overcome them, the solution lies not in rejecting religious instruction in elementary stages, but in imparting sound and healthy religious education under our direct supervision so that misguided credence may not affect the children in their plastic stage".

On the occasion of Convocation at A.M.U. Aligarh, he emphasised the need of secular education. He further added, "Sir Syed laid the foundation of the educational institution with a specific object. He had been impressed by the spirit of English education and realised that its excellence lay not merely in imparting instruction but in training of a special kind."

Azad's Philosophy

Azad as a philosopher is not easy to be understood. He was a religious and socio-political philosopher. His philosophy can be a nice combination of axiology, metaphysics, epistomology and aesthetics. He was an idealist but there are ample evidences of progmatism in him.

There were three basic metaphysical concepts of Azad: God, universe and man. The concept of God is the most important of all. This concept has here and there, a reference to the idea that only God is immortal. This faith had never influenced, however, negatively the intellectual advancement, which had been made clear in Holy Quran that man should apply 'intelligence'. While defending his religious stands, Maulana had been found to be scientific in approach.

The concept of universe follows from Maulana's concept of God, the universe manifests all his attributes. It has an evident relation to the Islamic foundation that man is created out of light of God and God is omnipresent. While, the concept of man evolves from two preceding concepts. In the creative process, man has been the best of all, who by virtue of his inborn qualities undertakes the responsibilities as desired by God. The concept of man as the 'best creature of all' reflects in Maulana's philosophy. He does not follow theory of evolution therefore, he has emphasised the word 'creation' most of the time.

Maulana's Tarjuman-e-Quran (1947) depicts well the concept of his religious faith in Islam as a whole, the concept of "Taqdir' (Luck) etc. While explaining the term 'Taqdir', Maulana dealt with 'freedom cum accountability'. This outlook of man's freedom and accountability is by no means reconcilable with the doctrine of his having transferred any thing from his ancestry. Rather, one has been gifted with something pure, good and perfect.

Maulana dealt, however, delicately with 'Wahi' (Revelation), the supreme kind of inspiration learning that man is endowed with. It has a relation to his idealism and mystic outlook. He says that revelation is the supreme faculty guiding man in this direction. He has also tried to throw light upon 'Din' (religion) and 'Sharia' (Islamic laws).

As regard the role of religion, Azad brought forth the secrets of universalization as an essence of every religious system. Thus, he proved himself to have respect for every religion. This once again comes to support the Sufism of Maulana.

In Azad's philosophy, there are five universal values which one must try to achieve in order to claim to be a full fledged man. These are: Maruf (Good); Haq (Truth), Jamal (beauty), Love and Adl (Justice).

While explaining the concept 'Maruf' he referred to the spirit that pervades the scheme of creation and that which guides man towards his advancement in the course of history. 'Maruf' is opposite of 'Munkar' or evil. The concept of right and wrong is attached to these words which is nothing but the outcome of his religious belief.

'Jehad' involves all type of human sacrifice including giving one's life for the noble cause of truth and justice. The second value of greater importance is Haq 'Truth'. In order that the man is equipped to discharge the role entrusted to him. 'Haq' must fulfill two basic requirements: the indivisibility of its identity and the consistency of essence. Bringing Quranic evidence, Maulana has put forth that 'Huq' is immutable and unalterable (which has universality) while its antonym, 'Batil' lacks sustenance and can't have universal appeal.

As a matter of fact, 'Jamal' has generated the climate of beauty and harmony in the physical as well as mental aspect. 'Beauty' itself is a philosophical idea which basically depends upon the perception. He refers to eternal beauty. Love is closely associated with beauty. Beauty is said to be truth and truth, beauty. God is truth and nothing else, because it is God that is immortal, therefore, he loves God, his creations etc. The unimpaired love for God, on the part of man, has of course, to be routed through his love for his fellow beings and others. Maulana's concept of love is not like romantics but can be found to be related to 'love' as found in the English poets like Milton, Tennyson, Wordsworth etc.

The fifth value 'Adl' (Justice) brings the creative process to its completion. It introduces equilibrium and harmony in the process of creation. 'Adl', therefore, can be substituted by balance. By virtue of its harmonising function, the concept combines number of forces together.

Azad and Education

Maulana's philosophy as a whole can be utilized in the field of Education under the following heads:

- Aims & objectives of Education.
- Curriculum
- Textbooks
- Methodology
- Teacher
- Discipline

Azad and Aims of Education

As it is said that philosophy and Education are the two sides of the same coin. Philosophy is the theoretical side and education is the practical side of life. It means what one professes as philosophy is practiced and achieved through education.

Azad's philosophical ideas can help a lot in the evolution and fixing of educational aims. The gist of his philosophy leads to the following aims of education.

Development of a balanced personality

The term balanced personality will obviously include his idealism that is the attainment of ultimate aim: spiritual and intellectual height. The aim would also target at achieving the five basic criteria to claim a balanced man: Maruf (Good); Huq (Truth) Jamal (beauty) love and Adl (Justice).

The mentioned five characteristics some how or the other, are inter-related. The chronological presentation also has some significance. Character-building holds very important place in Azad's philosophy.

Azad and Curriculum

In no other problem is this dependence of education on philosophy more marked than in that of the curriculum. It is probably the means and the tools of achieving educational goals.

Curriculum is the blue print of entire teaching and learning activities. Different philosophers differs in their opinions and recommend curriculum according to their beliefs.

Since Maulana was basically an idealist Soofi he does not profess like Pragmatist Dewey or Naturalist Tagore etc. But, the curriculum should be, according to Azad's philosophy, somewhat idealistic in nature which will obviously lay emphasis on spiritual and religious or value based education for the achievement of ultimate truth. It would enable an individual to discriminate between good and bad, to known good ways, to love beautiful things and ensure justice.

Any activity that guarantees the idealistic postulates to be inculcated among students should be included and given due emphasis in the curriculum.

Azad and Text-books

. The choice of text-books which apparently looks a puerile

task involves philosophy. Text-books are the real means of imparting knowledge. Teacher plays the role of interpreter and narrator of the thoughts presented in a book.

A text-book, according to Azad's philosophy should be scientific and value oriented. Lessons shall be written on secularism, value education, morality, humanity, socialism, democracy, justice etc. He has suggested the following areas of specialization — language, religion, craft, social studies, general science, maths, Indian culture and spiritualism, etc.

Azad and Methods of Teaching

Method of Teaching is the outcome of teacher's educational concept, his outlook towards man and society etc. Social integration and world integration are the concepts that are emphasised in Azad's philosophy.

The concept of 'nation' and 'man' should be well taught and must be attempted to include in the method of teaching. *Education for education* should not be the aim rather education for betterment should be the ultimate target.

The 'Method of teaching' employed by the teachers must ensure the character-building process. Integration of knowledge for the achievement of betterment or development of society or universe must be used. The concept of global unity is emphasised in Azad's philosophy. Besides, development of citizenship should also be ensured while teaching.

Home as informal agency need not be neglected while teaching. Mass Media can be used as very important devices and techniques for teaching effectively.

Maulana Azad knows about he psychological controversy 'Nature-Nurture'. Therefore, it must be kept in the teachers' mind while teaching. Environment plays, thus, very important role in the process of Education. 'Experimentalism' has been empahsised by Azad while teaching a concept. It may not be exactly the same as Dewey proposed under 'learning by doing' but, some how or other, it has some close connection.

The principle of sharing borrowed by Azad form 'Democratic school of thoughts' opens up the chamber of Question-and-answer or discussion method in the classroom teaching.

Student's own observation and the concept of self-learning and exploration has been given priority by Maulana Azad. 'School' in Azad's view is a miniature society.

Principle of freedom guides the entire teaching process. The cultivation of the intellect in the individual is related to the culture of the heart. It is correctly known as spiritual refinement, and is found solely at the disposal of methods of teaching.

Azad and Teacher

If we try to imagine about the role of a teacher according to Azad's philosophy, it would not be much different from the role assigned by an idealist that of a gardener for flowers. It is the responsibility of the teachers to guide the students to the desired path and ensure their harmonious development to personality. But, self-learning also holds an important role in education.

Azad and Discipline

The concept of freedom provides an opportunity to discuss discipline according to Azad's philosophy.

There is a concept of freedom and sharing experiences. This does not mean that it would cross the boundry of discipline. Those who are free they are accountable but if one can't prove one self to be accountable, can not be left free to do any thing. Here comes the role of the teacher. First they will make the student understand his/her responsibility then they will be free to learn/have experiences in the field of education.

* * * * *

GANDHI AND EDUCATION: SYNONYMOUS TO EACH OTHER

Education as defined by Mahatma Gandhi is an 'all-round development of personality'. By the term 'all round' he meant social, psychological, political, economic and philosophical dimensions of human personality. He further supported his idea of education by giving another concept of 'Harmonious Development' which is conceived as nothing but a nice and balanced combination of mind, body and soul.

Philosophy and education are the two sides of the same coin. Education being the practical side plays more important role in the upbringing of a person. Life is the practical side of education. What we visualise or conceive as educationists or educationalists we try to follow in our life. This is perhaps the actual function of education. Gandhi said, "My philosophy is my life". This idea supports the relationship between philosophy and life. A philosopher should practice the same what he professes. It is philosophy that lays a solid foundation of life, and education enables us to understand the life situations and the ultimate life is perhaps the outcome of both philosophy and education.

Educational thoughts were in fact the outcome of Gandhi's experience of life. He always found himself associated with education in India before independence. Had Gandhi lived for some years after India's independence the scenario of education would have been practically different. He, in particular, associated himself with Wardha Scheme (1937) for the establishment and promotion of Basic Education. Consequently, he deputed Dr. Zakir Hussain for Basic Education Committee. Jamia Millia Islamia first launched this idea in 1938 as a start of Teachers' College which tried to follow Gandhian concept by emphasising craft education and teaching through Mother-tongue. 'Education programme for Gandhi has always been an amalgam of both formal and non-formal Education means. Character-building process was considered synonymous with Education process. Making of good citizen, secularism, democracy, socialism, self-sacrifice, tolerance, unity, etc. were the socio-political aims of Education in India, Gandhiji was perhaps the one who attempted to lay a foundation stone for each educational targets.

Making even a modest attempt towards Gandhian contribution of Education and Educational philosophy is a challenging task. However, the present chapter would refer to some of the statements that Gandhi made in his autobiography, "My Experiments with Truth". These statements would exhibit the glimpses of Educational and philosophical thoughts presented by Gandhi.

"What I want to achieve – what I have been striving and pining to achieve these thirty years is self-realisation, to see God face to face to attain Moksha".

This statement is the gist of Gandhi's aim of life – the life which is temporary. What he aspires to attain through living life here is the attainment of salvation – permanent life that is the life here after. The idea of self-realisation, though, a spiritual concept, it enables an individual to lead a good life free from corruption, sin, vice, etc. Self-realisation is the first step towards developing faith in religion or any other noble concept.

Gandhi on other occasion stated, "I have gone through and through, and examined, analysed every psychological situation".

This perception of Gandhi gives an idea that an educated man's responsibility is to search himself introspectively and examine himself well so that he can arrive at a conclusion that is desired by the society.

Going a step ahead, Gandhi stated his concept of 'Truth' which is perhaps the backbone of his general philosophy. "I have had faint glimpses of the Absolute Truth, God and daily the conviction is growing upon me that the above is real and all else is unreal," God and Truth have almost same meaning for Gandhi. Truth as the concept was understood by Gandhi with the help of Gita. He was found to have been truly loyal and faithful to the creator or maker of the universe. He expresses a sense of gratitude towards God which can be felt in the lines by Surdas that always received an applause by Gandhi. Once he said, "I must exclaim with Surdas".

Where is there a wrath
So wicked and loathsome as I ?
I have forsaken my Maker,
So faithless have I been".

For an all round development of personality, for a harmonious development and character-building, it is very important that one is spiritual and religious by nature. Having faith in Creator leads to development of faith in creatures. These concepts are interrelated and as an educated person one has to unify such related things.

Gandhi was very honest, bold and straight forward. He while talking about his father, honestly wrote, 'My father was a lover of his clam, truthful, brave and generous but short tempered," "My father never had any ambition to accumulate riches and left us very little property." It is really interesting to see how honestly he talks about his father and himself also. He does not have a complain against his father having no desire of riches or wealth. It seems as if his father had inherited him the idea of satisfaction and self-sacrifice. He further said, "He had no education, save that of experience.... of history and Geography he was innocent". The word innocent has been deliberately used because when a son talks about his father being deprived of education for various reasons he should avoid words rather sympathise the case. On the other hand, he talks about his father's genuine and real experience that helped him lead a contented and peaceful life in a systematic manner.

Regarding his wife, Gandhi wrote, "I have already said that Kasturba was illiterate, I was very anxious to teach her, but lustful love left me no time." It must be appreciated that Gandhi was very blunt consequently he did not hide the illiteracy of his wife, his own interest of educating her and his being boastful which shows his sense of devotion and love that was his wife's right even though Gandhi's hectic socio-political schedule.

Giving secular lessons, Gandhi has written and spoken a lot. The following sentences would provide us a platform to think about his secular approach in his life situations.

"He (father), besides, Musalmans and Parsi friends, who would talk to him about their own faiths, and he would listen to them always with respect, and often with interest. "He further said, "These many things combined to inculcate in me a toleration for all faiths." "Only Christianity was at that time an exception, I developed a sort of dislike for it, and for a reason. In those days, Christian missionaries used to stand in a corner near the high school and hold forth, pouring abuse on Hindus and their gods".

Gandhiji has mentioned his presence in a session of Muslim league conducted by Ali brothers in Calcutta. Later, he was taken to Aligarh College at Aligarh (U.P.). The issue of Khilafat Movement was to be settled. Moreover, a reference in his autobiography is made that shows his positive involvement in his issue of Khilafat as well as similar other cases. In order to overcome problems arising due to difference of religion he always had been secular in his approach and that only helped him to fight against such non-secular forces.

Gandhi being the messenger of unity worked throughout his life with an open mind and positive thinking, however, a few people might not appreciate his endeavour.

Gandhi has also tried to provide a lesson that a person being in even England can maintain his culture and traditions and may live an ideal life if he is interested. He referred to the incidence of his own when he was about to go to England to pursue his studies.

"My mother, however, was still unwilling. She had begun making minute inquiries. Someone had told her that young men got lost in England, someone had said that they took to meat; and yet another that they could not live without liquor."

Once Gandhiji was convicted of lying which hurt him a lot. He wrote: "I was convicted of lying that deeply pained me," Gandhi was not a person who could lie. Similarly, he was not of a kind who could cheat either. He mentioned some where about an incidence where teachers were helping their students to cheat and he could not score good marks while rest of the students did. It resulted due to the fact that he only could not copy.

Gandhi while commenting on early marriage, said, however, very humbly: Heaven knows how many youths are in the same plight as he. Only in our present Hindu Society do studies and marriage go thus hand in hand."

He has always been a supporter of real educational system. Only in his early days he might not be so visionary, but, he always had a clear and practical notion. He wrote, "I then had the false notion that gymnastic had nothing to do with education. I know that physical training should have a much place in the curriculum as mental training."

As regards Education, in general, once he pointed out, "If our Education were more systematic, and the boys free from burden of having to learn their subjects through foreign medium, I am sure learning all these languages would not be an irksome task, but a perfect pleasure.

Regarding the practical difficulty in pursuing education, he pointed out about himself; "English became the medium of instruction in most subjects from IVth standard, I found myself completely at sea. Often I would lose heart and think of going back to IIIrd standard. "He further added, "Sanskrit, however, proved a harder task. The teacher was a hard task master. It is now my opinion that in all Indian curricula of higher education there should be a place of Hindi, Sanskrit, Persian, Arabic and English, besides of course the vernacular".

In connection with the education of his children, Gandhiji referred to (in the context of Durban, Africa) his experience in the following manner:

"I could have sent them to the Schools for European children but only as a matter of favour and exception. No other Indian children were allowed to attend them. For these, there were schools established by Christian missions, but I was not prepared to send my children there as I did not like the Education imparted in those schools. For one thing, the medium of instruction would be only in English, or perhaps incorrect Tamil or Hindi."

As a matter of fact, Gandhiji engaged an English governess so that he could oversea what was going on. He was of the opinion that there should be parents' involvement. Moreover, he further said. "These experiments were all inadequate. I could not devote to the children all the time." This consequently led the children to the feeling. However, at higher level, that they seemed to "feel the handicap of a want of school education, "in this way, we may conclude that Gandhiji was well aware of the relevance of formal, informal and non-formal system of Education. Besides, he was having a deep rooted cultural factor in him. He wanted, thus to retain the same apart form the fact he was in England and Africa for some time.

Gandhiji directly or indirectly recommended the right place of mother-tongue, classical language and an international language (English). If we properly analyse we would find that there is a hint for 'Bilingual Approach.' He has also emphasised the role of a teacher who is not a taskmaster rather fatherly and friendly, simultaneously he is highly well equipped.

He was always of opinion that teaching should be done in mother-tongue. He did it practically when teacher-training programme started in Jamia in 1938 after Wardha Scheme. He was also in favour of comparative learning of language.

Besides, Gandhiji also had a perception about even handwriting. He said, "I saw that bad handwriting should be regarded as a sign of an imperfect education".

There are plenty other occasions where Gandhiji proved his life as completely synonymous with Education. He believed in the notion that education begins from birth and goes until death. His experience of travelling in third class compartment gave him immense pleasure except the fact that the passengers were selfish, intolerant, less accommodating and narrow minded.

We may conclude that what Gandhiji preached he

practised and lived even by rejection of his own clothes for the sake of equality.

He talked about non-violence, he practiced the same and did something unbelievable in the form of India's independence. He put forth the concept of peace education before the entire world and humanity. He dealt with modernization and proved that a man is modern by his thoughts and not by mere appearance or Westernization. He claimed himself to be a worshipper of truth and lived his life in search of it. For the sake of Hindu-Muslim unity, he did every thing to maintain before and after the freedom, however, he was killed for that only reason because some of us did not like the same. He talked about non-cooperation and Swedeshi movement and as a matter of fact, he wore 'Khadi' spinned by himself. He kept 'fasts' in order to show grievances through self control and restrains. He eventually succeeded. He initially talked about uplifting of scheduled classes, consequently, the mass was educated.

These are some glimpses of Gandhi's Education through his life experiences. In other words, his life is an outcome of his philosophy and Education.

* * * * *

EDUCATION AND MORALITY: THE PRESENT CONTEXT

Education has been defined by learned people in different ways. For some people, it is means of life but for many educated persons it is itself the 'end'. The two notions determine the action of the people who are involved in the process of education. It is education that lays the very foundations of philosophy that lays foundation of the life of people.

The present age is categorically explained as the age of materialism and money-mindedness.

Ethics and morality like concepts are almost forgotten in this society. Sometimes, people do not know about such noble concepts and more often they do not want to know.

Ethics is a science about morality (morals), its nature and essence, structure and functions, origin and development. Marxism-Leninism believes that morality like other forms of ideology is of a class character and is manifested in people's behaviour in different ways in different historical conditions in accordance with the interests of what classes or social strata a person advocates. Others believe that morality is the norms, principles and rules of behaviour, human conduct itself (motives, results of activity), feelings and judgements which express the normative regulation of people's relations with each other and with social entities (collective, class, nation, society). In other words, morality is nothing but humanity in more than a sense of the term.

Morality is an integrated part of philosophy which now-a-days are found to be mostly misunderstood. Philosophers too are wrongly considered to be inhabitant of other worlds having nothing to do with the world of reality. Interestingly, the present generation forgets, however, deliberately that no man can be truly great unless he is a philosopher.

Philosophy, according to Dr. Radhakrishnan is "A Logical Enquiry into the nature of Reality". Mahatma Gandhi opines, "My life is my Philosophy". In other words, Philosophy is nothing but a rational outlook of an individual to live his life in a systematic way.

The following definitions of philosophy would enable us to realize its importance for a human life. Bertrand Russel states, "Philosophy, like all other studies, aims primarily at knowledge." Weber opines, "Philosophy is a search for a comprehensive view of nature, an attempt at a universal explanation of the nature of things". Raymont believes, "Philosophy is an unceasing effort to discern the general truth that lies behind the particular facts, to discern also the reality that lies behind appearances."

Thus, one may conclude that philosophy is basically related to the ultimate answer to basic questions pertaining to human life, the answers that can not be found unless one discovers fact, truth, reality; the ultimate knowledge to discriminate between good and bad; vice and virtue, proper and improper; modest and immodest, right and wrong etc. The ultimate purpose of life can only be explained in the light of philosophy. Those who have through of such basic questions are said to be philosophers, and those who are philosophers are moral and spiritual beings.

Aristotle's idea of man as social, political and gregarious animal; Marx's concept of man as productive animal an further be modified as a spirituo-moral being from the view point of a philosopher. And, such philosopher is not a saint, a hermit or an ascetic, but, a normal human being who has wisdom and sensibility. The present society is noticing a disastrous change. Selfishness has occupied the place of top priority in the present society. People by and large are found to be indifferent towards noble concept like humanity, brotherhood, fraternity, togetherness, solidarity, selfless love, sacrifice, patriotism, equality, help and cooperation etc. Human code of conduct and ultimate behaviour of an individual has acquired a different shape that can't be appreciated by any sensible man.

'Morality' and 'Religion' are interrelated

People by an large do not have faith in abstract or spiritual phenomenon. They are not ready to pray to God or worship gods and goddesses and claim that such things are unimportant. They are thus not afraid of anything now. If they are powerful, they do not hesitate in harming others.

Islam also emphasise 'Ethics' and 'Morality' and considers this place for action which determines the line of a person will live beyond this world. This world is a place of action and the other is the place of reward.

There are plenty issues in ones life. Man is a social and political animal. Economic aspects are also important for a human being. One can't live without money. In order to achieve worldly goals, people generally are found to look for some ways to earn money in any manner. This tendency leads to some sorts of materialism basically because of excess love for money. In other words, 'Materialism' is at peak at present basic due to the greed and ambition which prove to be deadly sins for good people. The prophet (PBUH) said: 'Man will not feel satisfied even if he has two dales of gold. He will hanker after the third one. Nothing but soil, dust or earth can satisfy man. (nothing but death can end mans greed for wealth).

"Greed is the web to one's heart and fetters to one's feet. If one blacks out great expectations from one's heart, one's feet will be automatically unfettered. Thus, one will be free from greed for wealth".

Ironically enough, these luxuries are temporary. They turn us away from the remembrance of our creator, noble acts, humane feeling and other noble qualities. The Quraan says very clearly :

Say : " Short
Is the enjoyment of this world:
The Hereafter is the best
For those who do right:

Never will you be
Dealt with unjustly
In the very least !"

....

Know you (all), that
The life of this world
Is but a play and a pastime,
Adornment and mutual boosting.
And multiplying, (inrivalry)
Among ourselves, riches
And children.
Here is a similitude:
How rain and the growth
Which it brings forth, delight
(The hearts of) the fillers;
Soon it withers, then
Will see it grow yellow;
Then it becomes dry
And crumbles away
But in the hereafter
Is a chastisement severe
(For the devotee of wrong)
And Forgiveness from Allah
And (His, good pleasure
For the devotees of Allah)
And what is the life
of this world, but
Goods and chattles
of deception ?

In Islam, worship is very important rather obligatory.

Without these fundamentals of Islam (Prayer, fasting, charity and pilgrimage), follower can not claim to be a real muslim. But,, without development of socio-moral values, he can also not claim to follow Islam in true sense.

Prayer is performed as a matter of relation between the follower and Almighty and if someone does not pray the Almighty may forgive but if one is not moral or social or human he/she has to explain on the day of judgement. For example, if a muslim does not have a good and healthy relation with his neighbour he is responsible for it and he will have to explain the same. Thus, if one is a practising muslim he must be truly socio-moral being. Similarly, religious and other scholars have explained the importance of morality be it the emergence of society or now the 21st century.

Politics is also considered to be responsible, however partly, for decline of morality. Politics is a noble concept that is "a welfare activity." But, ironically it is now found to be a nasty game played for encroaching chair of power.

The present age has been categorically called as of Computers. The society has been noticing, for many years, rapid advancement due to scientific applications of some sophisticated innovations in the field of science-technology. The entire world has been reduced to 'map of paper' due to the effectiveness of telecommunication. Transportation, communication, education and everything attached to these have achieved the optimum height. In other words, science-technology and education have risen to the top most level.

On the other hand, if one tries to peep into the internal aspect of personality or look at the other side of the coin, this society may notice that the 'Man' has declined a lot. A good example of sharp contrast may be found as luxuries and comforts have received the utmost state of 'Rise' while humanity / morality and 'man' have met the ultimate 'Fall'.

It has been a long journey which the mankind has travelled. It has consumed thousand of years. Many small stations might have come on the way to the goal-destiny. But, pity on thy fate who could not know their ultimate destiny. They were told to progress, prosper and develop, but in this sheer attempt they went down, met disasters and finally declined.

In this society, humanity is such a notion which is always treated synonymous to philosophy, however, wrongly and negatively. Even it is philosophy as others believe which can be professed only, it bears truth and one must not hesitate in saying that without it one can't visualise a human world or a society.

Materialism has been ironically considered to be the best appreciated policy of the present society. People are selfish. No one bothers about any body. And, if one sacrifices something for the noble cause or for the sake of a human being, he can be strangely stamped as a fool, however, religiously he can be wiser and finer than many so-called wise people.

Materialism is of course a curse on the society. It is something that has separated a son from father; a husband from wife; a man from his relatives and the worst of all, a lover from his beloved. It is nothing but a selfish attitude of an individual that has resulted from the notion which postulates that 'believe that which you can see and have'. Thus, the root of idealism and spiritualism has been trampled under the foot. For the sake of clarity, it can be outrightly stated that there are plenty of abstract and spiritual things which can't have standard parameter to measure and evaluate. On the other hand, such things can better be felt, realised and practised by an individual to make his life better, peaceful, satisfied and perfect.

There are be many correlates of 'Materialism', but 'Money-mindedness's is the root of materialism. The modern people have wrongly understood money and wealth to be the most important thing in this world. Had it been the fact then crores of people living in well furnished multistoryed buildings or staying in five star hotels would have claimed to be happier than many monitarily poor people who are living in cottages and enjoying almost all happiness of an ideal life.

One can only pray to God that our society becomes educated thus it may realise that the ultimate purpose of one's life is to worship (Islam), to work that is worship (Gita) and to serve family, society and state (sociology and politics).

The loss of moral values occurs particularly due to the lack of proper education, lack of parental guidance and guardianship, lack o teacher's accountability, fall of societal norms, money-mindedness, selfishness, development of inhuman behaviour, machine type tendency and due to functional relation with human beings.

Education is a process that helps us to change from an impolite state to civilisation. Thus, Education refines us in many ways. It makes an individual political, philosophical, social and spiritual being. Education is the instrument that can give an individual the desired shape.

Education is basically of two types: Quantity and Quality Education. Nowadays, many people are found to have many degrees but strangely they are not fully educated. Therefore, sometime ago, there has been a debate over delinking degrees from the jobs. Therefore, we have to prove now that we are educated in real sense of the term of Education that is an 'All round development of the personality'.

* * * * *

GANDHIJI AND ZAKIR SAHEB

Mahatma Gandhi was born in a Hindu family in Gujarat in India and Zakir Hussain in a Muslim family at Hyderabad and brought up in Farokhabad, U.P.

Gandhi received formal education and even travelled to South Africa. Zakir Saheb also got formal education and got Ph.D. from Berlin.

Gandhiji was an advocate by profession and Zakir Saheb was an academician and educationist. Gandhi had done pioneering work to establish the 'Congress' and Zakir was a staunch supporter and stalwart of Gandhian mission, particularly in Educational Sector.

Gandhi had a fair acquaintance with all important scriptures and paid due respect to all religions. Dr. Zakir was a simple Muslim and had fashioned his socio-moral values and his life, on the whole, on its teachings that bestowed him with a sense of respect for people on the basis of his secular outlook.

Dr. Zakir got involved in students' politics from AMU, Aligarh and earned him fame. Gandhiji's philosophical and socio-political excellence emerged when he had attained the age of majority but Zakir Saheb academic excellence proved him even for the highest post of Indian Republic. Both were brilliant and had prodigiously sharp memory. Gandhiji was the maker of politicians and Dr. Zakir was a true leader and an administrator. Both were well versed in every field of study: Philosophy, Education and Politics. They were logical, imaginative and pragmatist.

Gandhiji was a secular Hindu and broad-minded Indian whereas Dr. Zakir a secular Muslim. Gandhiji's economic background was good enough and Dr. Zakir was also from a good background. Both Gandhi and Zakir were fair in their personal dealings. Gandhiji used to be immaculately dressed before he plunged into the arena of Indian Politics, later he opted for the dress that became his mark. He did so for his socialistic thoughts. Zakir had a good taste for dress and used to wear Sherwani, Pajama and a goggle. He had a taste and choice for his outfit. Gandhi was able to enjoy his life even in Ashram but Zakir was different. Zakir was very fond of eating good and delicious food. He was not able to resist his hunger even in Parties. Gandhiji was a true vegetarian.

Both Gandhi and Zakir possessed visionary thoughts. They were able to foresee even distant future. They never spoke high of themselves. Besides, they never reacted violently against their opponents even if they had been in the wrong.

Socio-Political Philosophy

It is said that a man's socio-political outlook is formed by his individual efforts and social surroundings. Zakir's educational activities got momentum even in his prime of leadership. Though he studied Economics, he was able to read, understand, practise and promote socio-political ideology. Gandhiji's personal experiences and philosophical outlook gave birth to his socio-political ideology. As Gandhi was a philosopher he was more aware of social problems. He believed in Kabir's concept, 'Sadhu aisa chhahiye jaisa soop subhaye, sar saar ko gahi rahe thotha deye urhaye' (A good man is one who takes every thing that is useful and discards useless things). Both were real politicians therefore, they naturally had some goals to achieve and many dreams to materialize. Both were products of British rule in India and had witnessed many socio-political, economical and educational ups and downs.

Tolerance

Both Gandhi and Zakir possessed the virtue of tolerance and patience. In fact, Zakir was governed by his personal traits. As a result of his humble and modest approach, he believed in patience. Once he said, "...I have a firm conviction that no good cause has suffered unduly or for too long because of lack of resources. It seems to be a quality of the wisdom of providence not to fulfill needs as they arise, to try the patience of us human being but complete deprivation is also not something that appeals to providence". It was Gandhi was gave the message to the nation to put restraints on their emotions, to tolerate and bear the rude things sensibly and act accordingly.

Tolerance is associated with other concepts like self-restraints, self sacrifice, democracy, peace and non-violence. Tolerance may be personal or socio-political. Gandhiji exhibited both kind of tolerance.

In short, both the politicians were blamed for many things by their fellow community men. Zakir Saheb being basically an educationist did not receive many complaints but Gandhi was blamed for many things which he was not responsible for. He was even killed by a Hindu. Both were highly tolerant and had forgiving nature.

Peace

Islam has been etymologically derived from the Arabic word 'Salaam' that means peace or surrender before God. Thus, Islam is the religion of peace. Religiously Zakir Hussain was a Muslim and a peace lover; politically he was like Gandhiji. Both of them did not want violence. Religiously Gandhiji believed in Hindu-mystic philosophy that rests on the pillar 'Om Shanti Om'. Besides, Gandhiji followed the message preached by lord Krishna in Mahabharata that the path of Peace is the path of salvation'.

Zakir Hussain's Philosophy of Peace can be ascertained through his following statement: "World Peace today depends largely upon the marriage of religion and science. Religion should be enabled to find the means by which world society can move forward towards a united, prosperous, happy and peaceful world community.

Peace for the Muslim and the Hindu is very important as it the basis of the sustenance of human life, for worship and prayer or even for ordinary work. In Islam, it is of religious significance, as prophet Mohammed (PBUH) once said, 'The least charity is to make peace amongst men'.

Gandhi was a true follower of peace-philosophy. Zakir Saheb was always a follower of Gandhian thought atleast in Politics for the upliftment of a secular society like India. They even did not allow any body to fight in the state of crisis.

Unity

Gandhiji was very much determined with his concept of unity. As a matter of fact, he tried his level best not to disintegrate India before 1947. Both Gandhi and Zakir used to believe that unity among people is the most important requirement for the development of the nation. People can be divided on the basis of caste, creed, belief, custom etc. because these are personal things. On the whole, all the people of a country are interlinked and united. Zakir once stated about cultural synthesis, "....Something deep down in me seems to furnish me with the belief that providence has destined India to be the laboratory in which the greatest experiment of cultural synthesis will be undertaken and successfully completed".

In the Indian context, even if all Indians are not from the same community but, generally it is said that India is a community, however, there live Muslim community and Hindu as well. Though we maintain differences of customs, practice, beliefs etc., we in more than one way, share a lot of cultural phenomena. And maintenance of these differences is our strength. Even if we are not culturally the same we may maintain oneness, and unity was the foremost target of the leaders in general and Gandhi and Zakir in particular. They were the spokesmen of such noble concepts.

Patriotism

There is no doubt that both Gandhi and Zakir were true patriotic in nature. Both were devout Indians. Gandhi's patriotism can not be questioned for the simple reason that he was the leader of freedom movement being a Hindu by birth and loyal to motherland through out his lifetime. Zakir Hussain, right from his student leadership always tried to achieve his goal for the upliftment of the nation. It was high time for any educated Muslim leader to shift to Pakistan and get a suitable post in 1948. But, he has not even imagined about the same.

For Gandhi, Patriotism was a selfless love for one's country and desire for its welfare. It crosses the boundaries of all religion, caste or creed. Gandhiji believed in the doctrine, 'One's mother and motherland (Country) are greater than even the heven.' Iqbal's line, 'Sare Jahan Se acchchha Hindustan Hamara' 'Hindi hain hum watan hai Hindustan Hamara', expresses the actual feeling that every true countryman should have if he wants to prove his patriotism. It was perhaps the testimony of Zakir's patriotism that he became the first Muslim President of Free India.

Non-Violence

Non-violence is the most prominent philosophy of Mahatma Gandhi. He even won the movement of freedom following this noble doctrine. Many people were against him saying that they would be able to attain freedom if they followed 'himsa'. But, the 'Sadhu' looking man proved what he preached. He strictly followed the philosophy of 'Ahimsa parmo dharmah' that means non-violence is the greatest religion or the best way of life. Though Zakir did not preach any such idea, he was a staunch supporter of Gandhi. In Islam too, it is not allowed to kill even a bird without a prescribed reason. It is the philosophy of non-violence that provides that platform for self-restraint, self sacrifice, tolerance, fraternity, equality and peace. Therefore, the importance of non-violence for the establishment and promotion of world order can not be denied.

Dr. Zakir stated about non-violence "Whether or not non-violence is accepted as a religion, creed, it has to be accepted by all as a postulate for civilized behaviour or expression of respect for human personality. Again, it was stated, "If the people of India eschew non-violence there is no hope for them. Dr. Zakir con inued, "Non-violence, which Gandhi preached, was not a metaphysical doctrine and a religion truth to him, but it was an act of statesmanship.

Religio-Moral Philosophy

According to Gandhi, 'Religion is a personal matter which should not have a place in politics'. For Gandhi, it was a good guide for conduct and not a game for power. He was having a secular concept about it and he believed in the philosophy, 'Iswar Allah tere naam'. His approach towards looking at different religion might be of Kabir's type as the latter conceived it as different means of reaching one goal that is – God. He further said that different religions are like different flowers of the same grand tree of the garden. This concept of religion leas to harmony. Iqbal's idea of religion if interpreted nicely in his line. 'Mazhab nahin sikhata aapas main bair rakhna' (Religion does not teach to harbour enmity amongst one another), leads to beautiful doctrine of national integration.

Gandhiji's concept of religion was not confined to his personal relation with the divine power rather it was basically concerned with his philosophy of life when he himself came out with an idea. 'My philosophy is my life'. This statement leads to many interpretation and can be summed up as the way he conceived and visualized his life actually lived in practice. He once said, 'Truth is my religion and Ahimsa is the only way for its realization. Mokshya is the realization of the truth and belief in one God is the corner stone of all religion'. Gandhian Truth has an impact of Indian classical doctrine, 'Satyam Shivam Sundaram'.

Thus, it may be inferred that religion for Gandhi was not an impulsive attachment with the divine power rather it was his own way of life during which he tried throughout to be non-violent and attempted to attain Truth as a means to salvation – the only end of this temporary life.

Dr. Zakir was not a philosopher. But he was a muslim. He had a very practical aspect of thinking. About religion, he said, "It is spiritual experience. Those who are authentically religious undergo an inner transformation and they radiate peace, harmony and goodwill.... The religious spirit is the foundation-lead of the aspiration of man to serve his fellowmen, to establish equality and justice, to abolish ignorance, pain and sorrow."

About 'Self', Dr. Zakir said, "Be yourself-think for yourself. Judge things for yours. Feel responsible and own responsibility for your action. If you must look for faults, look for them not in others but in yourself." About his concept of service or worship, be said, "we can serve him (God) by serving people, our neighbour, our fellowmen".

Regarding spirituality, Zakir Saheb said, "I maintain that the concern of education, and therefore of the university, is with the individual and the spiritual, and the university can not do too much to refuse to deviate from its responsibility in this regard".

Educational Philosophy

Gandhi was a philosopher, therefore, his educational thoughts were influenced by his philosophical outlook. Gandhi associated himself with education in general and teacher education in particular in 1938. The Wardha Scheme was initiated for Basic education when a committee was constituted under the chairmanship of Dr Zakir Hussain. Simultaneously a teacher training college in Jamia Millia Islamia was established and the concepts of Gandhian philosophy came into practice. The importance of Craft education was realized and mother-tongue was considered suitable as the medium of instruction. Thus, an all round development of personality was ensured by providing a combination of formal and non-formal education progamme. As a whole, the ultimate purpose of education revolves around character building and making good citizen. In addition, education process aims at the concept of equality, secularism, democracy, self-sacrifice, etc.

It will consume a lot of pages if we start dealing with almost all aspects of Gandhian concept of education and educational philosophy. But, in short, we may conclude that Gandhiji wanted to develop one's all round personality by providing a good and effective curricular programme. The teacher becomes the most vital component in the entire process.

As mentioned earlier that Zakir Hussain was basically an educaitonist and later on educational administrator, he wanted to improve the entire system of education. He has therefore suggested many fruitful concepts in many areas of Education. Dr. Zakir was basically associated with 'Basic Education'. He has referred to four activities for the development of a child: play activity, sport activity, casual occupational activity and work activity. Work activity was later focussed by him as work experience. It was to some extent similar to Dewey's ideas of 'Learning by Doing' and Mahatma Gandhi's 'Manual work'. Dr. Zakir defines education of a mind is essentially a process of reifying in it the latent values continued in cultural goods'.

About 'book' he said, 'The book is a wonderful companion. It is a wonderful companion for those who are lonely, it is a wonderful teacher for those who wish to learn and it is a wonderful source of enjoyment.

As most of us know that Dr. Zakir was basically a teacher therefore, he was very particular abut Discipline. He states, 'Democracy postulates a self-imposed discipline. Democracy allows full freedom of discussion. Everyone of us participating in the democratic process should constantly put himself the question if he is imposing this democratic discipline on himself."

On other occasion, Dr. Zakir pointed out about education, 'The justification of good education is an enrichment of life for individual human being and the full development of their spiritual potential".

Having gone through some of the dimensions of the philosophy of Gandhi and Zakir Saheb were in position to infer that the ideas put forth in their writings and speeches are worth following. Particularly, at this stage when this world is heading towards non-violence and war. The people of twenty first century are in need of peace for education, industry, economy and other kind of development. The mass needs to be really educated so that concepts like philosophy and education can be strengthened and later achieved by practising the same in our life. Otherwise, it is felt that there is no actual achievement of such aims of education and life that Gandhi and Zakir professed and lived.

* * * *

INDIAN TEACHER AND PEACE: THE 21ST CENTURY CONTEXT

Education has generally been defined as an "All round Development of Personality" and "Betterment of Society". Philosophy, being theoretical side of Education lays emphasis on setting goals: socio-cultural, political, economic, moral and last but not least, 'Educational' aims.

Teaching is a 'process of Interaction' by which educational aims are attained by a group involved in educational institutions. Teacher is an individual that is considered as the most important source of achieving different targets. Therefore, philosophy of a teacher plays very important role in forming a clear cut vision to understand educational goal in a particular socio-political set up and evolve better strategy to attain the same for fruitful implementation. The role of a teacher in multi-lingual and pluro-cultural society like India is much more important and crucial than countries with simple and open social patterns.

Philosophers, Educationalists and Planners have some genuine expectations from the teachers in the beginning of the new era. Philosophers think that teachers would act as they wish them to do. While the fact is little different because the teachers of today are not always philosophers. On the other hand, every educationalist is a philosopher, therefore, he has some thoughts and visions to be professed and implemented.

We have some names of learned personalities or philosophers who ruled the minds of many teachers after independence. Gandhi being the first and most influential, successfully attempted to reform the socio-educational set up as a politician-philosopher. He is rightly considered as a true educationalist-philosopher who initiated the idea of 'Non-cooperation Movement during which some Indian institutions emerged with philosophical basis of Indian origin. Gandhiji advocated the idea of teaching in schools through mother-tongue and as an activity subject, 'Craft Education' was given due importance. It became very popular under 'Teacher training programme'. Gandhi was not a teacher by qualification and career. But, he wanted Indian teachers to develop a vision of Education so that they can try to achieve some objectives based on the philosophy of the Individual. It is a well known fact that Gandhiji was a staunch supporter of 'Ahimsa' (non-violence). Thus, it may be inferred that he might expect from his teachers to be admirers of a noble concept like this. Ahimsa leads to 'Peace' in more than one way. Peace requires simplicity and nobility of thought and action. Being the follower of peace, he even agreed to the proposal for partition of India. He expected peace from the people of the two nations but his expectations went wrong due to the fact that they were very angry with each other as they also did not want any such division. Considering many events in his life, it may be inferred that he professed and practised peace in more than one sense.

Azad (Abul Kalam) was one of the greatest politicians of Pre-independent and post-independent India. He was known as 'Maulana' because he came from an Islamic background. He was said to be a highly learned man. His philosophy of knowledge, secularism and national integration makes us think about his vision towards 'Peace' because an integration is not possible without peace. Therefore, he was not in favour of partition of India. Azad was also not a teacher but a great philosopher and educationist. His speeches as Education Minister of free India gives us impression that he was a peace lover. He tried to hold Hindus and Muslims till he could. But, some negative forces were working behind which succeeded finally and disintegration took place. Consequently India witnessed hatred and blood shed.

Tagore, one of the greatest poets and Educational thinkers of India was the epitome of 'Peace'. His educational institution known as 'Shanti Niketan' is the right example of 'Shanti', a Hindi word that is roughly translated as 'Peace'. Tagore was apparently a 'Sadhu' (saint) and a follower of 'Mysticism'. He was highly spiritual by temperament and a philosopher of Indian type.

Tagore started his school in a different way following his own philosophy of teaching and interaction that was basically based on the idea of 'Peace'. The concept proposed through Tagore's 'Naturalism' may be interpreted as the actual interaction of a child with 'Nature'. Children too have been considered as part of nature as if they were flowers in one garden and teachers were gardeners. We may well imagine the relationship between flowers, garden and a gardener. The idea is noble and the environment is rather nobler and peaceful. Thus, Tagore was a teacher, a poet, a philosopher and an advocate of peace.

Dr. Zakir Hussain was a spokesman of Gandhi. As an educationist, he became popular when he came into Gandhiji's contact in 1938, for 'Wardha Scheme' to launce 'Basic Education Programme'. Craft Education under 'Basic Education' scheme was the practical side of Gandhiji's own style of life. Dr. Zakir was also an Educationst, politician and a peace loving person.

He endeavoured hard to give a vision of education which is the embodiment of harmony, peace and human development as a whole because in their unconscious state of mind or suppressed consciousness they did not cherish the idea of partition.

Having seen the crucial responsibilities of important personalities who have been discharging significant functions we can now easily sum up teacher's role who is simultaneously a philosopher, an educationalist, a politician, a social reformer and a moral guide. The following is a bird-eyeview of the roles of an ideal teacher.

Teacher as a Gardener

The role of a teacher is highly critical. It is said that a teacher is the same as a gardener. The philosophical status of a teacher as gardner explains the role of a child as a flower. A flower is very soft, supple and sensitive. It has to be nourished, watered and looked after properly. It may wither away against rough wind. Therefore, a teacher has a keep in his mind all the adverse factors that may affect a blossoming flower and be vigilant so that the flower may be protected in time and subsequently grow and maintain its beauty and charm and spread its fragrance.

Teacher as a Pot-maker

A pot-maker prepares clay for a pot and tries to giver a desired shape. If a pot-maker is not well experienced and suitably trained he may to be ale to succeed I his targets. However, the same lump of clay be used to make another one, on the other hand, while in the process of making of a student, another chance may not be utilised as sometimes, it is too late to mend. Therefore, a teacher deals with more delicate material.

Teacher as a Diamond-maker

Teacher's responsibility as a diamond-maker is to sharpen and use the inherent potential of the students. A diamond maker polishes a stone untill it becomes a diamond – a precious stone. He can not do this crucial task unless he is well trained while processing it, the stone may be broken and the entire effort may prove to be futile and a resource may be wasted. Similar job is done by a teacher. When a student is admitted he is an ordinary stone, however, the potential to convert him into a diamond exists there. After the teacher provides the academic treatment and required training the same student modifies his behavior and in the end, it shines like a diamond and becomes a valuable person. The process of making a diamond is very difficult. It is to be seen whether which stone has the quality to be converted into a diamond and how much polish is needed. If it is polished less it remains a stone and if polished carelessly it may be broken. Therefore, a teacher as a diamond-maker performs a very crucial role and a valuable duty to change an ordinary man in to human beings, a person into a responsible citizen, a child into an intelligent scholar or a human resource.

Teacher as a Maker of Future Generation

It is highly crucial concept to consider a teacher as *maker of future generation*. In fact, students are treated as future generation and he teacher is morally and socially responsible for imparting knowledge for personality development. If a teacher is not good and well equipped the outputs (the students) may not be able to become what one expects from them. He is supposed to make or spoil thirty six generations, simply because he is employed at the age of 24 and serves for thirty six years until he retires. Therefore, a teacher is responsible for good or bad career of the students. Each society expects change and development in the future and the role and responsibility of a teacher in the entire process of change and development is evident. A teacher is rightly said to be a social reformer because it is the teacher who visualizes an ideal society. He tries to give shape to a student as he desires according to need and requirement of the future. There are two kinds of teacher: a teacher by choice and a teacher by chance. There is a good percentage of teachers who wanted to become doctors, engineers or managers but they could not materialise their dream. On the contrary, they opted for teaching positions which happened only by a chance. Such teachers do not have any interest in teaching because they are not properly motivated towards their jobs and they only pass their time in order to get money at the end of the month.

Teacher as an Instructor

According to the new theories of Teaching/Learning, the role of a teacher is more like an Instructor, however, there are some philosophical limitations with this concept. A teacher supervises students as if they were doing some experiment and in order that they may not to 'Trial-Error' which leads to waste, he instructs them from time to time. This idea is highly technical but sometime, may not be applied to outside class-room situation that is also not less important than classroom activity.

By instructing less experienced lot (students), a more experienced person (instructor) brings about some changes, in the students' personalities. Moreover, it is also one of the teacher's roles in the form of some practical knowledge.

Teacher as a Guardian

Many people having philosophical blend of thoughts believe that a teacher is a social-moral guardian of students. It can not be denied for various reasons that teachers have been providing guardianship for students for a very long time. They have been leading them towards the right and the prosperous path. The teachers have been acting like fathers and the students have also been paying reverent and showing great respect to the them consequently learning more from the teachers than anybody else. There is no denying the fact that teachers have been the role model or ideal for most students.

These points bear an implication that is right and ideal, therefore, an important responsibility may successfully be discharged by no other eminent personality than a teacher.

Keeping his status in view, a teacher is expected to develop his personality on the principles suitable for him. It is also important for the reason that he is a model and the students are going to copy him in totality or in part in near future. A teacher must have philosophy of life. He can later try to achieve the same through philosophy of life so that he can try to achieve the same through philosophy of teaching and education. He should know moral values which are important for the development of human beings. He should have a clear cut vision of objectives of education/teaching.

Teacher as a Peace-lover

In the foregoing pages, we have seen the crucial duties being discharged by the teachers in general and Indian teachers in particular. The tasks of a teacher are determined by philosophy, sociology and psychology. Psychologically, a teacher is a motivator and an instructor. Sociologically he is one who provides guidance and guardianship by virtue of being senior and more experienced. Philosophically, a teacher is one who guides students morally, inspires and inculcates some values in the students. Value system is something very important for human life. It is the value system which distinguishes man from animal. Peace has become very important aim to be achieved by philosophers due to the fact that it is missing from the socio-philosophic dimensions of one's life. Peace can be defined as a state of mind and soul that gives extreme unmixed pleasure to an individual. It is the condition that provides ease and comfort. Peace is far from the madding crowd and a ray of hope in the present big buzzing confusion. Peace as noble and philosophically idealistic concept can be rightly contrasted with money based achievements of human beings. Peace can not be had by even those who are multimillionaires. It is something internal. Peace is the ultimate ambition of many sensible people in the crowds of men who are more machines than human beings.

Peace is important for one and all a student, a teacher, a painter, an artist, a poet, a novelist , a philosopher, a wife, a husband, a boss and a worker.

The role of a teacher starts from imparting knowledge. In India, knowledge is rather subjective and can operationally be defied. 'Knowledge of Life' may include all the dimensions-social, psychological, political, economic, moral or even educational. Knowledge enables one to differentiate the right and the wrong, good and bad, vice and virtue etc. It is therefore, the potential of the teacher that leads one to the right path-social or religious. A stanza written in Sanskrit may here be rightly quoted:

"Yesham na vidya na tapo na danam
    Gyanam na sheelam na gurho na dharmah
Tey mirttyu lokey bhui bhar bhuta
    Manushya ruperh mrigyash charanti."

It is translated as: "The one who has neither knowledge (Education), not worship, nor charity, nor knowledge (depth), nor character, nor religion, roams like a deer in search of 'kastury' (a kind of fragrance) that is dispensed by its body only. It can further he inferred that those who do not have 'knowledge' may not know the importance of worship and the faith required. They may not dispense charity as they may never know the noble purpose behind it. Similarly if some one does not have the knowledge of the these, he does not know himself, his potential and capabilities, thus wastes one's fruitful life for no sensible reasons.

A teacher gives knowledge. If he is responsible for all these dimensions and aims of life, it is his duty to acquaint his taught in the way that they learn about life the real manner. When students are in the educational process they should ultimately know about he aims and objectives of their lives, their different roles in the society as well. While getting education under the supervision of a teacher, they should develop knowledge about different aspects of life, problems and the way in which one can cope with. It is a well known fact that only philosophy determines one's aim in life and it is education that builds up and changes the philosophical aspect of one's life.

Thus, the person involved for the attainment of educational targets is the most important one in the life of a student. A teacher holds this prestigious post and enjoys the position of an ideal. Thus, an ideal teacher in India bears a lot of responsibility on his shoulder.

The present century is going to be tougher than the previous one, however, for some years, it is just a technical change from twentieth to twenty first century. It is expected that every one would be in a great hurry, with the heat of hope and ambition, thus, making his life functional like a 'machine'. He may get comfort and material satisfaction by dint of money but 'Peace', the most important target will be missing. Therefore, the teacher, being the maker of future generation, builder of the nation and founder of a real personality, is forced to take up the responsibility to establish 'Peace' and restore the same among the young children, adults and even senior people of the country. The society is deteriorating basically because the teachers are becoming indifferent towards their tasks. Therefore, the teachers of the modern century are expected to come forward with renewed zeal to maintain their image. The society lacks in moral values and peace just because the teachers are growing unmindful of their duties in relation to value education and furthering peace.

* * * * *

PEACE: THE ULTIMATE PURPOSE OF LIFE

The concept of 'Peace is highly philosophical. It may however, be related to socio-political context also. Socially, it is the most needed condition while politically, peace is usually a post-war scenario.

In this context, peace has been dealt with philosophically or spiritually. Yet, the ultimate postulates of the same do not differ much.

The important of 'Peace' need not be emphasized. It is perhaps the most desired achievement of a human life. In Hindu philosophy, 'Shanti' holds very important place. A devotee normally prays for Shanti (peace).

The Greek philosophy advocates the concept of 'Truth' and 'Beauty' which, somehow or the other, is related to the concept 'peace'. In India, the same philosophy covers a broader dimension as it states, 'Satyam, Shivam, Sundram'. Satya (truth) is shiv (god); and a god is always sundar (beautiful), and one that is beautiful is always truth. Truth is also a philosophical concept. It does not have any physical entity as it is believed that a thing that has a physical shape is always mortal.

Peace is never related to a mortal world. It does not have a determined criterion. For example it cannot be found in a Five Star hotel that provides luxuries and comforts. These facilities can not lead to attainment of peace. It can rather be had even in small huts in a garden or at a river side. Attainment of peace however differs from individual to individual. Some people can get it by reading of Holy Qur'an or Ramayana or by other modes of prayers. Namaz offered by Muslims, Puja by Hindus can be named as finding out means to get peace. In yoga also, mental as well as spiritual peace has been emphasized. Aesthetics in philosophy has been much emphasized by philosophers like Rabindra Nath

Tagore. 'Shanti Niketan' can be said to be the means to attain peace through education.

Plato advocated the concept of Ideal State. That too had the same notion. The attempts made by organization like SAARC primarily aims at peace. UNO is the organization that had been established to maintain peace all the world over.

In English poetry, a lot of emphasis had been put on the concept 'Peace'. William Wordsworth while describing the beauty of Nature, in some Lucy poems particularly, expressed his sentiments and plan. An example:

'Hers shall be the breathing balm
and Hers the silence and the calm
of mute insensate things'.

The poet in the same poem, wishes that his adopted child 'Lucy' would live in the happy dell where peace prevails. He further plans for his child 'Lucy' who would enjoy secret place where there are many rivulets, and the fall of water with a musical sound that would make Lucy's childhood enjoyable.

Many other mystic poets have dealt with this concept. Some of them have left the buzzing society in search of peace. This society as a whole is lacking this noble idea. There can be many factors involved i.e. over-population, transportation, pollution, industrialization, business and above all materialistic philosophy of the people of the world.

Philosophy of Peace is not an easy concept to understand and to practise the same is more difficult. Mystic personalities like lord Buddha. Vivekanand and Tagore etc. have always advocated 'peace', however, the methods of preaching might differ.

If we exemplify evidences existing in the present society, still most people are in search of peace. It is a difficult issue whether such people are aware of the importance of the same or not. Usually, it is seen that youngsters and other people go to picnic spots or mountain sides. This is an attempt to have a change from the machine life to a peaceful state where one feels about other dimensions of life.

Peace can be an important factor for students, teachers, family members, businessmen, industrialists or any human being. Without it, one cannot do any work. Creative writing or a piece of art is never possible unless there is 'tranquillity'. Interestingly, disturbance has become a part and parcel of our daily life. A sensitive man, a literary figure, a fine artist, a thinker or philosopher can not be happy if this condition prevails any longer. Intelligentsia can also hampered to a great extent.

Man is of course not a machine. Even in the case of machines, the 'Rest' is the ultimate requirement. For human mind too, 'Rest' is a prime factor for healthy creation.

Everywhere a state of restlessness is pravailing. Natural settings have been encroached by the industrial expansions. Instead of listening and enjoying the songs of nightingales, cuckoo and skylark we are used to listen sirens, whistles, unpleasant sounds produced by different machines etc.

Terrorism and extremism have become integral parts of human life. Scholars and intellectuals are highly against it. They wish to restore peace. Human life is very important . If it is not given by a human being, must not be attempted to take by any one. Even if one is alive he is unhappy due to disturbance and state of restlessness for many reasons. Ass human being, we must also try to establish peace and improve upon the prevailing situation. It would be a modest contribution towards humanity. Service offered to society or humanity is in other way, a service to God.

Politicians have been trying their level best to fight against terrorism or extremism. But, the attempts are insufficient as it is felt that the endeavours are politics-based. Had we been trying to work for the spread of real peace in order to promote society by defending the most fundamental right of a man to live a peaceful life.

Such kinds of teaching can never be possible unless the Indians are really educated. The people are biased and jealous. Sometimes they are found to be highly against other people. They fight due to casteism, racism, religion, political affiliations and so on, and forget the oneness and unity. The feeling of togetherness, solidarity, brotherhood, we-feeling, nationalism and above all humanism have been missing from the hearts of most people. The bad shape of the present society is just because of such factors.

Education is the means of inculcating values. As regards value education, peace should also hold a very significant role in the process of education. If the present educational system really wishes to achieve its targets, it has to train its teachers properly to impart knowledge about humanity, national feeling, democracy, secularism, socialism, equality of opportunities etc. or, we have to face such problems throughout the existing society. And, peace would obviously become a dream.

* * * * *

PEACE EDUCATION: PHILOSOPHICAL VIEWPOINT

Concepts like Philosophy, Art and Education are almost forgotten in this society. No one wants to know about such noble concepts. The level of right kind of education is very low. Those who are educated have different purposes of their education that consequently affect their targets of lives. Philosophy, misunderstood by many, is something that has to do anything with realities of life. As believed by many Art is the domain of those who belong to another world. Education is treated by majority of illiterates as wastage of time. Such attitude among people is really a serious issue for future. People's thinking and ideologies generally lead to practical aspect of life. In other words, what we think we generally act and accordingly achieve.

Art is the outcome of Philosophy. What one professes one wants to exhibit the same in an artistic piece whatever the form or type: novel, drama, poetry or fine arts like painting sculpture of photography.

Art is the preserver of beauty and beauty according to John Keats (an eminent Romantic poet) is Truth and Truth is perhaps synonymous to God. Every beautiful thing attracts an individual, however, parameter of beauty varies. Art and philosophy are correlated as one depends on the other. It is said that every artist is a good philosopher. On the other hand, a individual may have some ideas but it is not necessary that he is a philosopher.

Education is the greatest achievement for an individual. It also depends on people's Philosophy. Education is now considered as status symbol. Besides, it is a necessity, pursued for employment and also for the sake of an all round development.

Education has many dimensions. It is related to sociology, politics, economics, psychology, philosophy and religion. Sociologically, it is betterment of society. Politically, it is process of making of citizens. From economic point of view, it is an investment while from viewpoint of psychology, it is a development of personality. From the viewpoint of philosophy, it is attainment of truth while religious point of view differs a bit and focuses on the attainment of spiritual advancement.

If one delves deep all the definitions share one thing common as they highlight the centrality of an individual. Betterment of society is not possible without amelioration of human being. Making of citizenship is not possible without education of human being. Right investment remain a dream unless individuals are rightly educated. Development of personality is not possible unless an individual fulfills requirements. Attainment of Truth is only possible when an individual has a philosophical outlook and penetrating insights into certain social issues. Similarly, spiritual advancement can't be achieved if a man does not have socio-moral education and the knowledge of the purpose of the creation of he world.

Thus, it may be said that an individual is the most important part. Now the purpose of an individuals' life needs elaboration. An individual does a lot of thing in this fast progressing society. He is awfully busy and works like a machine. The questions why does an individual involves himself in so many activities if he is mortal. If we ponder we get frustrated. Why does a man get education? Why does one earn money? Why does he worship? Why does he serve his parents? Why does one aspire to get a good life partner? And why does an individual wish to go to a hill station? There is one and only answer: PEACE.

A man earns money to get physical comforts, to provide better life standard to family members and children, to attain desired social status, to have some peaceful moment. One gets education to understand the ultimate purpose of life. A man worships God in order to please Him, thus gets peace. He wishes to marry a good partner so that a mental understanding can be attained and life may be proved to be peaceful. In all these activities, one consciously or unconsciously responds for the attainment of Peace.

An artist, by making a creative piece does nothing except satisfying his artistic zeal. He may/may not have some pre-conceived notions. As said by an English poet/critic. It may be a 'spontaneous overflow of powerful feelings and emotions; recollected in tranquility'. An artist creates or recreates something in order to get peaceful state of mind but he can't do it unless his mind is peaceful. So, peace and creation are the cause and effect. Similarly, a student can't achieve educational target if he does not have peace. The entire society would be reduced to chaos in the absence of peace and human beings will live wild life. And Peace is possible only if the society is rightly educated. Industrialization is causing a lot of problem to restoration of peace and we are not able to control or check industrialization for our worldly needs and achievements. Machines and Technological developments have pushed a man away from a peaceful place.

Villages in the past were very peaceful. Still there exists greater peace than in towns or cities. Homes are now quite disturbed. There seems to be a chaos every place. A peace loving man seems to be disturbed and unable to do much for the restoration of peace. There is sound of machines, horns of vehicles, sirens of factories, sounds of audio-visuals in place of chirping of birds and singing of nightingale or skylarks. Sometimes an ordinary voice of a man seems to be bothering due to the fact that a man seeks some peaceful state of mind and body. Man would to be senseless if this situation prevails for a long time.

The present age is faced with a lot of political geographical disputes. It may lead to destruction of an ideal situation that a human being needs. Psychologically, there is no mental rest. From spiritual point of view, every one feels that there is lack of harmony and peace conducive to spiritual advancement. In short, in almost all the spheres of social life, there is an urgent need of peace. Thus, Peace Education is a must, keeping the present socio-political and spiritual sates in view.

Peace Education may be defined as a kind or mode of Education for the attainment of Peace Like other types of Education i.e. Science Education, health Education, Language Education etc. Peace Education is also connected with different aspects of Education. The aspects may be summed up as : Educational objectives, curriculum and textbooks, Methodology, Teacher and Evaluation etc.

Educational Objectives

In order to attain Peace, Educational objectives should accordingly be formulated. And, the question what, why and how Peace Education should properly be linked.

Curriculum

Curriculum includes all the educational activities that are carried out for the attainment of the objectives laid down by the policy makers. Curricular or Extracurricular activities may lead to the attainment of the Educational targets. However, activities within the classroom may impart Peace Education in a more appropriate manner. Therefore, curriculum should be designed in such a manner so that the objectives of achieving peace should be attained by those who are involved in the entire process.

Textbooks

Textbooks are the means of achieving educational targets. These should be nicely written keeping the general as well as specific objectives in view. Peace and its related topics may be included in the books of politics/civics. It is also a fact that certain general topics have already been attempted in such books but it is needed to improve. Books of language and literature, sociology etc. may include some good topics pertaining to peace. Later, at higher stage, philosophy and anthropology can have some good books dealing with mental and spiritual peace. In short, social studies and social sciences, in particular, can deal with the area of peace Education, therefore, good books with such topics may be provided for the attainment of objectives of Peace.

Methodology

Methodology is another very important educational activity. If it is not upto the mark, the objectives of Education can't be achieved even if the textbooks – designing and planning is very good. It is not always important that a lesson emphasizing Peace is directly included in the textbooks, but, the same may indirectly be taught through appropriate methodology. Methodology can be updated by latest innovations. Besides, teaching experience as well as appropriate training with innovative blend may be utilised suitably.

Teacher

Teacher is perhaps the most important factor in all educational activities. It is certainly the hub of the mechanism. Educational administration including teacher achieve the targets laid down by the policy makers. Teacher, if he tries, can impart knowledge pertaining to 'Peace' with the help of certain topics included in the textbooks prescribed for particular level of students. Besides, a teacher can make use of other teaching and non-teaching materials and opportunities to infuse with the sense of peace.

The teacher should be peace-loving. He must understand the concept of Gandhi's 'Ahimsa' and Wordsworthian 'solitude'. He should be highly philosophical in nature, spiritual by heart and an idealist by temperament. Classroom discipline is also related to peace.

Evaluation

It is the last activity of the whole teaching/ learning or educational activity. Evaluation of Peace Education is as difficult as the evaluation of any other philosophical dimension. However, it can indirectly be done in most cases. Indirect techniques may surely help the evaluation of attainment of those objectives that are directly or indirectly related to Peace Education. Attitude test or projective techniques may be provided to be helpful in the process of evaluation of the achievement of targets.

In sum, Peace Education is the most urgent demand of the present society. It is imperative from philosophical, political and social point of view. Without attainment of Peace, the humanity may face a tough time. The entire educational process particularly textbooks and teachers may be found to be more important agent than any other for the promotion of peace among human beings.

* * * *

JEHAD AND PEACE IN ISLAM

Islam has many contexts. Etymologically, it has been derived from the Arabic word 'Salaam' that means 'peace'. Thus, Islam means a concept related to peace. Many scholars are of the view that Islam is the religion of peace.

Philosophically, it is a noble doctrine, a chosen way of life. Sociologically, Islam depends on togetherness, solidarity and 'we feeling'. From the view point of politics, there are evidence in Islamic history about the concept of politics and the way noble companions handled the situation after holy Prophet Mohammad (PBUH) left this world.

Educationally, Islam is very strong. The very first revelation from Almighty Allah is about 'Reading' and later, it was supported by Prophet Mohammad (PBUH) when he advised people to receive education even if one had to go to China. In Islam, Education is considered synonymous to light and illiteracy to darkness.

The concept of 'Tolerance' in Islam is very popular. Once a noble companion was fighting with a disbeliever. While doing so, he overcame his opponent and sat on his chest. In order to take revenge, the disbeliever spit on him consequently the noble companion got down. It was known later that he did so because that matter had become personal. Indirectly this incidence showed personal tolerance. In Islam, it is allowed to take revenge but those who tolerate and forgive are greater people.

The criticism that Islam receives is mostly due to concept of Jihad, however, this noble concept is normally misunderstood. And, this kind of misunderstanding is not only found among non-Muslims but also among many Muslims. 'Jihad' comes from the word 'Jahada' that literally means 'to endeavour'. Literally 'Jihad' can be defined as a fighting against wrong doers who came on the way of right and virtuous deeds. Undoubtedly, Jihad may lead to killings but it should have a sound reason. Otherwise, in Islam it is strictly prohibited even to kill an animal or a bird without a real reason.

The idea of revenge and the concept of force may be found to be related to 'Jihad'. In Islam, only self-defence is allowed. A man can't be forcefully handled without a reason. Even a man is not allowed to take his life because it is believed that Allah has given life to people so one has no right to kill oneself.

Going back to Jihad again, it is clearly stated to have patience before going to war.

> "And for the sake of your lord be patient" (LXX IV:7)

Another time *Quran* says

> "And whoever is patient and forgiving, that most surely is of the affairs the doing of which should be determined upon". (XLII : 42, 43)

Not only has patience been so strongly recommended to avoid hasty action but has been discouraged also. Hasty action has been considered as the action of Satan.

> "Yet surely your lord with respect to those who fly after they are persecuted, then they struggle hard and are patient, most surely your Lord after that is Forgiving, Merciful". (X VI: 110)

Quran is not silent. It speaks boldly as follow:

> "These shall be rewarded with high places because they were patient, and shall be met herein with greetings and salutation".

> "Abiding therein, goodly the abode and the resting place!" (XXV : 75, 76).

Quran is very clear about war and peace. It orders to avoid war if possible and induce others to avoid it. But, if one is forced, can fight.

> "And fight in the way of Allah with those who fight with you, and do not exceed the limits, surely Allah does not love those who exceed the limits". (II,190)

As regard self-defence, *Quran* says clearly, "And kill them (who fight against you) wherever you find them and drive them out from where they drove your out and persecution is severer than slaughter...." (II, 191)

A Muslim is supposed to fight always for justice, he is not worth his salt if he fights for injustice.

> "Those who believe fight in the way of Allah, and those who disbelieve fight in the way of Devil. Fight therefore against the friends of Devil; surely the struggle of Devil is but weak" (IV : 76)

It is said in Islam to be moderate before joining a cause because it might be unjust. It is also suggested that one should not consider every disbeliever as the enemy of Islam. Rather doubts should be cleared and removed.

> "One you who believe! When you go to war in Allah's way, make investigations, and do not say to any one who offers you peace. (IV : 94)

If we interpret the orders of Quran it will be quite clear that before going to war, a muslim must be clear about his aims and objectives. Every war can not be Jihad. Peace has been considerably emphasised, and a peace loving Muslim does not enjoy less prestigious reputation and status than a Muslim who joins a war without a mission. As we have seen in the opening paragraphs of this paper that Islam is a peaceful religion, and whatever war was fought, it was for the sake of restoration of peace and an ideal society. The wars of Islamic concepts were fought for making the people better and society based on humanitarian values. Prophet Mohammad (PBUH), the leader of muslims had never been aggressive throughout his life

An example of neighborhood can be cited here. It is said in Islam that a person's food is illegal if his neighbour is hungry. It is never said that the neighbour should be a muslim only. General behaviour should be good so that even a disbeliever would be bound to think about good principles of Islam, consequently he may embrace the same.

At the time of Prophet Mohammad (PBUH), when he used to walk down the street, an old woman used to through garbage on him. Once she did not do. Prophet Mohammad (PBUH) asked the people of that locality about the woman. He was told about her sickness. People would be surprised to know that he went to ask after her health and finally the lady was so impressed that she embraced Islam then and there.

Islam is the religion that has duly praised and recommended Equality, Socialism, Democracy, Brotherhood, Neighbourhood, Sacrifice etc. so that people of the Nation can restore unity and peace.

Peace is the ultimate purpose of life. It is highly philosophical in nature. Every muslim is asked to shower peace on other mulsim in the form of Assalam-O-Elaikum.

When we talk about even prophets we wish them peace (peace be upon him/them) Besides, a muslim is ordered to wish peace for those who are resting in graveyards.

Finally, when Allah asks muslim to follow right path, in return, He promises heaven/ paradise. Heaven is believed to be a peaceful place. Therefore, it can be said that peace is the highest reward even from Almighty Allah's side. In this world even, every individual is interested in having peace of mind and spirit. If a muslim is a true follower of Islam he will be peace loving. He should try his level best to ensure and enforce peace in the country and the entire world.

* * * * *

ISLAM, PHILOSOPHY AND PEACE

The concept of Islam according to many people is highly philosophical, however, Philosophy itself is not even properly understood by a particular group of Muslims. They perhaps think the two being contradicting while the fact is something entirely different.

Philosophy can be roughly defined as 'The way of life' which also includes religion. Besides, if we consider even the technical definition of Philosophy as 'The logical enquiry into the nature of Reality', it does not go against Islam. In Quran, it has been stated that one may use brain or positive logical thinking to decide what is right and what is wrong. Moreover, the philosophical dimension of any thought must not make any attempt to contradict however, deliberately the noblest ideas that exist in holy Quran. And, any kind of such thinking is not allowed to question for the sake of only questions, but, obviously possible for the purpose of reaching near God or the ultimate 'Truth'.

Peace, a philosophical concept, received momentum in the recent past. Since then, it has been dealt morally and spiritually by plenty philosophers and literary figures. It is highly philosophical in nature and very much dealt with in Islam as well. Peace has many aspects: individual and social/political; physical and spiritual; peace-here and life here after. Peace can be considered as an eternal phenomenon and also a state/condition after a war of destruction. It could have prevailed even before the creation of the world and it may be found after the process of making was over. Besides, it is a post-destruction scenario.

Many articles/papers have been attempted in the recent past both in general field as well as keeping the Islamic considerations in view. Etymologically, the words-Islam and Muslim are derived from the root of the term 'salam' that means soundness, well being, peace, peacefulness, safety, security (Dictionary of Modern Written Arabic by Hans Wehr: 1976).

It is needed here to enlist a few words that are perhaps from the same root word 'salaam'. Istilam means 'takingover' or 'acceptance' while Istislam means 'surrender' or 'submission'. Islam also means 'submission', resignation 'reconciliation' (to the will of God). In Arabic, Al-Islam is the religion that is characterised by a particular belief or faith professed or preached by the last Prophet Mohammed (PBUH). Further, to talk about the etymological significance of the word 'Muslim' we have to see and understand a few words of the same family like 'Musalim' and 'Musallam'. The former means peaceable, peaceful, peace-loving, mild, tempered lenient, gentle etc. while latter means unimpaired, intact, flawless and a Muslim (the follower of Islam) etymologically symbolises peace and submission. It might have been in the recent past, a very peaceful place. In addition, Dar-As salaam (place of peace) symbolises Paradise. 'Ya salaam' is an exclamation of dismay that means Good Lord! or Good Heavens! Assalam-o-Elaikum, the ordinary salutation of Muslims means 'peace be with you'.

It is said that a muslim should say 'Salaam-o-Elaikum' when he goes to or passes by any graveyard because it helps in attaining spiritual peace for those who have been buried long ago or even before a few days. It serves the same purpose of wishing peace for a dead or an alive.

Mayas-salaam is a greeting of farewell (goodbye), is philosophically based on the idea of peace, safety and security. In addition, peace is the basis of the respected words used for prophets before Mohammed (PBUH) and himself. For prophets before him, people used to say 'Alaihe-As-Salaam (upon him be peace) and for Mohammed (PBUH) Sallalaḥ-u-Alaihe-Wasallam that is a respected word which means peace be upon him.

If one tries to go deeper into all the greetings of Muslims

or salutations or the words used to honour and respect, peace (salaam) is common in all. An ordinary muslim wishes peace for another muslim, a muslim greets/wishes or respects prophets including Mohammed (PBUH) by wishing peace. When a muslim sees/welcomes a muslim he wishes peace and when he says good bye to any one he wishes the same. Therefore, it may be said that peace is the ultimate purpose of one's life.

Thus, in Islam, the concept 'Peace' bears a great significance. Peace in society is important from individual point of view when he has a physical entity. When he departs from here, peace becomes more important therefore, a muslim wants to offer 'namaz' to his Almighty and tries to fulfill other Islamic requirements so that there is peace in his grave. A muslim finally worries about the day of judgement. He, therefore, wishes an utmost peaceful place which is none other than 'paradise' that has been promised by Allah for only virtuous mulsims. When a muislim says good bye to this material world a lot of his friends and family members recites holy Quraan so that his/her soul may further be blessed by Almighty's mercy and enjoys complete peace and serenity. Thus, peace is important in either of the case. Now, it depends on an individual to choose his ways. It would be one's own target to facilitate his worldly life or life hereafter.

The concept 'Jehad' is often contrasted to the vision of Peace. Both have equal importance in Islam. Quraan and Hadith have treated these concepts differently in different contexts.

Jehad is basically supported in Islam as a matter of revenge or reaction. However, it has been vividly mentioned at almost all places to forgive than to take revenge. It is only permissible when there is no other option.

Quraan says, "And for the sake of your Lord patient" (LXX IV:7)

One other occasion, Quraan sates, "One you who believe! When you go to war in Allahs way, make investigation, and do not say to any one who offers you peace. (IV:94).

These can be plently other examples that can be cited in this regard. The only thing is to understand the noble concept of peace which is preferred to Jehad many times in Quraan and Hadith. However, it has been felt that in order to establish an eternal peace one is free to adapt measures of temporary violence. Therefore, one can fight primarily for one's religion and also for nation.

Brotherhood and universality in Islam enjoy a great reputation as holy Quraan often addresses by calling, 'O! the people of he world' or 'O! People'. Besides, it also referred at more than one place, to prophet Mohammed that he was sent as 'blessing'(Rahmat) for worlds.

Neighborhood in Islam also bears great significance. It is clearly mentioned that food eaten by a neighbour will be 'Haraam' (disallowed) if there is no food to eat in neighbour's house. It may point towards importance of neighbourhood. There is no reference of caste, creed, race or religion of neighbours. Thus, it is evident that man to man relation; neighbour to neighbour relation is more important because the entire social life is an accord, an agreement and the life is synonymous to peace. There is no concept of life without peace. Besides, peace is also synonymous to agreement or accord.

The concept of justice is closely related to peace. Without it peace may appear to be a far fetched concept. In order to promote justice and peace, Islam issued a few very strong recommendations. About a thief, it is legal in Islam to punish him even by chopping off his hand or hands. Similarly, if one kills someone without a reason he will be killed by the judiciary of the Islamic country. However, there is a process that ensures the evidence against the accused whether right, and only if it is proved, the action of legal justice is taken. The action seems to be very cruel but the idea is highly noble. People are afraid to commit any crime because of the thought of the action usually taken by Islamic judiciary.

Thus, we may say that at he time of the last prophet and even now muslims follow some strict laws that can take life of the sinner or criminal. If it is a matter of religion one may even kill the evil character. Some example of this kind of action may be found during he time of Lord Rama. During the exile period, he had to fight against a very powerful king 'Ravana' who symbolises 'evil' and in order to teach him a lesson for his action noble wife of Rama a battle was fought. Finally, Rama won the battle because he was right. However, he was supported by his brother 'Lakshman' and a great admirer 'Hanuman'.

The above mentioned facts do not go against the philosophical concept of 'Ahimsa'. What prophet Mohammed (PBUH), lord Rama and lord Krishna did was the need of the time and the only solution to such problems. In fact, Ahimsa' prohibits the killing of a living being for no genuine reason. It is also in every religion that one must not kill any living being for no reason but, if there is a reason one can be aggressive even violent in order to eradicate the root of the evil. And, this is religion. This kind of consideration were the basis of the battle of 'Mahabharata' and the battle fought by lord Rama because Ravana symbolised 'evil'.

While summing up, it may be stated that Islam is an agreement – between creatures and the Creator; the followers and the God; the help seeking and the Almighty; the sinners and the Divine who forgives. Peace is an agreement between people and society and nation. Philosophy is the search of knowledge – knowledge of the ultimate reality which constitute the demand of life. And, an individual is believed to demand 'Peace' from his life what ever type he is living.

Politically, Islam includes the concept of war and peace. There has been many wars (battles) in Islamic history for the betterment of society or for the making of an ideal society. The term 'ideal' may symbolise a peaceful state or country. Similarly, the concept 'war for peace' is also available in Islam. There have been many wrong doers at a particular time, therefore, Islamic people fought temporary wars in order to restore permanent or atleast long term peace. Peace after war is but natural. It is both physical and spiritual. After each war, there is a deathly calm and silence and later in the life of people. If the purpose of the war is achieved, peace prevails.

To be very precise, peace is synonymous to well being, satisfaction, contentment, serenity etc. In Islam, 'Peace' has a greater significance. It deals with all the three dimensions of peace—peace in society, peace in grave and peace hereafter (in Heaven). Peace is a philosophical concept. Philosophy is the way of life. One developes a philosophical outlook on the basis of life experiences. Islam is also a way of life adapted by Muslims so it includes many concepts related to philosophy. There are many noble ideas in Islam as found in Quraan and Hadith, reflected through the life activities of the last prophet Mohammed (PBUH). The following is an example of philosophy of Islam which can be explained as a contribution to the field of Education. "Al-Eilm khairan men-al maal" (Education is better than money/property). This sentence indirectly serves a socio-economic purpose of control over people who are greedy and wish to earn and save money and do not want to get education, and prefer saving money.

In this context, if we follow the noble sayings of prophet and other noble Islamic personalities, money is considered a material achievement which can give comfort only. It may make an individual highly competitive that may lead to corruptions and evil activities. While, there can be peace of mind even without money and other material achievements. Education can be considered as one of the means of getting satisfaction and peace.

Education appears to be a process and sometimes a target itself. Thus, it may be concluded that without education nothing can be achieved in this world. It is education that leads to the philosophical considerations which ultimately focus on the final and the most important achievement of life and that is peace.

* * * * *

EDUCATION, PEACE AND DEVELOPMENT

In order to study the relation between the above three concepts it is required to know the definitions and scopes of the same.

Education has been defined in many ways. The attempt of defining depends on the background of the person who looks at it.

Basically there are five contexts of education: Social, psychological, political, economic and philosophical.

Sociologically, education is betterment of Society. From the view point of a psychologist, it is development of personality. Politically, it is making of better and efficient citizenship while an economist considers 'Education as an investment'. A philosopher looks at it in a different way and defines it by saying 'development of inner and spiritual self'.

Moreover, all these definitions of education has one thing common development. Thus, development is a very important concept. It is rather qualitative in nature that is the ultimate aim of Education and life.

In the opinion of many educational scholars, life and education are synonymous. The approach is highly philosophical. It can be interpreted that life without Education is worthless which can be compared with the life of animals. Further, education is the means of life. It gives insight to live a proper life. It enables an individual to discriminate between good and bad, right and wrong, proper and improper, vice and virtue, legal and illegal, legitimate and illegitimate, just and unjust etc. It is education that discriminates between a man and animal. Man has been considered in Islam as the superior most creature obviously because of his life style. And, style of life can not be understood without an ability to think about it. And, this ability can not be developed without proper education.

The concept, 'Peace' is highly philosophical, however, it has also five contexts. Each concept will be dealt in detail, later in this paper but, let us first define the concept 'Peace'.

Peace is a mental and spiritual state or condition. It is probably the most ideal condition which every human being wishes to enjoy.

In Islam, Peace (Salaam) is highly significant. Interestingly to note, the concept Islam has been derived from the word 'Salaam' (Peace). Thus, Islam as religion, etymologically, is peaceful. In Hinduism, 'Shanti' is also duly emphasised. Usually in temples, peace prevails and worshippers get peace while worshipping. Spiritually, the concept 'Peace' is highly significant. Ravindera Nath Tagore, a Poet and a Philosopher lived a life in search of peace. In order to realise goals related to peace, he even founded 'Shanti-Niketan' in order to get peace through education and education in peaceful environment.

Wordsworth, an eminent romantic-mystic poet of English also aspired to get peace. He tried to find out a perfectly serene and content place where he could place his beloved innocent girl 'lucy'. However, all the places discovered by him were truly 'Nature-oriented'.

Lord Tennyson has also referred to such places and wished to abandon worldly life particularly after so much experience of life. Thomas Gray has been found to be a great admirer of peace and 'Natural' scenery. In his attempt towards 'Elegy Written in Country Churchyard', there is a clear description and admiration of peace.

The life that a 'Sadhu' lives on mountains is not less important than a life in a 5-star hotel. What matters is the perception and attitude of a person. There is no denying the fact that the mystic's life attains peace and one who lives in luxurious buildings and hotels get comfort. Bodily comforts are important but not more required than the sheer peace of mind and soul.

People who are businessman earning lot of money can't promise to have peace—the ultimate purpose of human life. He, however, can get apparent satisfaction of his needs as he fulfills his day to day requirement. These daily needs are self-created. If there is a check on such ambitions and worldly hopes, a person having nothing can attain mental peace and satisfaction. Satisfaction has been mentioned in Holy Quran that states, "Allah is with those who are satisfied". In Hinduism, a lot of such references can be cited. Lord Kirshna has delivered many instructions relating such noble concepts in Mahabharta. Poets like Wordsworth opine that poetry is 'Spantaneous overflow of powerful feelings and emotions recollected in Tranquality". By 'Tranquality' he meant Peace.

Refering to Islam again, it has been agreed that Islam assures everyone's security and peace at every place. Islam is the message of peace, security and prosperity. It is the message of brotherhood of Adam's generation. Brotherhood in Islam is the means of Peace. Prophet Mohammad (PBUH) used to treat, look after and ask about the health and welfare of even non-believers.

While preaching the noble concepts of Islam at Makkah the Prophet was forced to migrate then even he prayed for peace and welfare of the people of the locality. The prophet gave the message of Universal brotherhood, peace, security, welfare and humanity to each and everyone. In the court of prophet Mohammed, everyone occupied the same place and importance, be an Arab or a non-Arab, be a white or a black. Quran confirms Allah as 'Lord of the worlds'. For Prophet Mohammed (PBUH) it (Quran) says, 'Rah-mat-ul-lil-Alameen' (light and mercy of the worlds). Everywhere in Quran and Islam, there exists a noble concept of 'Oneness' and that leads to universal brotherhood.

Further, Islam accepts thousands of Prophets before the last prophet, Mohammed (PBUH). It gives respects to Christ, Moses, Noah, Ibrahim, Ismael, Ishaq, Yusuf, Yaqoob etc. (PBUT). And, it gives order to the followers of Islam to respect those messengers and their preachings. This sentiments and ideologies lead to respect for others, togetherness, solidarity, brotherhood etc. Moreover, Allah does not want disturbances, fights etc. therefore, we the offspring of Adam must also try to maintain peace.

In sum, Islam is a name and expression of peace, security, good deeds, affection and respect of others and nice behaviour towards fellow beings.

In other religions too, as it has been referred earlier, peace occupies a very important place. The concept of Ashram where lord Rama got training under the supervision of Kul-Guru (family Teacher) is an example of peace education. However, they got training to fight for the sake o defending 'Right' against 'Wrong' in order to restore and maintain Peace. Besides, Lord Rama was always an admirer of peace. If we compare him with his brother Laxman we will find him a young blood and aggressive. But, Rama never out bursted in emotion and remained calm. Such expressions are evident in Ramayana.

Other sacred scriptures of India are also not silent on Peace. The last hymn of the Rigveda has the following words to remind us of the need for untiy and peace among human beings:

"Sam gacchhadhavam Sam Vadadram
Sam Vo manamst janatam
Samani Va akutih, Samana hrdayanivah
Yatha VahSusha Sati."

(Translation: Walk together, speak in harmony, let your mind receive/ comprehend alike, let you be unite while doing something, let your hearts be in agreements, let our thinking be united, that we all may be happy).

There are many Hindu Mystics, philosophers and poets who have been primarily a 'peace-lover'. Pt. Ravindra Nath Tagore can be exemplified as the pioneer of peace-philosophy. Shanti Niketan in Bengal is the practical side of his philosophy.

Christianity, maybe considered as the most popular religion of the world. We cannot neglect the importance of the prophet who preached his noble concepts of philosophy of religion. Jesus Christ in this respect can be referred who said "Love all hate none". This leads to his peace loving philosophy for which he has been rightly considered as the Prince of Peace. He came to this world to materialise some noble mission, he achieved. Peace is an aspect of his noble mission.

Jesus is Peace, Peace is his name, announced the Peace-prophecies that proceeded his birth. "For to us a child is born, to us a son is given, and the government will be upon his shoulder and his name will be called wonderful counselor, Mighty God, ever lasting father, Prince of Peace" (Isaiah 9:6).

The actions and deeds of Peace that Jesus initiated went beyond any race, religion, caste, creed and political boundaries. If we attempt to discuss about Peace mission of Jesus we must go through His Gospels which are full of his message of Peace and unity. Jesus lived in Gospels as the source of Peace. Therefore, the peace and forgiveness of Jesus never even failed the worst sinner.

Jesus Christ's education to offer another cheek to one who hits some one's cheek was an example of tolerance and peace-loving mind. Jesus Christ's gesture proved the education of peace in a noble manner presenting oneself very humble, polite and tolerant. He was even crucified and did not complain. More or less all the noble creatures particularly saints, mystics, messengers, prophets etc. have been found to be peace-loving and humanitarian in nature. What ever they did was for the betterment of the society and development of mankind.

It is now time of discuss 'Development'. It is a substantial change in behaviour, society or economy. It is rather qualitative in nature and results as an effect.

Development of peace has been one of the major themes and aims of education. Sociologists, anthropologists, politicians are .concerned with restoration of peace. Spiritual people,.

right from the beginning until now aspire to attain peace. Thus, peace and development of peace is the ultimate purpose of society.

Educational Development has been the target since the independence struggle. In 1944, Sargent plan for Educational Development was a comprehensive blue-print for the development of education at every stage. After Independence, education and literacy was given top priority. In 1948, Mudaliar Commission, Radhakrishnan Commission in 1952, Indian Education Commission (1964), New Education Policy (1986), Program of Action (1990) and later Rama Murthi Commission etc. are the documents of the planning and policies of Indian government to develop the status of Education in India.

In spite of all the attempts that Indian government has been making from time to time to raise the educational standard in India, the country could not realise its aims. It remains a target what the country conceived in 1944. There can be a little difference in the ratio or percentage of literate / educated people but as a whole almost all of the population still is ignorant of education.

The Government of India has been trying to achieve the desired level of Science Education, Technical Education, Computer Education, Value Education etc. On the other hand, Peace Education has been felt to be much more important for many reasons. Education of Peace is the most desired aim in this fast moving society which is characterised by materialism.

There are many factors that affect peace: personal factor, socio-psychological factor, economic factor, political factor, educational factor, religious factor and philosophical factor etc.

Peace is itself a factor that affects one's personality and over all development. It is a very prominent factor that leads to economic and industrial development. It is also a factor that is responsible for political stability. Peace is rightly said to be a factor that leads to spiritual attainment. It enriches poetic excellence.

Peace and Politics: A new dimension—Peace in relation to politics is very crucial in this atomic age. UNO's function has primarily been in the direction of restoration and establishment of peace all the world over. A nation can't develop without Peace. Therefore, world-development is also not possible without establishment of peace. Peace is a boon to any country on the other hand, war is a curse which may be either internal or external.

The entire world is interested in establishing peace in South Asia because there are some crucial issues that every socially aware person knows. And, nations have developed difference of thoughts and policies for many reasons. In addition, terrorism is also one of the main issues prevailing in this society. Whatever is the mission behind the act it affects a lot and the effects are evident. Such kinds of problems may cordially be resolved with the intervention of the third party preferably UNO.

Peace and Society: The Urgent Need—A society is a group of human beings. A man can't live without peace. He can work actively, he can be highly productive, he can be truly creative only if he is in peaceful condition. If one is restless or disturbed he may not be able to put his efforts and prove his talents in proper direction and his abilities may be wasted to some extent.

Peace within a man, peace in the group or family and peace in society or community is the urgent need of time. It can be achieved with a proper understanding and harmony.

Peace and Religion: A Philosophy—Religion is itself a

philosophy. It primarily depends on a peaceful, spiritual and mental state/ condition. 'Muslims' namaaz or Hindu's worship can never be possible without peace. In Christianity also, peace enjoys a great importance. Lord Budha was also great admirer of peace. In short, in all the religious beliefs, Peace is the basic condition.

Religion is also defined as a way of life. And life is no life without Peace of mind. Bodily Comforts may be very important but mental and spiritual peace is much more important than any other thing.

A religious man gets peace when he prostrate before Allah or bows down before an idol.

The Ultimate Aims of Life

Life is the outcome of a philosophy. It is highly complicated concept to understand. The operational definition of life depends on one's education, background and experiences. It may be sweet for one man or sour for another person.

In order to become a complete man, (a man with healthy body and healthy soul), one's life requires 'Education'. Without education, one is not able to discriminate between good and bad, right and wrong, virtue and vice etc. one needs to have proper education. It may lead to the following: personality development, psychological development, moral development, spiritual development, philosophical development etc. Education may lead to development of peace also.

Peace is supposed to be the most important achievement in this century. Every organisation is trying its level best to go ahead for restoration of peace all the world over. Peace processes are initiated everywhere mainly because tension is prevailing everywhere. People are hoping for a congenial situation so that they can live peacefully. Peace is a necessary and primarily condition for human life. Without it, a man can't achieve either education or develop economically or worship or pray properly or even live together.

Development is the top priority. Education is aiming at all kinds of development. Educational institutions are trying to achieve the aim none other than development – the over all development. Education is the means of all kind of development. Economic development helps educational process to achieve other kinds of development. Development of nation includes development of individual, family, society, economy, political development, moral development etc. Governmental agencies aspire to develop nation through various means.

Besides, peace development is also one of the major tasks of the government as well as educational process.

2

Sociology and Education

Sociology is the science of Society and Education is the betterment of the society. Therefore, both of the concepts depend on each other. Sociology as descriptive field of study developed in seventeenth century in the writings of August Comte.

It was later influenced by the French Revolution particularly with the emergence of the concepts like liberty, equality and fraternity. These concepts were later utilised in the area of Education. The industrial and professional revolution drew the attention of the people to the labour class, and it was found that education was necessary for it. Social consciousness also emerged in various classes, and this led to a reduction in the impulse for individualism. This also encouraged the sociological tendency.

SOCIOLOGICAL TENDENCY

Educationists as Pestalozzi, Herbart and Froebel, admitted the influence of sociological factors in the child's development. According to Herbart, the aim of education is the moral development of the individual. Both Herbart and Pestalozzi wanted to educate the child for social welfare. Even Froebel reflects some sociological inclination, for he conceives of the school as a miniature society.

Characteristics of Sociological Tendency

1. *Emphasis on professional or vocational education:* The sociological tendency lays stress on enabling the child to earn his livelihood through professional or vocational education.

2. *Revolt against individualism:* The sociological tendency was born out of reaction to individualism. It lays emphasis on the importance of collective society.

3. *Social Development as the ultimate aim of education:* Social welfare is the aim ascribed to education by the sociological tendency. Children should be trained only for this through a system of free compulsory education. This should make them useful members of society.

4. *Faith in democracy:* The sociological tendency also evinces faith in democracy. In a democracy, education is based on the cooperation between the state and society, and besides, the success of democracy depends upon the education of its members.

5. *Upliftment of the standard:* The ultimate sociological aim is to raise the standard of social life by achieving the child's overall development. Education process must inculcate the individual the value to achieve his social responsibilities.

6. *Importance to social sciences:* The presence of the sociological tendency in education has led to greater importance being attached to the social sciences, so that the child can understand social phenomena and problems, and thus be enabled to make some positive contribution to social welfare.

7. *Education as an agency of social progress:* According to sociologists, education is the best means of social control, social change and thus, finally, of social

progress can be easily brought about through education. Social control becomes a measure of self control through education because education socializes the individual.

Impact of Sociological Tendency

It is clear that education that sociology has had vital influence upon the meaning, objectives, functions of education upon the curriculum, the methods of teaching, the administration etc. These influence can be summarised as under:

1. *Meaning of education:* According to educational sociologists, education is a social process which socializes the child and causes certain charges in his behaviour.
2. *Objective of education:* The objective or aim of education is to evolve those social standard and a social responsibility in the child.
3. *Functions of education:* The educational sociologists have stressed the following functions of education, spread of knowledge, social control, protection of social heritage, social development, curriculum organisation etc.

IMPORTANCE OF SOCIOLOGY IN EDUCATION

Man is a social animal because he is bound to live in a society. He learns and changes his behaviour in relation to the rest of the people. In other words, the existence of a man is not possible without a group of people – society. Therefore, it is important to study the discipline that deals with society and related aspects.

Sociology as a separate branch of knowledge took birth around 1837 from the speeches of August Comte. Thereafter

Herbert Spencer made special contribution to the progress of Sociology in 1876. Writers like Frederic Le Play, Moore, Cole, Duncan, McIver and Merril wrote on various aspects of Sociology. Today, Sociology has become an important discipline.

Sociology deals with the nature of society and man. Scientific method is applied for the study of society. Sociology is regarded as a science because of its scientific nature. In sociology, we study group behaviour. Sociology studies how a man behaves when coming in contact with the other beings. Therefore, it is said that Sociology mainly provides the knowledge of social interaction and relationship.

Since Man lives in a society and shares some behaviour of the group, it influences man's behaviour. Man's personality is developed under these influences. Sociology is the discipline that can explain this sort of characteristics.

There are many branches of Sociology. One of them is educational sociology. George Payne wanted to solve the problems of education on the basis of the principles and facts of sociology. According to him, it would be difficult to determine the aims of education without a knowledge of social interaction. Education is a powerful source of social control, therefore, the knowledge of social control is necessary.

Sociologists like John Dewey, George Counts, Taba and Havighurst have thrown enough light on Educational Sociology. Durkheim in France, Clark and Ottaway in England and Max Weber in Germany worked in the field of Educational Sociology. Educational sociology is a very relevant branch of Education. A country like India where there are different castes, creeds, sects, religion, language and regions etc. A branch like Educational Sociology may help us solve many problems in this country.

The study of Educational Sociology is necessary for every educator, trainer, pedagogue and teacher. The function of education is to make an all-round development of the student's personality. This development is impossible in isolation. Development is always influenced by social contacts. The environment of the child's family influences developments. The impact of the school environment is also important. The culture and environment of the student leaves its picture on his personality. We study all these things in Educational Sociology. Some principles of sociology have proved themselves to be very useful to education. Education is a means of social development. It facilitates healthy social interaction. There is a close relationship between culture and education. All these relationship are analysed in educational sociology.

SCHOOL AND SOCIETY

Society is a group of people and a school is an institution set/established by the society in order to meet some important needs of the same. Plato had also analysed society and presented the background of education accordingly but all educators from Plato and Aristotle down to Hegel emphasized intellect and defined the aim of education as the development of intelligence. Intelligence of human beings are always in demand for the sake of the development and promotion of the society. In their opinion, refinement of intelligence is the ultimate aim of education. According to Darwin's theory of evolution, intelligence developed as a much later process of man's evolution. Persons like Dewey paid attention to the need of adaptation and they admitted adaptation of environment as the fundamental principle of education. The existence of man depends upon his ability of adaptation. His survival would be endangered if he did not establish relationship with social environment.

Psychology has made great contribution to Education. Psychology has given us the knowledge of child's interests and needs. The teacher takes advantage of this knowledge. That is why educational psychology has made progress but unfortunately Educational Psychology has given birth to individualism in education. It has put individual differences before us in a fine way and has advised us to take up educational problems from a scientific point of view. But now it is being experienced that individual outlook would not do.

The existence and progress of society depend on proper education of the coming generations. There is need for an analysis of the ideals and values of society. These ideals and values should be developed in future for the future existence of society. For this the future members of society should have a knowledge of those ideals. Therefore, society takes much interest in education. The role of society in the establishment and manipulation of schools is natural. Sometimes school is called a miniature society. All this proves that there is close relationship between school and society.

The Concept of Society

Society is dynamic. It is progressive and changeable. Stagnation in society is its downfall. Society is a kind of community. A sociologist uses the world 'community' in a specific meaning. According to Cook, "Community is a configuration of land, people and culture, a structured pattern of human relations within a geographic area." Brownell defining a community says, "By a community I mean a small, diversified group of people, young and old, male and female, with different skills and abilities, living together as kin neighbours. It is a face-to-face, primary group, in which many of the major functions of life are carried on co-operatively within the group itself. It is a small group where people know one another as whole persons, not as specialized fragments, and in which they have a sense of 'belonging'. This normal community has been the setting or matrix in which human activities have taken place since immemorial time. To it the human-being is adapted; he is, indeed, a community animal. When this community is dissolved, human life breaks down biologically, morally, even intellectually, and human education becomes futile." An association takes the form of society when its members are awakened towards their style of life and march ahead towards unity being stimulated by common aims and ideals.

There is no significance of the number of members in a society or community. Two or more persons may construct society. Political and economic factors are every important forces in a society. These factors influence the functioning of society. Public opinion and religious views are also effective factors. All these factors help construct society. Now we shall consider something about culture.

EDUCATION AND CULTURE

The study of the culture of a society is necessary in order to understand that society. The whole system of social life is called 'culture. Therefore, it is said that the style of social life is culture. Anthropology makes special study of culture. A sociologist shows special interest in anthropology. In his book 'Sociology', Cuber has defined culture in these words, "In terms of anthropology culture is a continually changing pattern of learned behaviour, including attitudes, values, knowledge and material objects which are shared by and transmitted amongst the members of society."

Since culture is the style of social living. Some aspects of culture remains constant whereas other aspects of culture are in the state of flux. At a particular moment of the history of a nation culture remains in the melting pot. "Culture is constant yet always changing – constant is that certain of its elements, such as language and law persist without major alteration for long periods of time; changing in that all its elements, however gradually and subtly, are undergoing a continuous metamorphosis. Cultural change can take place in at least three ways: (1) New practices may be invented within the culture itself, e.g., progressive education developed within the state (2) Practices may be borrowed from other cultures, (3) Existing practices may be modified to meet fresh circumstances, e.g., extension of aid to education."

Man has got many kinds of needs. There is a method of satisfying these needs. It is this method that makes culture The needs of the individual may be divided mainly in two parts:

(1) Biological needs, and
(2) Psychological needs.

Education and Kinship: Both education and kinship are important institutions of socialisation in the society. Every society introduces gradual socialisation of a child through complex processes which give the child individual identity and the ability to acquire social status and fulfil roles according to it. In the kinship system, the most important role towards socialistion is performed by parental family. The school transfers knowledge from one generation to another and develops intellectual ability. Both kinship and educational institutions develop the value system in a society.

Family is an enduring association of parents and children. Its primary functions are the satisfaction of the members and the socialization of the child. It is a social agency for the education and protection of the race. It is in the family that the child acquires such important qualities as sincerity, sympathy, self submission and consciousness of responsibility, etc. It is the character developed in the family which helps the child in becoming an important and responsible member of any society. In every family, the child gets an opportunity for free expression of thoughts and development of his entire personality. Psychologists have proved that the proper development of the child is impossible without a good environment in the family. The child's first school is his home so family can't be ignored. The child's education should be in the hands of the parents. The parents should participate in all the child's activities. A child learns much by imitating his superiors.

The School as a Social System: After the home, the child exposed to the school which also influences him, for the school is nothing less than a miniature society to him. It socializes him, gives him an opportunity to manifest his qualities, instincts, drives and motives and helps to develop his personality. For the child, the educator's personality and character provide a model which he strives to copy, thereby consciously or unconsciously changing his personality. This is true only of those teachers who succeed arousing in the child's mind an attachment and love for themselves. Even little action, every movement, speech, etc., impresses itself on the child's mind. On the other hand, he is often repelled by some teachers, and he was to contradict them through every act. During the process of education, the child's personality develops under the impact of the other personalities with whom he comes into contact. In the school, the child is disciplined. He is aware that disobedience brings immediate punishment, but too strict a system of discipline restricts the child's mental growth and may even drive him to negative activity. On the other hand, complete absence of control may either make him liberal, free and independent or impulsive. Besides, the cultural programmes of the school also help to refine his attitudes.

In this manner, the human personality is profoundly influenced both by the home and the school. Of the two, the family influence lasts for a longer time and is more comprehensive.

EDUCATION AND SOCIAL STRATIFICATION

Social stratification whether open or close, is very much concerned with education. Social mobility is very much influenced by castes, religious groups and classes. All these influence the mental progress of the child through education. Thus social stratification governs the type of education which a particular individual will be able to secure. This is clear from the influence of castes, religious groups and classes upon education in India.

(i) Influence of Castes: It is sometimes the caste which determines the individual's status and position in the social hierarchy. One finds elements of the caste system even among the Muslims. In the caste, the professions and occupations of the lower castes are predetermined and fixed, and the child aims at adopting the occupation of his own caste. Since the child is almost compelled to adopt the same profession as his forefathers, he is inevitably exposed to the rules of untouchability which operate between his caste and a superior caste. This creates very undesirable prejudices and gives rise to narrow mindedness in the child. The caste system has had the effect of splitting the society into many small segments, and this fragmentation obviously hinders the development of national unity. Besides, it is also responsible for the child's awareness of discrimination and distinction between individuals and the consequent feelings of superiority and inferiority. In this way, the presence of many different castes hinders the child's mental progress.

(ii) Impact of Religious Groups: India is plurocultural state. In India one can see many religious groups such as Hindus,

Muslims, Christians, Buddhists, Sikhs and Jains, etc. Most of these religious groups have established and are maintaining many religious schools in which general religion is taught, along with their own respective religious teachings. Most of these schools try to inculcate a particular set of religious principles in the educand. In many ways, the teaching of religious principles can be of benefit to the child and the community, but when teaching in the school contradicts or ridicules teaching in another school, it naturally gives rise to a consciousness of differences between one religion and another. The best course is to inculcate the general principle of religion, stressing the fact that the purpose of all the religions are one and the same, for without this, religion, can only lead to narrow minded thinking.

(iii) Impact of Classes: Social class has the most potent influence on the child. On the one hand, we find some sort of discrimination based on religion and caste, but on the other, we find a growing consciousness of the class one comes from, thus intensifying the feeling of difference. This awareness, that one belongs to the lower, middle or upper class is communicated to the child also. Consequently, children coming from the lower classes start with the feeling of inferiority of being poor, of deprivation of the good things of life. In reaction to this inferiority many of them turn to bad activity, because children from the upper classes find pleasure in displaying their superiority which has already created in them pride and vanity and a number of other igoistis emotions. The emotion of superiority on the one hand is reduced by consciousness of inferiority on the other, and this explains the reason why most middle class children show better performances in academic work than children from either of the two other classes.

Education and the Political System: In the modern age, one finds that education is provided in government controlled institutions as well as privately managed institutions. Many educational institutions are also controlled and managed by religious institutions. And even among the government or state controlled institutions, one finds that some are administered by the central authority and others by state or local self governing bodies. Another aspect of the state control of education is to determine the spheres which the state should take under its own areas which can be safely left to the control of the people. In the present day, every form of government, be it autocratic or democratic, must contribute to education.

EDUCATION AND DEMOCRACY

Democracy can never be successful without education. Wherever democracy has been unsuccessful, it has been because of the lack of education. In a democracy the government is composed of the elected representatives of the people and if the people are uneducated they can never elect the right leaders and consequently can never create the right kind of government. It fact, it is impossible even to hope for democracy in the absence of education. It is difficult to expect a citizen to behave in a responsible way if he is not even aware of his rights and duties. The truth of the matter is that education is a prerequisite of democracy. Only after proper education should the citizen be invested with his democratic rights. Education is a necessary condition for establishing a democratic society. Dewey has pointed out that democracy is inconceivable without education, because education alone can generate and instill the qualities which democracy demands as a prerequisite. Philosophers of the ancient Greek city state were aware of the significance of education. Both Plato and Aristotle laid stress on the importance of education for the success of democracy. Plato, in his famous text, 'The Republic', stressed not only the importance of education for democracy but even formulated a plan for the education of men and women which made possible all kinds of development physical, mental, moral and aesthetic. Aristotle was of the opinion that the aim of the state is to make possible the achievement of the highest moral level and this can be reached through education alone. Thus, education is the most important function of the state. From one point of view, the state itself is a school in which the individual learns citizenship. Aristotle suggested that the aim of education was to produce good citizens. These truths were known not only to the Ancient Greeks but also to Indian thinkers of ancient times.

Education and the Attitude to Knowledge: The sociologists are interested in the social attitudes towards the sources, the limits and the validity of knowledge. With the change in these social attitudes, one finds a considerable interest in the interaction among educators and the educated in educational institutions. In the ancient times, knowledge was limited and attained through some limited means. The teacher was highly respected and his words were the law. People refused admission to a student purely on personal grounds. The student, on the other hand, considered knowledge to be a treasure deposited with few persons who must be obeyed in order to learn. He had high respect for knowledge since most of the knowledgeable persons belonged to high caste or high social status. Thus the teacher-taught relationship in ancient India was very much governed by attitude to knowledge.

This attitude to knowledge has considerably changed in the modern times. The growth of knowledge in all directions, the substitution of new and sometimes absolutely opposite theories for the older ones, have led to the growing relation that no knowledge is final. Knowledge is unlimited and can be achieved by innumerable means. The one single factor that has come out to be the most certain concerning knowledge in our own time is the realisation that no knowledge is final and the only means of knowledge. Most of the scholars today are realising that the knowledge attained by non-scientific, intuitive, psychic or spiritual methods is no less or ore valid than scientific knowledge. The world of knowledge is drifting towards a pluralistic, catholic, agnostic, mystic, holistic and integral approach. Therefore, the student's approach towards knowledge has greatly changed.

Interaction: The most important area in the scope of sociology of education is however, social interaction within the educational system. The educational system involves three social constituents-teachers, students, administrators and in a small measure the society or the community at large. All these aspects constantly change within themselves and in their interaction. The educational sociologist analyse the factors of this change, observes the direction of change and finds out cause-affect relationship. An in depth analysis of the social interactions within the educational system will give a better insight in the scope of sociology of education.

(i) Teacher-Administrator relationship: Teacher-Administration relation is very important. The administrator is the employer or the agent of the employer. He is the leader, the supervisor and the guide of the teacher. With the authority vested in him, he gives rewards and punishments for successes and failures. Therefore, the personality and the way of teaching is very much influenced by teacher-administrator relationship. The nature of the administrator changes according to the types of management. In government institutions, the government officer is the administrator. In aided institutions the management is constituted by a president; a secretary, a nominee of the government and influential members elected by the donors constituting the

general body of management. Moreover, administration at all level should try to maintain a good functional relation with the teacher.

(ii) Teacher-teacher relationship: In every educational institution, today there are more than one teachers. Therefore, the educational sociologist is interested in knowing teacher-teacher relationship. Even in small institutions or university or college departments two or more camps may be found among teachers giving opportuity to jealousy and rivalry against each other. The groups are based upon castes, religion, region, language, nationality, seniority, qualification or cadre. These groups may be seen from primary to university level involving differences or groupism among students seeking favour from this or that camp.

(iii) Student-Student interaction: The interaction among students is governed by age, classes, sex, study habits, extra curricular activities and so many other factors. The most intimate interaction is provided by the classroom situation. Interaction everywhere may be cohesive or divisive. It may increase cooperation or conflict. The most important dimension for improving interaction is provided by extra-curricular activities, the debating societies, the dramatic clubs, literary associations, teams for sports and games and batches of excursions. The educational sociologist analyse the conditions of student-student interaction, divisive sources, the consequences, the factors, of social change and social control etc.

(iv) Teacher-Student relationship: The most important field of interaction within an educational system is the teacher-taught relationship. Formerly, the teacher himself laid down the rules of admission, syllabi, teaching schedule, teaching methods and practically every detail of education. Today, the rules and syllabi are framed by experts or the government bodies while teaching schedule is prescribed by the principal

or the time table incharge. Therefore, the teacher is confined only to teaching of his subject according to time table. He is appointed on his job on a particular salary scale and under certain conditions. Teaching today is a profession with all its advantages and limitations. The following are the factors governing teacher-taught relationship.

(a) *Age:* The distinction of age creates respects on the part of the younger and leadership on the part of the elder. In teacher-taught relationship the distinction of age is in inverse correlation with the level of education. Thus it is maximum at the primary level and minimum at the university level. The bigger age gap allows for the development of teacher-taught relationship based upon respect, fear and reverence. The smaller age gap makes for more intimacy, love, affection and more interaction between the teacher and taught.

(b) *Teacher's status:* In some societies, the status of the teacher is high. He is considered as an all knowing person. He may punish or reward according to his own judgement. In modern democratic societies, however, the authority of the teacher is eroded along with the authority of the administrator. Therefore, there are more interaction in the present day institutions in comparison to the institutions of ancient past.

(c) *Status and attitude of knowledge:* If these are marked by a certain finality the teacher exercises more authority over the students. If these are tentative and probable, as it is today, the authority of the teacher is proportionately eroded.

(d) *Mode of acquiring knowledge:* Formerly, teacher's words were unquestionable. He commanded total loyalty. Today, however the mode of acquiring knowledge is multiple, tentative and creative. Therefore, teacher-taught relationship has become more informal, less based upon fear and more intimate.

(e) *Image of the teacher in society:* Formerly, the image of the teacher was almost the highest in the society. Therefore, even the princes used to touch feet of their teachers. If a scholar came to a court even the king used to leave his seat. Today, with the contractual system of education, the teacher is a professional person if not a poor member of the society. With the change of the image of the teacher in society, the interaction between the teacher and taught has considerably changed.

(f) *Self image of the teacher and the student:* The self image of today's teacher is professional person delivering goods, making out his living and at the most pursuing knowledge. He is one among equals, never superior and occasionally even inferior. The self image of the student on the other hand, is no more of a submissive disciple obeying his teacher but an individual making the best of education to further his own aim in life.

(g) *Role of the teacher:* The teacher-taught relationship usually change according to change in the teacher's role in education. Formerly, he was independent and sovereign. Today, he is subordinate and dependent upon the management, the government, the wider community and even the student. This role again changes on various levels of education such as primary, secondary and university. It also changes according to the type of management of the educational institutions, the private, the religious or the government management. Besides, this role is also governed by personal traits, seniority, qualifications, cadre, economic condition and innumerable other factors. The educational sociologists analyse the change of role and the consequent changes in the teacher-taught relationships.

(h) *Mode of Standardization:* As most of the educational institutions today receive financial aid the government lays down uniform modes of standardization about the syllabi, the teaching methods and the evaluation techniques at various levels of education. Some times, there is an examining body governing all the students in a state such as U.P. Board of Secondary Education. Each university arranges for examinations and evaluation of all the students of all the colleges affiliated to it. This mode of standardization has eliminated the value of personal qualities and scholarship of the teachers. The teachers and the students now concentrate upon text books and even notes; books with the ultimate aim of preparing for the examination and achieving more success.

In the end, it may be noted that the scope and type of interaction between the educators and the educand is today becoming more and more complex. It is changing fast for various reason. This requires an occasional review by the sociologists of education so that the educational system may be improved according to the need and requirements.

3

Psychology and Education

(Relevance of Psychology in the Field of Education)

Human psychology is a complex field of knowledge. Every one is interested in understanding human behaviour. As a result of continuous research in the field of education and psychology, the subject of educational psychology has subsequently assumed importance. Teaching-learning today, is to a great extent determined by the principles of psychology. The theories and principles of psychology are being increasingly used in the field of Education. On the basis of the understanding of a student's behaviour, one can plan, arrange and modify the process of education. A student faces a variety of problems in the process of education. The principles and techniques of educational psychology help to solve these problems. Besides all teaching and learning activities are organised by the principles and techniques of psychology. Educational psychology is naturally that branch of psychology which is concerned or related to the understanding of the problems of Education in general and teaching-learning in particular. Educational psychology is an applied branch of general psychology. With a view to have proper understanding of the meaning, nature and scope of educational psychology it should be quite worth while to study a few definitions of some popular educational psychologists.

"Educational psychology is the study of the

psychological aspects of educational situations." (Trow)

"Educational psychology describes and explains the learning experiences of the individual from birth to old age." (Crow and Crow)

"Educational psychology is that branch of science which deals with teaching and learning." (Skinner)

On the basis of above definitions, we can conclude that educational psychology is that scientific knowledge which deals with teaching and learning process. Further it may be operationally defined that Educational Psychology is the practical side of certain psychological principles. It is the application of some general principle of psychology to the context of Education and Teaching.

NATURE OF EDUCATIONAL PSYCHOLOGY

Human behaviour is the core of educational psychology. Now-a-days it is being taught as subject of training. Ordinarily the nature of educational psychology is the subject matter of discussion. The unanimous opinion about it is that educational psychology may be considered as the science of education, but in order to understand the nature of educational psychology, the following facts and points may be kept in mind to have better ideas.

The behaviouristic aspect of an individual is studied through the study of educational psychology. The principles and theories of psychology are used for this purpose. Educational psychology studies the behaviour of students, but it only takes into consideration the behaviour in educational situation.

Educational psychology is an applied science. It deals with some pertinent theories within the scope of educational psychology. Besides, it helps in understanding the teaching skills and techniques. It explains how the knowledge of Educational Psychology helps the teacher to carry out his responsibility, in the context of teaching and learning.

EDUCATIONAL PSYCHOLOGY AND THE TEACHER

Educational Psychology helps a teacher in different aspects of teaching-learning process. That is why the knowledge of educational psychology is found to be useful in making a teacher more effective. It helps the teacher not only in the classroom or outside the classroom but also to develop a better understanding of the total teaching-learning process. The knowledge of scientific aspects and his approach to the education of the child justifies the reasons as to why educational psychology has been given due importance in the curriculum of the Teacher's Training Colleges.

1. *Knowledge of Individual Differences:* The knowledge of educational psychology makes the teacher understand that all students are not equal. There are individual differences for various reasons.
2. *Knowledge of Unconscious Mind:* To understand the unconscious mind of the student is very essential, because the personality of the child can be ascertained through his unconscious mind. The knowledge of educational psychology, therefore, helps him to become a more effective teacher.
3. *Helps in Measurement and Evaluation:* The teacher comes to know the new methods and techniques of measurement and evaluation through the study of educational psychology. As a result he becomes an efficient and effective teacher.
4. *Helps in Improvement in Teaching Methods:* The use of audio-visual material and technology in the teaching-

learning process helps in improving the quality of teaching methods. The concept of the use of audio-visual aids is based on the principles of educational psychology. Therefore, in order to modernize the teaching methods and also to make them more effective, it becomes imperative to include the subject of Educational psychology in the Teacher's Training institutions or Faculties of Education.

5. *Improvement in Discipline:* The repressive techniques of discipline must be replaced by the techniques based on psychological principles. Educational psychology helps the teacher in overcoming the social, mental, emotional problems of students and as a result of the solution of these problems, the likelihood of students becoming more disciplined increase.
6. *Improvement in Curriculum:* The new curriculum has replaced the traditional curriculum. Educational Psychology has brought about many changes in the curriculum. The curriculum should be based on the needs, interests, aptitudes and abilities of children. The effectiveness of the curriculum for the child is assessed with the help of educational psychology. So in this way the knowledge of educational psychology is helpful for the teacher in the construction of the curriculum.
7. *Rapport among the Teachers and the Taughts:* With the help of the knowledge of educational psychology, teacher can establish rapport with students. Interests and abilities of the students can also be known by assessing the personality of his students that leads to development of better human relations.
8. *Helpful in Guidance:* For understanding the need, concept and methods of educational guidance and counseling, the knowledge of educational psychology

is a prerequisite. Without the knowledge of educational and vocational guidance, a teacher may not be able to guide his students properly. As for as guidance purposes are concerned, the knowledge of the principles of psychology is a must.

9. *Helpful in Learning:* Educational psychology is an important component of teaching learning process. Without the knowledge of educational psychology, a teacher cannot make teaching-learning process effective. In other words, he cannot be a successful teacher if he lacks knowledge of educational psychology. A teacher knows about the motivation techniques, learning theories, techniques of teaching special/exceptional children etc. through the study of educational psychology. It helps a teacher to teach interestingly and effectively.
10. *Helping the Problem Children:* Educational psychology helps a great deal in tackling the problem children in the class. The effective use of the principles of educational psychology can help the teacher to treat the problem children effectively and thereby help them to adjust in the climate as normally as possible.

EMOTIONAL CHARACTERISTICS OF ADOLESCENTS

1. *Period of Emotion:* The adolescence stage is the stage of emotional revolution. At this stage many ups and downs occur in the adolescents with regards to emotions. These ups and downs in the adolescents are due to their physical, sexual and emotional changes. During this period their emotions are so intense that the adolescents can do any activity under the effect of these emotions. If an adolescent loves any body he or she shows immense love for the individual. Similarly, if her or she has hatred for

some one he or she will exhibit maximum dismay for that individual. In short, during this period the emotions reach their limits.

2. *Uncontrolled Emotions:* The emotions of this period are not under the control of adolescents. Tension and anxiety persists among them. There may be variety of reasons for them. They are emotionally unstable.

3. *Variations in Emotions:* There are distinct fluctuation in the emotions during the adolescence period. The adolescents are happy at one moment and become depressed at the other moment. The extreme of their emotions is that sometimes they decide to even commit suicide. Their mental state does not remain the same for all the times. Therefore this stage of the adolescents is called a stage of stresses and strains.

4. *Loyalty:* At the adolescent stage, the male and female adolescents show loyalty towards their groups or institutions etc. These people remains more loyal for their class mates and friends.

5. *Feeling of Sexuality:* At this stage the feeling homosexuality and hetero-sexuality develops. In the beginning of this stage the males and females establish relationship with each other and these adolescents attract towards each other. This is called hetero-sexuality. At this age, boys ad girls try to attract each other by using various methods. This includes the make up of girls too. The boys also observe themselves in front of a mirror.

6. *Emotion of Anger:* At this stage the adolescents do not tolerate their criticisms. They don't like joking. If they are kept away from their rights or they are forced to do something the emotion of anger arouses intensely.

7. *Emotion of Jealousy:* During this period the emotion of jealously arouses very quickly. This starts competition among adolescents. Sometimes these emotions arouse as a result of neglecting boys ad girls.

8. *Emotion of Anxiety:* At this stage, the adolescents remain affected by different kinds of anxieties. These anxieties are caused by the problems regarding adjustment in the future or examinations or due to economic conditions of the family. The girls are more anxious as compared to the boys. The anxieties of the girls are mostly concerned with matrimonial affairs. Boys are anxious about their future. Sometimes these anxieties are so intense that they affect the minds of the adolescents and the adolescents may lose their mental balance.

Educational Implications or Significance

It is essential to pay attention towards the various aspects of adolescent period. Otherwise, a danger of deviation may always prevail. For this following steps may be taken:

1. *Democratic Environment:* A democratic environment is essential in the school and at home so that they may get full opportunities for the development of their personality.
2. *Co-curricular Activities:* There should be provisions for the development of various activities like Poetic competitions, Symposium, Arts, Paintings, Music, Drama, N.C.C., Scouting etc.
3. *Sympathetic and Affectionate Behaviour:* In view of the unstable emotional state of the adolescents, the parents and teachers should have a sympathetic and affectionate behaviour with them.
4. *Respective Individuality:* The characteristics of personality of the adolescents should be respected

and they should be allowed opportunities for participating in the domestic and school function.

5. *Physical Exercise:* There should be arrangements for physical exercise of adolescents at home and in the schools so that they may have the proper occasion to develop their physique. By doing this, they should get the chances of races, gymnastics etc. or other activities.
6. *Teachers' Positive Attitude:* The attitude of the teacher is very crucial in the process of attaining the educational targets set by the policy makers. It has been felt that unless there is a positive attitude the optimum level of achievement may not be yielded.

Factors Affecting 'Learning'

Learning is not affected by one factor but many factors. There are many factors that make learning speedy and some there are factors which hinder the learning process. In this case, the positive factors are adopted and the factors which make learning process slow should be controlled. The factors affecting the learning are described as under.

1. *Motivation:* It is a process in which one is pushed towards achieving some specific goals. Motives like reward, success, competition, level of aspiration, punishment are powerful incentives to the learner for better learning.
2. *Learning Method:* It depends upon the teacher to select methods to make learning process effective. Teacher should select the methods according to the age of children. Apart from this, he should adopt psychological teaching methods.
3. *Proper Environment:* Learning is also affected by environment. Environment is of many kinds such as: external environment, internal environment, home

or community, class or school environment etc. Environment is created in the class room by light, air, sitting arrangement, and cleanliness etc.

4. *Maturation:* Learning depends upon maturation. If the individual is enough to learn a particular activity, he will learn easily effectively. If the individual is not mature, learning will not be effective.
5. *Distribution of Practice:* 'Practice makes a man perfect' is a well known proverb. Learning is more efficient when practice is distributed at intervals over a period of time than when it is considered in one period as in the case of cramming.
6. *Curriculum Construction:* Curriculum should be based on principles of 'easy to difficult'. This principle makes learning easier.
7. *Fatigue:* Fatigue causes boredom consequently has negative effect on learning.
8. *Teacher Behaviour:* The whole process of learning is considerably affected with the teacher behaviour. The teacher behaviour should be interesting and sympathetic. Teacher should give particular attention to individual differences. Then only the learning becomes effective. Teacher should gain new knowledge through magazines, news papers etc.
9. *Will Power:* Will power is a necessary factor in the process of learning. Teacher should have his will power strong in the process of learning as well as teaching. If any student is reluctant to learn, he should not be compelled.
10. *Mental Health:* A child who is mentally healthy i.e. free from frustrations, conflicts, anxieties and worries will learn better.

11. *Sensation and Perception:* Sensation and perception are the foundations of all cognitive learning. The stronger the power of perception, the greater the amount of learning.

CHARACTERISTICS OF ACQUIRED BEHAVIOUR OF LEARNING

Learning has got the following characteristics:

1. *Learning is universal in nature:* Learning is universal process. Every living being learns one thing or the other. Man is rational being so he learns more.
2. *Learning is a life long process:* Man always desires that he should learn as much as he can. One achievement motivates for more efforts and achievements. Learning is continuing activity. It starts from birth and lasts till death.
3. *Learning is the response:* It is a response of the individual to the total situation. It means that a man is always conscious to situations of learning. His activities are also directed towards learning.
4. *Learning is goal directed behaviour:* When the aim and objective of the task is exact and clear, learning becomes purposive and the student is benefited more by it.
5. *Learning is motivated:* Man has to adjust himself according to the new environment. In this way learning is a kind of adjustment.
6. *Learning is aroused by individual and social needs:* Learning depends upon our social needs, problems, desires and ideals. There are certain persons, who learn very fast, certain others are slow in learning. It should be noticed that social environment affects learning. It is impossible to learn in the absence of environment.

7. *Learning is transferable:* It means that learning may change place but the amount of change in the place may be different. Change of place takes place from one field of education to the other field and from one class to other class.

MAIN PRINCIPLES/THEORIES OF LEARNING

1. Theory of Trial and Error

This theory is also known as Simulus Response Theory or Pleasure Pain Theory. This theory was indoctrinated by Thorndike of America in 1968. According to this theory, human beings and animals learn through trial and error method or they learn through the link established between a particular stimulus and corresponding responses i.e. through connectionism. An individual works through trials and as a result of it his learning process goes on. After every trial, the errors go on decreasing. Sometimes we say that an individual learns after committing mistakes. Actually this notion is the simplified version of this very theory. Learning through trial and error theory needs certain elements such as motivation, some suitable responses and achievement of goals. Only then the individual can learn through this theory.

In the context of connectionism, it would be important to say that in this theory, relation between stimulus and response is established. Therefore, to understand this theory it is essential to know the stimulus and response. The equations 'stimulus response' mean stimulus is connected with response. Our behaviour is a direct outcome of a factor that causes an activity. In our nervous system the relationship are formed. These relationships are expressed by the equations S.R. These relationship are also known as 'Bonds'.

This theory has certain demerits also. Through this method of learning, intelligence is not used infrequently. This method suits the backward children only. Gifted children do not get benefit from it.

2. Theory of Learning by Insight

The theory of learning by insight was indoctrinated by a German psychologist Kohler. To understand this theory, experiments were conducted on animals. Later on, these experiments were conducted on the human behaviour. Kohler conducted experiments on chimpanzees. He experimented on their intelligence by keeping them in natural conditions and he concluded from these experiments that the animals also use intelligence. If a human being is placed in similar condition he will be also behave in that manner.

3. Theory of Conditioned Response

In this theory, learning occurs through classical conditioning. This was indoctrinated by Pavlov and Watson. According to this theory, learning takes place with the help of related situations. In other words, conditioned response means producing natural activities as a result of artificial stimulus. Russian scientist Pavlov after experimenting on dogs and Watson after experimenting on rats have proved that animals can learn a lot through a condition response. If the human beings are put in the same situation, they will also learn in the same way.

Educational Implications of Trail and Error

(a) *From easy to difficult:* By this theory, the task can take place from the easier to more difficult way. This will benefit the weaker and backward children.

(b) *Learning of Skills:* A small child learn some skills through trial and error method only such as sitting, standing, walking running etc. In teaching also, the child rectifies the writing and other mistakes.

(c) *Emphasis on motivation:* In this theory, motivation has been emphasized in the process of learning. The motivation of the children is found most essential, for any activity even learning.

(d) *Learning by Insight:* In trial and error method also insight as a theory is also used in the form of mixture of the two as a matter of requirements.

(e) *Learning by Practice:* Practice leads a man towards materialising the goal. Practice is the main feature of trial and error method. Practice reduces the errors of the child.

(f) *Repetition:* To learn any task, its repetition is essential. In trial and error method the activities are repeated.

(g) *Basis of Habits:* Habits are formed as a results of repetition. With this the learning behaviour of the children can be modified and may be directed towards the achievements of the desired goals.

Educational Implications of Conditional Response Theory

The following is the summary of the educational implications of the Conditioned Response theory:

(a) *Reward and Punishment:* Reward and punishment depend on conditioning of the child. It is sometimes essential to punish him for his misdeeds and give him reward for good efforts. A punishment or reward at appropriate time changes or modifies the behaviour of the child.

(b) *Useful in Learning Training:* Conditioning is much useful in language training. The correct use of the language gets the child conditioned for the use of that language.

(c) *Removal of Superstitions:* This method should be used to remove the superstitions. Certain superstitions like sneezing and cat crossing your way etc. can be removed by this method.

(d) *Use of Audio-Visual Aids:* By using audio visual aids in teaching man things can be taught through first hand experience such as by showing the picture to the child and by writing or telling about that picture. In this way, he can be conditioned. After this the written words without picture are shown to the child. In the absence of pictures the child reads the words and derives meaning of that word, depending of he previous application of the audio-visual aid and learning out of it.

(e) *Arousal of Fear, Love, Jealousy:* By this method the feelings of fear, love and jealousy can be aroused among the children and the teacher. If a teacher beats any student that student will develop hatred even for the name of that teacher. This would be an example of conditioning.

Educational Implications of Thorndike's Laws of Learning

1. *Law of Readiness:* Woodworth has named this law as Law of Mental Set. Therefore, it is also known as the Law of Mental Set. Some people call it as Law of Motivation Educational utility of this law is given below:

(a) *Arousing Attention and Interest:* The main utility of this law is to arouse the attention and interest in the students.

(b) *Arousing Curiosity:* A teacher should try to arouse curiosity for a particular task among the children. The use of this law is very beneficial.

(c) *Motivation of Children:* For teaching in the class room the motivation of the children is very essential. The execution of this law makes it possible. If the children are mentally and physically prepared then the children can be motivated to learn.

2. *Law of Effect:* This is also known as law of satisfaction and annoyance. The learning of some tasks provides pleasure and some task provide displeasure and are disliked. The educational implications of this law are mentioned below:

(a) *Increase in Memory:* Law of effect is related to the remembering power. Integrating tasks are remembered by the students for a long time and dis-interesting jobs are forgotten

(b) *Increase in Interests:* Like memory, interests are also directly related to this law. The satisfaction and pleasure arousing activities give birth to the interest o the children.

(c) *Use of Reward and Punishment:* The effects of reward and punishment also affect the learning. The use of reward and punishment is based upon this law.

(d) *Formation of Good Habits:* The teacher can produce good habits and attractive behaviour by using stimulation efforts.

(e) *Treatment of Delinquents:* The teacher can change the behaviour of the delinquent children by using this law. He should modify the behaviour of such children by using this method.

(f) *Control of Emotions:* With the help of this law the teacher can control the negative emotions of the children such as anger, jealously etc.

(g) *Improvement in Teaching Methods:* The teacher can improve his teaching methods with the help of this law. He should see the effects of his teaching methods on the students. If he think it proper he should not hesitate to make necessary change in them.

(h) *Care of Mental Level:* The teacher should show more interest in the activities being performed according to the mental level of the children.

3. *Law of Exercise:* The leaning will increase if we repeat the task for many times. In psychological language its images go on strengthening. The educational implications of this principle are mentioned below:

(a) *Formation of Habits:* If a correct activity is repeated again and again that activity gets stabilized. This leads to the formation of good habits.

(b) *Improvement in Handwriting:* There can be improvement in hand writing by doing practice. This is more appropriate in case of small children.

(c) *Less Forgetfulness:* Repeated revisions of the activities decrease the forgetting.

(d) *Development of Skills and Correct Responses:* Development of skills and correct responses is possible by using this porinciple.

(e) *Oral Drill:* The teacher should conduct oral drill of the contents, that have been taught. This strengthens the learning process.

Operant Vs Classical Conditioning

How and why conditioning Occurs: To know this it is proper and essential to go through the various experiments conducted by the psychologist I.P. Pavlov in 1904.

Pavlov experimented on dogs. He took a dog and it was kept hungry. Then it was tied with an experimentation table. There was a provision of measuring the level of the salvia secreted by the dog. The dog was served with meals through an automatic device. Pavlov rang the bell while the dog was served with meals. On looking the meals the dog's mouth was watered i.e. saliva was secreted. This salvia was collected in a tube and measured. This experiment was repeated many times and the collected salvia was measured.

In the last stages of the experiment Pavlov rang the bell only and did not serve the meals. By doing this the dog again secreted saliva. This salvia was collected and measured. In this experiment the meals was the natural stimulus and the bell was artificial stimulus.

This experiment resulted in the learning of the dog that when at the time of ringing of the bell the food is served. After learning this its mouth started salivation. This type of learning is called learning by conditioning. In the learning by conditioning artificial stimulus is also presented along with the natural stimulus. After sometime natural stimulus is withdrawn. Artificial stimulus produces the same response as that natural stimulus. In this way, along with artificial stimulus the response gets conditioned.

B.F. Skinner (Operant Conditioning)

Skinner was born in 1904 and received Ph.D. in Psychology from Harvard in 1931. He published a book, 'The Behaviour of Organism' in 1938. His influence increased gradually and he became the most talked about and most important learning of Psychologist of 1970's. His work resembles that of Thorndike. Both connectionist theorists emphasize reinforcement as a basic factor in learning.

B.F. Skinner is a practical psychologist who conducted several experiments on different reflexs existing in rats and pigeons.

He developed his own apparatus and method of observation to study and analyse behaviour in a systematic objective way. His method has become so viable that most of the American psychologists adopted his method of research in their studies.

The two kinds of learning: Skinner recongizes two kinds of learning that are produced by different experimented procedures. Respondent behaviour is elicited by specific stimuli. Given the stimulus the response occurs automatically. This is what we have earlier discussed as classical conditioning by Pavlov.

Skinner maintains that most behaviour of a different kind. He called his own procedure as operant conditioning in which the response occurs spontaneously in the absence of any stimulation with which it may be specifically co-related. The term operant emphasizes the fact that behaviour operates upon the environment to generate its own consequences. If the consequences are rewarding, the response will be repeated and will grow in strength. The relationship between response and reward is the essence of operant conditioning.

The Operant Method

A laboratory rat is placed in a conditioning apparatus called Skinner's box. The rat roams in the box in an exploratory manner. Eventually it presses a bar which triggers a good delivery system, and a pellet of food becomes available. After gaining this reward the subject continues its random activity but sooner of later presses the lever again it receives food as a reward. As the time passes the bar is pressed more frequently and then a point is reached where the rat presses the bar consistently in order to receive the reward.

When a food deprived rat has learned this response and is placed in Skinners box, it usually begins pressing the bar immediately and continues to do so many times, provided that it continues to receive awards.

Initiating Stimulus	Response	Reinforcing Stimulus
S_1 ————————	R ————————	S_2
(Unknown)	(Bar Press)	(Food)

Operations in Operant Conditioning

Several Operations are involved in the process of Operant Conditioning.

(1) *Shaping:* This is the most important mechanism used in operant conditioning. It refers to the use of selective reinforcement to bring certain desirable changes in the behaviour of the organism.

Principles involved in shaping:- There are some principles involved in shaping of behaviour.

(a) *Generalization*: Application of knowledge from the previously learned situation to the similar situation, it can be repeated, they are likely to vary over a range of more or less similar acts.

Stimulus generalization: stimulus generalization occurs when a particular response elicited by a particular stimulus is also elicited by other similar stimulus.

(b) *Charming*

(c) Habit Competition

(2) *Extinction:* The rate of responding decreases when reinforcement is consistently absent. Complete absence of reinforcement is followed by eventually by extinction of response e.g. formation of habits etc.

(3) *Spontaneous Recovery:* If an organism is removed from a situation for a while after extinction and then returned and again presented with S_2 his performance will be better than the his performance at the end of preceding extinction.

(4) *Concept of Reinforcement*: Skinner has presented two types of reinforcement. Positive and Negative.

(a) Positive Reinforcement: It is any stimulus which an individual will work to obtain e.g. food, money.

A reinforce serves to strengthen or maintain the response.

(b) Negative reinforcement: It is that unpleasant stimulus which the learner will readily terminate if given the opportunity to do so. e.g. a child who is not interested in doing his homework will do the homework to avaid the displeasure of his parents. So this reinforcement is a means of forcing behviour to occur more frequently.

Applications of Operant Conditioning: It is applied in school situation. Skinner has developed a system of learning known as programmed learning or programmed instruction.

- Use of reinforcement in scheduled manner has been found to be very effective.
- It has been used as a Behaviour modification technique to bring about desired changes in behaviour of exceptional children and mentally ill people.

* * * * *

MEANING AND CONCEPT OF MOTIVATION

Motivation is the energy within a person, which direct him to perform his work sincerely.

"Anything that initiates activity whether internal or external is motivation".

English word 'Motivation' originated from 'movere' which mean 'to move'. In the field of education, the word 'motivation' is interpreted in the form of interest of the pupils for learning and encouragement.

"Motivation is the influence of general pattern of activities indicating and directing the behaviour of the organism". (Johnson)

"Motivation is an energy change within the person characteised by affective arousal and anticipatory goal relations". (McDonald)

A motive can be defined as any particular internal factor or condition that appears to initiate and to maintain activity.

In the nature of motivation, needs are considered to be important. Therefore, psychologist like Blair, Jones and Simpson have considered the need as a basic source of motivation.

What are Motives

Motivation is the state of mind, which emerges within a person and directs him towards the goal or the achievement of desired result. All these initial basic behaviours are motives. These may be primary or secondary motives in nature.

Technology and Devices for Motivating the Learner

Motivation is of two types – external and internal motivation. These both types of motivation are essential for the students in the class rooms. External motivation is concerned with the external environment while internal motivation is related to the interest aptitudes, growth etc. of the students. External motivation is also known as artificial motivation and internal motivation is known as natural motivation. Motivation is very essential whether it is external or internal. For this purpose, the selection of various techniques is essential, the description of which is given as under:

(1) *Reward and Punishment:* The use of reward and punishment is of great importance to motivate the students in the class. Both reward and punishment mobilize energy in the students. These rewards can be in the form of objects or in form of words. The reward given in the form of words can be appreciation. This technique is very useful for small children. In the home assignments, when they get rewards,

as 'good' 'very good' they feel glad. Later, they are compelled to complete their home assignments double excitement in future.

But, sometimes the excessive use of motivation proves harmful as it tends to lead to no improvement in the target child.

The students become opponent-type. Sometimes punishment to the wrong student in an appropriate time lead to better results. Hence more the restricted use of punishment more it would be better. The use of reward should also be made more intelligently. Sometimes, the use of this technique of reward develops jealousy among students. The students who fail to get rewards develop ill-feeling for the teacher concerned. Therefore, this method should be used very carefully.

(2) *Fixation of Goals:* The fixation of goals also provides good opportunity to the students. Unless and until there are clear goals before the students, they will not be motivated to learn anything. There will be neither external nor internal motivation in them. Similarly, if the teacher's are also not clear about teaching goals, they will also not get motivation for their task. Hence for teaching and learning, the objectives must be clear and pre-determined. Pre-determined objectives provide direction to as well as teachers the students to do something.

(3) *Teaching Methods:* The teacher should pay attention towards his teaching methods in order to achieve his goals as well as motivate his students in the class. He can select his teaching methods keeping in view the individual differences. The selection of teaching methods in the class can produce or develop motivation of students or may contribute maximum extent. In the light of new concepts of teaching, only the modern teaching methods can produce motivation.

(4) *Praise and Reproof:* The word of praise and reproof uttered by the teacher in the class-room affect deeply the minds of the students, Praise and reproof are a forms of reward and punishment. Like rewards and punishments, the use of praise and reproof should also be made very carefully. Like rewards the students are always curious to win the praise of the teachers. Sometimes the students get motivated to learn something as a result of the reproof of the teacher. Praise and proof are very advantageous for the talented as well as the backward children as per the situations.

(5) *Novelty:* Novelty and change are also cause of motivation. In the classroom, the exhibition of novelty by the teacher is sufficient to motivate the students, especially in the lower classes. The teachers can motivate the students by introducing novelty in their teaching methods. The students are always essentially interested in novelty.

(6) *Success and Failure:* To motivate the students in the classroom, success and failure also play a prominent role. The students want to go on doing that very task in which they get success. Sometimes failure also mobilize energy in the students and the unsuccessful students work very hard to achieve the success. Hence, success and failure are also used as an important technique of motivation in the classroom.

* * * * *

INTELLIGENCE

Various theories have been presented to explain the nature of intelligence. Some of them follows:

1. *Unitary or Monarchic Theory:* This theory was indoctrinate by Johnson and Stern and according to them, the intelligence consists of only one factor. In other words,

intelligence is the ability to solve all types of problems. According to this theory, a man with intelligence can utilize it in any field of life to minimize or eliminate all the problems of the life and achieve the success. But this theory is not acceptable to all. This theory supports the idea, if a man is intelligent in one activity, he should also be intelligent in other activities. It can be related to the concept that, if a student is intelligent in science, he should also be intelligent in history. This may not be true in practice. A person who is intelligent in science may not show any interest in history.

2. *Group Factor Theory:* This theory is also known as the sampling theory of intelligence. According to this theory, the intellectual abilities are related to some groups and have mutual relationship. The abilities related to a single group are closely related with each other. According to this theory, if a child is intelligent in one group, then it is possible that he may not be intelligent in other group. For example, if a child is intelligent in the group of science, then there is a possibility that he may not be intelligent in arts group. He can be intelligent in the other subjects of the group, such as, if he is intelligent in physics he can be intelligent in chemistry, because both physics and chemistry belong to one group of study.

3. *Multi-Factor Theory:* The advocate of this theory was Thorndike. According to this theory, intelligence is a group of many elements. There is no peculiar relationship among these elements. It is difficult to predict the ability of the child in other field on the basis of his ability in one field only. For example, if a child is intelligent in literature it is difficult to predict about mathematics or other subjects.

4. *Spearman's two factor theory or Electric Theory:* This theory was presented by Spearman. According to him, intelligence consists of two factors – one is 'G' factor and the other is 'S' factor. 'G' factor means general ability and 'S'

factor means specific ability. Factor 'G' participates in all the intellectual activities. But the factor 'S' does not participate in all the intellectual activities. In all the persons, there are different 'S' factors for different tasks. In some tasks 'G' factors are required more in some tasks. In this way, according to this theory there exists a sort of general intelligence which exists in all the individuals. For example, for mathematics 'G' factors and for music 'G' factors are needed more. The advocates of this theory plead that the persons having 'G' factors are more successful in life because they can use the same in various field.

5. *Theory of Primary Mental Abilities:* According to this theory, intelligence consists of nine primary mental abilities. These abilities are – number abilities, inductive reasoning ability, deductive reasoning ability, word fluency ability, perceptual ability, spatial ability, memory ability, verbal ability, problem solving ability etc.

On the basis of above theories we can assess the nature of intelligence but due to lack of a definite theory, definite nature of intelligence has not been possible as yet.

Measurement of Intelligence

Intelligence test is administered to measure the mental ability of a person. Before discussing the various aspects of intelligence test, we must understand the utility of intelligence tests for schools and its significance in the modern world.

6. *For Promotions:* It is always proper to use the intelligence tests to promote the students to the next classes. In the vocational fields, the use of these tests is always advantageous the person who may be promoted according to his abilities.

7. *For Research Purposes:* The intelligence tests are used for many important research studies.

From the study of the above advantages, we can say that

importance of intelligence tests is increasing day by day in the modern educational set up. One cannot avoid the uses of these tests.

Intelligence Quotient (I.Q.) is called Mental Ratio also. First of all Wilhelm Stem, a German Psychologist used the term intelligence Quotient in 1912. In 1916, the idea of I.Q. was utilised in the Standard Binet test. Intelligence Quotient is the Index of Intelligence. It is the ratio between Mental Age (M.A.) and Chronological Age (C.A.). By mental we mean the age received on the test and by chronological age we mean the actual age.

Uses of Intelligence Tests in Schools

There is much importance of intelligence tests in the schools. The description of the uses of these tests are given below:

1. *For Classification:* In schools, to classify the students these tests are used. This classification is done on the basis of intelligence. The classes of the students with higher intelligence can be arranged separately and with that of lower intelligence separately. In this way the education an be made effective.
2. *For Guidance Purposes:* Intelligence tests are needed for educational and vocational guidance to the students. On the basis of these tests, it is possible to provide proper guidance to them.
3. *For selection purpose:* The intelligence tests are selected for the selection of various subjects, scholarships or co-curricular activities. The children are selected on the basis of I.Q.
4. *To know the individuals:* The intelligence tests are used to know the individuals and potentialities of the individuals. For child-centered education, it is essential to know the children and intelligence tests.

5. *To Establish Aspiration Level:* On the basis of results of intelligence tests, the aspiration levels of the individuals can be established. The establishment of higher aspiration of persons with lower intelligence would be injustice with the persons. In the same way for the persons with higher intelligence, lower aspiration levels would be improper.
6. *For Promotions:* It is always proper to use the intelligence tests to promote the students to the next classes. In the vocational fields, the use of these tests is always advantageous for the persons who may be promoted to higher classes or positions.

   Formula for finding I.Q.:

$$\text{I.Q.} \quad \frac{\text{M.A.}}{\text{C.A.}} \times 100$$

To explain, for example, a child who is 4 years old but possesses M.A. of 5 years his I.Q. will be calculated with the help of the following equation:

$$\text{I.Q.} = \frac{5 \times 100 \quad 125}{4}$$

Classification according to I.Q.

Garret in his book, "Great Experiments in Psychology" has classified people according to their I.Q. and shown their percentage it he population as under:

I.Q.	*Classification*	*Percentage*
140 or above	Very superior	1.5
120 to 139	Superior	11.0
110 to 119	Bright	18.0
90 to 109	Average or normal	48.0
80 to 89	Dull or back ward	14.0
70 to 79	Very dull	5.0
0 to 69	Feeble minded	2.5

Constancy of Intelligence Quotient

The Intelligence Quotient of an individual remains fairly constant from age to age. Proof of constancy of I.Q. comes from the fact that a dull child will grow up as a dull adult and a bright child will grow as a bright adult. Moreover, earlier experiments had indicated that the I.Q. of an individual remains exactly the same from age to age, and that no changes whatsoever took place in its value.

Characteristics of Good Intelligence Tests

"A good psychological test is essentially a purposeful standardized tool of observing the sample of individual behaviour objectively and comprehensively". (Dr. M. Bhargav)

We have to use many criteria to know about a test. If a test proves appropriate against that criteria that test will be considered a good test. Similar criteria are also used in the context of intelligence tests. Therefore, we should use these criteria to evaluate the characteristics of intelligence tests. The description of good intelligence tests or criteria are given below:

1. *Reliability:* Reliability means a test gives what types of results on using it repeatedly. If the results given are similar the test would be considered reliable.

   "The reliability of a test refers to the considency of scores obtained by the same individual on different occasions or with different sets of equivalent items. (Anastare)

   In other words, the stability in the results is called reliability. In the construction of any test there are different methods to determine the reliability, such as test-retest method, split half method and parallel from method etc.

2. *Validity:* The second characteristic of intelligence tests

is its validity i.e. whether a test measures that very characteristic for which the test has been constructed or not. This is called validity of the test. The validity of the test is done through various methods, such as, construct validity, content validity, concurrent validity, predictive validity, etc. A good intelligence test is always proved to be valid.

3. *Objectivity:* It is essential to be objective for an intelligence test or any other test. The objectivity of any test depends on two things. First, the test should include those test items or statements which are according to the level of the testees. The test items include should in a test should bear a definite response. One question should have the possibility of one answer only. If it is not so then the test cannot be valid and a non valid test cannot be reliable because the test cannot measure that ability correctly and meaningfully which it is made to measure.

   Second, the administration and evaluation of the test should be in an objective way. For this, a key of definite responses is prepared and according to that key, the students get the scores.

4. *Economical:* The test should be economical. It is also a very important characteristic of a good test. Intelligence test will be good if these are economical with regard to time, finance and manual efforts. It would be very difficult to use those tests which are costly enough and not feasible.

5. *Scorability:* Intelligence tests should have one more characteristic that the scoring method of these should be simple. The scoring methods should be such that these can be used by every person. If the scoring method is easy, then the interpretation of secured sores will also be very easy.

6. *Acceptability:* Good intelligence tests should also be acceptable. These tests should be such that these can be used by every person and in all the situations. For example, Bines Simon Intelligence Sale is included in the category of acceptable tests.
7. *Representativeness:* Good intelligence tests have the characteristic of representativeness. Those aspects for which the intelligence tests are constructed are measured in a representative manner.

* * * * *

PERSONALITY

The word 'Personality' is being emphasised in this modern age. In the field of education, 'personality' is considered a central point. The main objective of present education is basically the over all development of human personality. But what the term 'personality' means, various view points are as under.

Meaning of Personality

Various scholars have expressed their view points in their different definitions to explain the meaning of 'personality'.

> "Personality is the sum of the activities that can be discovered by actual observation over a long enough period of time to give reliable information." (Watson)

> "Personality is a dynamic organization within the individual of those psycho-physical systems that determine his unique adjustment to his environment." (Allport)

"Personality is that which permits a prediction of what person will do in a given situation." (Cattel)

"Personality is the more or less stable and enduring organisation of a person's character, temperament, intellect, and physique which determine his unique adjustment to the environment." (Eysenck)

In his definition, Eysenck has emphasized more on the organization of physique and a constitution of an individual instead of his behaviour. In this definition both the references of heredity and environment are present. According to this definition the measurement and evaluation of personality is possible as its study is based on scientific principles. In this way, due to the mention of various aspects o personality this definition of Eysenck is considered very comprehensive. But the main problem of this definition is due to its consideration as definite and static.

The English word 'personality' has been derived from Latin word 'Personal which means 'Mask'. But 'mask' is considered a narrow aspect of personality i.e. the outer nature of the individual.

In addition to the above mentioned description, there are more views regarding the meaning to personality by the scholars of different categories:

- *Philosophical View:* The meaning of personality according to this philosophical view is 'completeness'. This ideal of completeness represents the personality.
- *Social View:* According to sociologists, the people are images of the society. The place of persons is main in the society and then comes the society. According to Faris, personality is the subjective side of culture. Personality is the social effectiveness.

- *Bio-physical View:* Whatever an individual possesses inside him represents his personality. The external behviour of the individual also expresses his internal aspect.

* * * * *

MEANING OF BACKWARD CHILDREN

"Backward child is one who is unable to do the work of the class which is normal for his age."

"Backward pupil is one who compared with other pupils of the chronological age shows marked educational deficiency.

- Schonelt

"Backwardness in general is applied to cases where other educational achievement falls below the level of other natural abilities."

- Burton Hall

Backward children have also been defined on the basis of Educational Quotient or academic scores. According to Burt, 'the children who have their E.Q. less than 85, they are backward children'. By Educational Quotient, we mean whether the knowledge of school subjects possessed by the pupils is according to his age group or not. The formula follows:

E.Q. - Educational Quotient.

E.A. - Educational age. (pupils average level of achievement)

C.A. – Chronological age.

To explain the same, the following example may be used. Suppose the chronological age of a child is 10 years. His mental age in Math is equal to the child of 8 years of age and in other studies is equal to the child of 6 years of age. In maths, the mental age and average mental age in other studies $\left(\text{E.A.}-\frac{8\times6}{2}-7\right)$ comes to be 7 years,

His

$$\frac{\text{E.Q.} - \text{E.A. (Educational Age} \quad \text{x } 100)}{\text{C.A. (Chronological age}}$$

$$=\frac{7}{10}\times100=70$$

Characteristics of Backward Children

1. Backward children learn slowly. In comparison to the backward children normal children learn rapidly and quickly. Due to this reason such children cannot adjust alongwith normal children. Backward children feel inconvenient to study with normal children.
2. In the academic field, such children are much backward in comparison to the children of their own age group. Due to this very reason, such students stagnate in one class. In the field of education this defect is termed as 'stagnation'. In addition to the problem of stagnation there can be more factors of backwardness.
3. A correlation is not necessary among backwardness and intelligence quotient. In backwardness, no level of I.Q. has been fixed on the basis of which backward children can be categorized.
4. Educational achievements of backward children seem to be inappropriate with regard to their abilities. An individual is unable to achieve for which he has the potentiality. Academically backward child is sometimes a complete failure.

5. Backward children are not of lower level in the academic field only in comparison to their own age group children but also find themselves incapable of working with the children of lower age group.

Causes of Backwardness

There can be various causes of backwardness. Some of them follows as under:

- Physical causes,
- Mental causes,
- Environmental causes,
- Social and cultural causes,
- Miscellaneous causes.

Education of Backward Children

In the class room, the teacher has to face the adjustment problems due to the presence of backward children. Therefore, to remove these problems special educational programmes are needed. What a school teacher can do in this regard has been described below:

1. *Individual Attention:* A special attention is needed for the backward children because these children lag behind too much as compared to the normal children and they do not understand the group instructions by the teacher. In addition to this, inferior complexes are also developed. Due to these complexes, these children show fear or hesitate to go to the children. Therefore, an individual attention may help in getting rid off their backwardness.
2. *Handicrafts:* Backward children lag behind academically. Hence they are not successful in achieving higher education. Therefore, they should be provided the training of handicrafts. With their

self confidence, they can start any vocation after the completion of school education.

3. *Search of Causes Responsible for Backwardness:* It is essential to find out the causes responsible for the backwardness prior to its remedy. We can inquire about the backwardness by intelligence tests, achievement tests, evaluation of specific abilities, physical capabilities and efficiencies, child's educational history, study of social and economical situation of child's family. After a proper inquiry is made, causes responsible for backwardness can be determined. As a result of this inquiry, any educational planning can be framed.

MEANING OF GIFTED CHILDREN

Gifted children need special attention because they have higher intelligence. Such children are so different from the normal children that they need special education, training and adjustment, otherwise they don't get adjusted with other children in the class. Sometimes negligence leads their deviation in the undesired direction.

Generally the students with higher I.Q. are considered talented. The term 'gifted child' has been commonly taken to mean a child with a high I.Q.

The gifted children are usually superior in physical development, educational achievement, intelligence and personality etc. Not only those children with higher I.Q. are included in the group of gifted children, but others are also included who are superior than others in any field, such as, Arts, Literature, Poetry etc.

The term gifted has been applied to every child who in age group is superior in some ability which may make him outstanding contributor to the welfare activity and quality of living in the society by any kind of useful activity.

Identification of Giften Children

Every school or class has gifted children. But their identification is not an easy job. In order to do this, a teacher will have to use various techniques. Therefore, the knowledge of all these method for a teacher is essential otherwise the talent of the student will suffer. To identify or to select these methods, the teacher can use the following techniques.

1. *Intelligence Tests:* The teacher can use various intelligence tests for the identification of these children. These intelligence tests can be administered to groups or to individuals. The tests administered to an individual are called individual tests and tests administered on a group are called group tests. The training of the teachers is essential for these tests.

2. *Achievement Tests:* In addition to intelligence tests, achievement tests can also be used to identify the gifted children. With these methods the achievement of the students can be known. Higher level of achievement arouses the hopes of being talented.

3. *Aptitude Tests:* Aptitudes express the nature of the children. Aptitudes can predict about the future of the children. Aptitudes are related to a specific ability. The Intelligence test is also a kind of aptitude test. In these tests too, the training of the teachers is essential, because the interpretation of the scores obtained in these tests is possible only by the trained teachers. Untrained teachers can interpret incorrectly hence training is essential.

Education of Gifted Children

The presence of talented children in the class creates

numerous problems. Such children need special education and special training for the teachers. The following are the description of some main methods:

1. *Equality of Opportunities:* The equality of opportunities means providing the opportunity for developing the abilities or talent of children like the normal children.
2. *Rapid Promotion:* Some psychologists and educationists recommend the rapid promotion of talented or gifted children. But this would be unpsychological. By doing so, the children go to those classes in which the children are more developed physically, mentally and socially. Rapid promotion of the children fears maladjustment. In this way, rapid promotion makes possible adverse effects on the children.
3. *Enrichment of Curriculum:* Gifted or talented children take less time in understanding the curriculum as compared to the normal children. The time span can be utilised in other activities. Hallingworth has prepared the following programmes for the enrichment of the curriculum.
   - (i) Study of Civilization,
   - (ii) Study of Biographies,
   - (iii) Study of modern languages,
   - (iv) Training in special abilities.
4. *Prevention of Bad Social Habits:* If the creative energy of talented children is not utilised properly they can join antisocial activities. Therefore, the teacher should provide such education to the talented children so that they must learn good habits.
5. *Education Based on Child Study:* The education of talented children should be based on the carefully-conducted child studies. For this their specific talents

should be taken into consideration. This is possible only if their education is child-centered.

6. *Special School and Classes:* There can be a provision of special schools for talented children. In these schools, sufficient facilities are provided according to the characteristics of such children to develop them. But this concept is not possible in reality. In schools, there are not sufficient talented children that separated schools may be opened for them. The students studying in these schools develop a feeling of pride due to which they consider other students as inferior. In addition to these problems, there are other financial problems which create hindrances in opening separate schools. Apart from the opening of separate schools is not feasible in a democratic country like India.

Development of Creativity Among Children

Creativity is universal. It is not the monopoly of certain gifted and intelligent persons. Everyone of us has certain creative ability in one way or the other. It is, therefore, necessary for the parents of creative children to create proper situations and environments for the development of the creativity of their children. This problem is difficult but not impossible. Creativity can be developed by proper motivation and environment. Originality, flexibility, fluent and varied thinking, self confidence, continuous work, sensitiveness, ability to develop relationship etc. are such qualities which help in the development of creativity. The following suggestions may be proved to be useful for the education of creative children.

1. *Developing healthy habits among children:* Self-dependence, confidence and hard work are such qualities which are helpful to creativity. These qualities should be found in children. In addition to it, they

should also be trained to stand up and face their own criticism by others for their creative expression. He should feel that whatever they have created is novel and it is communicating whatever he wants to express.

2. *Freedom to respond:* We should allow sufficient independence to the children to respond. They should be given sufficient time and be encouraged to think seriously about the solution of the problem.
3. *Opportunity for ego involvement:* Children can involve themselves with active behaviour, if they have their ego i.e. they should feel that certain creative works have been possible due to their efforts. Therefore, we should provide children such opportunities, wherein they should experience that the particular novel expression or task is their own creation.
4. *Encouraging originally and flexibility:* Originality of students, in whatever form must be encouraged. They should be allowed and encouraged, in the process of solving certain specific problems or while learning certain activities.
5. *Providing appropriate opportunities and atmosphere for creative expression:* Creative thinking should be developed among students. In order to develop creativity arrangement of healthy and proper atmosphere is a must. Sufficient adjustment should be made between learning and experimenting, getting passive knowledge or obtaining knowledge through private efforts and definite stability and risk. The curiosity eagerness and tolerance of children should not be suppressed in any way. In order to provide opportunities for the manifestation of creativity, co-curricular activities, social ceremonies, religious fairs, exhibition may also be used. Regular class work can

also be arranged and planned.

6. *Removal of hesitation and fear:* Hesitation caused by fear and inferiority complex is a hurdle on the way to the development of creativity. Every possible effort should be made to remove the causes responsible for fear and hesitation. The teacher and the parents should motivate such children to write.
7. *Presenting the self example and ideals:* Children always imitate others. Teachers and parents who follow the beaten track, do not experience any new thing or do not perform any new task or do not show originality cannot develop creativity in their children. Children can develop creativity if their teachers and parents manifest love for creativity in their behaviour.
8. *Using the creative resources of community:* Children should take a trip to creative art centres, scientific and industrial manufacturing centres. They will get incentive from these places and get motivated. Sometimes artists, scientists and other creative persons should be invited to the schools. It will help the increase of knowledge and encourage the development of creativity.

* * * * *

THE LEARNER

In a variety of settings Educators are responsible for the education of the students and the teaching staff. Several factors have made using principles of learning particularly challenging for the teacher educator to meet learners' needs for information. In the case of staff, many times the difficulty with meeting learners' needs is due to the various educational and experiential levels of staff and time constraints in the practice arena. To meet these challenges, the educator must know what determines how well a person learns. This is done by assessing the needs of the learner recognizing factors involved in the readiness to learn, and being able to correlate teaching interventions with learning styles to maximize opportunities for learning.

Educator's Role in Learning

The role of educating can be one of the most challenging and essential interventions a educator has to perform. To do it well, the teacher-educator must identify the information learners need as well as consider their readiness to learn and their styles of learning. It however, can't be denied that the learner is the single most important person in the education process. Learning can actually occur without an educator, but learning is enhanced by the addition of an educator who can serve as a facilitator. Just providing information to the learner, however does not mean that learning has occurred. Teaching is a bipolar activity therefore if there is any gap between the two poles there is no guarantee that the learner will learn the information given. But, there is more of an opportunity to learn if the educator assesses the determinants of learning.

Assessment enables the educator, to facilitate the process of learning by arranging experiences within the environment to help the learner find meaning and purpose for learning. As assessment of the determinants of learning enables the educator to present information in a variety of ways, which a learner cannot do alone. The educator manipulates the environment so that the learner's experience is put into meaningful parts and wholes to reach the learner's unique potential. This enables the learner to incorporate the information into behavior. The educator plays a crucial role in the learning process by (1) assessing problems or weaknesses, (2) providing appropriate information and presenting it in an appropriate manner, (3) identifying improvement being made, (4) giving feedback and follow up, (5) reinforcing learning in the acquisition of knowledge, a skill (6) to measure any change in attitude and behaviour, (7) evaluating learners' abilities.

The educator is vital in giving support, encouragement, and direction during the process of learning. Learners may make choices on their own but these choices may be limited or inappropriate. The educator can help to identify optimal learning approaches and then provide assistance in choosing learning activities that can both support and challenge the leaner based on individual learning needs, readiness to learn, and learning style.

Assessment of the Learner

The importance of assessment of the learner may seem self-evident, but often a special service is offered to the assessment phase of the educational process. It is not unusual to witness different learner groups with the same condition being taught with the same materials in the same way. Frequently the teacher is involved in teaching before considering all the determinants of learning. Educational assessment of needs, readiness, and styles of learning is the first and most important step in instructional design, but it is the one most often neglected. The effectiveness of teaching interventions is dependent on the scope accuracy, and comprehensiveness of assessment prior to interventions. But, one has to ask some questions as to why is assessment so significant and fundamental to the educational process, and why is it often overlooked or only partially carried out?

This initial step in the educational process helps validate the need for learning and the approach to be used in designing learning experiences. Persons who desire or require information to achieve optimal target to deliver quality education to the learners deserve to have an assessment done by the educator so that the needs of the leaner are appropriately targeted. There are many factors to consider with respect to the three determinants of learning, and assessments of all three should be based on theories, concepts, and principles. Assessments do more than identify and choose preference of information for purposes of setting behavioral goals and objectives, planning instructional interventions, and being able to evaluate in the long run if the goals and objectives have been met by the learner. Good assessments ensure that optimal learning is helpful in minimizing the chance of needless repetition of known material.

In addition, an assessment increases motivation to learn by addressing what the students or the teaching staff feel is most important to know or to be able to do. Lack of provisions or resource as a result of such factors affect the very process of teaching-learning. In addition, many educators although expected and required to instruct others, are unfamiliar with the concepts and techniques of teaching. The educator must become more familiar and comfortable with all the elements of instructional design, but particularly with the assessment phase because it provides the foundation for the rest of the educational process. Because of time constraints, which are a major concern when having to teach the teacher/educator must become skilled in accurately carrying out assessments to have reserve time left for actual teaching.

Assessment of the learner includes attending to the there determinants.

(What , When and how):

1. What the learner needs to learn.
2. When the leaner is receptive to learning.
3. How the learner best learns.

LEARNING NEEDS

Of the three determinants, learning needs (what does the leaner need to learn) must be examined first because there may be no reason to assess readiness to learn or learning styles if, by chance, learning needs are nonexistent. Assessment is essential to determine learning needs so that an instructional plan can be designed to address deficits in any of the cognitive, affective, or psychomotor domains. The purpose of assessing learning needs is to discover what has to be taught and to determine the extent of instruction or if instruction is necessary at all. Not every individual perceives a need for education. An assessment is used to identify and prioritize the needs and interests of the learner. This information is used to set objectives and plan appropriate and effective teaching methodologies whereby education can begin at a point suitable to the learner rather than from an unknown or inappropriate place.

Learning needs are defined as gaps in knowledge that exist between a desired level of performance and the actual level of performance. A learning need is the gap between what someone knows and what someone needs to know. These gaps exist because of a lack of knowledge, attitude, or skill.

Most learners, 90% to 95% of them according to the estimates of many educators in educational psychology (Bloom, 1968; Carroll, 1963; Burner, 1966; Skinner, 1954), can master a subject with a high degree of success if given sufficient time and appropriate types of help. It is the task of the educator to determine exactly what needs to be learnt and be able to identify an approach for presenting the material that will be best understood by the learner. That is to say the teacher first must discover what the needs of the leaner are and then find the most appropriate means of instruction that will enable the leaner to master the subject under consideration.

The following are important steps in the assessment of learning needs:

1. *Identify the learner*: Who is the audience? If the audience is one individual, is there a single need for many needs that have to be fulfilled? Is there more than one learner, and if so, are their needs congruent or diverse? The development of formal and informal education programs for students must be based on accurate identification of the learner and their immediate needs.
2. *Choose the right setting*: Establishing a trusting environment will help learners feel a sense of security in confiding information, believe their concerns are taken seriously and thought of as important, and feel respected.
3. *Collect data on the learner*: Once the leaner is identified, the educator can determine characteristic needs of the population by exploring typical educational problems or issues of interest to that population. Subsequently, a literature search can assist in identifying the type and extent of content to be included in teaching sessions as well as the educational strategies for teaching a specific learning group based on the analysis of needs.
4. *Include the learner as a source of information*: Leaners themselves are usually the most important source of needs assessment data. Allow the learners to identify what is important to them, what types of academic and other support systems are available or perceived to be available. If the audience for teaching is students, solicit them for information as to what areas of knowledge they feel they need new or additional information. Actively engaging learners in defining their own problems and needs allows them to learn

in the process and also motivates them to learn because they have an investment in planning for a program specifically tailored to their unique circumstances.

5. *Involve members of the administrative team*: Administration beside teachers may have insight into learners needs as a result of their frequent in the socio-political and economic set up. Teachers should also interact with those who so ever are related to the educational system. In addition, associations as well as NGOs should also be utilized for the same purpose.

Prioritize needs: A list of needs can become endless and seemingly impossible to accomplish. Maslow's (1970) hierarchy of human needs helps the educator prioritize identified learning needs. The educator can then assist the learner to meet basic needs first. Learning of other needs will be delayed if basic needs are not attended to first and foremost.

Setting priorities for learning is often difficult we faced with many learning needs in several areas. An effort to prioritize the identified needs will help the students or the teaching staff to set realistic and achievable learning goals. Choosing what information to cover is imperative, and choices must be deliberate. Learning needs must be prioritized based on those set.

Not all learners need to know everything, and assessment can help to discriminate the "need to know" from the "nice to know" information. If students want to know the factors that are responsible for their poor educational standard, that's fine, but it is not fundamental to learning how to cope with some such problem. Often, highly technical information will serve only to confuse and distract students from learning what they need to know. There may be needs that are not amenable to education. It is important to sort out types of learning needs from non-learning needs. This will help the educator know when action other than education would be more appropriate. Education in and of itself is not always the answer to a problem. Often, when something goes wrong, when something is not being done, when a student is not following a prescribed pattern or when a staff member does not adhere to protocol, it is believed that more education is necessary. Always look for other needs that are non-learning. For example, the educational expert discovers that the student is not doing his educational activities, not attempting self-learning etc. and may begin a teaching plan without adequate assessment.

6. *Determine availability of educational resources*: A need may be identified, but it may be useless to proceed with interventions if the proper educational resources are not available, are unrealistic to obtain, or do not match the learner's needs. In this case, it may be better to focus on the other identified needs at this point in time. For example, a student needs to develop proficiency in English. Educator determines that this student group learns best by the teacher's knowledge and practice of the same thrust area giving a demonstration. If the proper facility is not available for education/training at that moment in need and time, it might be better for the educator to concentrate on teaching the signs and weaknesses of the students might experience when having poor interaction than to cancel the facility altogether. Thereafter the educator would work immediately on obtaining the necessary resources for future interaction.

7. *Assess demands of the organization*: This will yield information hat reflects the climate of the organization. What is the organization's philosophy, objectives, strategic plan etc. The educator should be familiar with standards of performance required in various employee categories along with job descriptions in an institution, professional, and agency regulations. If the organization is focused on development of the student for future career versus educational problems and difficulties, then there likely will be a different educational focus or emphasis that dictates learning needs of the future opportunities.

Methods of Assess Learning Needs

The role of educator must ensure objective data about the leaner as well as subjective data for the learner. The following are various methods that can be used to assess learner needs and should be used in association with one another to yield the most reliable information.

Informal Conversations

Often learning needs will be discovered during informal conversations that take place between the teacher and the students or the family of the students. The educator must rely on active listening. Open-ended questions will encourage learners to reveal information about what they perceive their learning needs to be.

Structured Interviews

The structured interview is perhaps the most common form of needs assessment to solicit the learner's point of view. The teacher-educator asks the learner direct and often predetermined questions to gather information about learning needs. As with the gathering of any information from a learner in the assessment phase, the teacher should strive to establish a trusting environment, use open-ended questions, choose a setting that is free of distractions, and allow the learner to state what is believed to be the learning needs. It is important to remain non-judgmental when collecting information about the learner's strengths, beliefs, and motivations. Notes should be taken with the learner's permission, so important information is not lost. The telephone is a good tool to use for an interview if it is impossible to ask questions in person. The major drawback of a telephone interview, however is the inability on the part of the educator to perceive non-verbal clues from the learner.

Interviews yield answers that may reveal uncertainties, conflicts, inconsistencies, unexpected problems, anxieties, fears and present knowledge base. Examples of questions that could be asked of a student as learner are as follows: What do you think caused your problem? How severe is four earning difficulty? What does your course/education mean to you? Why do you want to be educated? What results do you hope to obtain from classes. What are your strengths and weaknesses? What do you think you will have the most problem in learning? Is there any skill that you have doubts you can perform? What problems have you encountered in the past? What to you see as your strengths and weaknesses? These types of questions help to determine the needs of the learner and serve as a foundation for beginning to plan for the education of the learner.

Focus Groups

Focus groups involve getting together a small number (4 to 12) of potential learners to determine areas of educational need by using group discussion to identify points of view or knowledge about a certain topic. A facilitator leads the discussion by asking questions. The questions are open-ended, and detailed discussion of each question is encouraged by the facilitator. These groups of potential learners should be same with similar characteristics such as age gender, and past experience with the topic under discussion. However, if the purpose of the focus group is to solicit attitudes about a particular subject or to discuss ethical issues, for example, it may not be necessary to have a homogeneous group.

Appraisal

Appraisal of the employees is one type of assessing learning needs. There may be many methods or steps that can be used in this process.

Readiness to Learn

Once the learning needs have been identified, the next step is to determine the learner's readiness to receive information. Readiness to learn can be defined as the time when the learner demonstrates an interest in learning the type or degree of information necessary to become more skillful in a job. Readiness to learn is when the learner is receptive to learning and is willing and able to participate in the learning process. The educator must never overuse the expression "the learner is not ready to learn." It is the responsibility of the educator to discover through assessment when exactly learners are ready to learn and what they want to learn. For example, the educator needs to adapt the content to be learned to fit with what the leaner is ready to learn. In preparing to teach a learner-group, the educator must determine what needs to be known about the teaching-learning process to assist the student to move toward independence in self study.

Assessing readiness to learn requires the educator to first understand what needs to be taught and to be competent in collecting and validating information. The same methods that were used to assess learning needs can also be used for assessing readiness to learn, such as making observations conducting interviews gathering information from the learner as well as other administrative team members, and reviewing the data.

An assessment of readiness to learn must be done prior to the time when actual learning is to occur. No matter how important the information is or how much the educator feels the recipient of teaching needs the information, if the learner is not ready, the information will not be absorbed. If educational objectives are set by the educator prior to assessing readiness to learn then both the educator's and the learner's time could very well be misused because the established objectives may be beyond the readiness of the leaner. The educator must give thought as to what is required of the learner that is what needs to be learnt, what the learning objectives should be, and in which domain and at what level of learning these objectives should be classified. The educator will then have an idea about what to focus on in the assessment of their learner's abilities.

Timing, that is, the point at which teaching should take place, is very important because anything that affects physical or psychological comfort can affect a learner's ability and willingness to learn. A learner who is unreceptive to information at one time may be more receptive to the same information at another time. Within the educational system, the educator often has limited contact with students and their family members. The student's readiness to learn is confined to that particular time and is based on learning being brief and basic. Timing is also an important factor with the teaching staff because readiness to learn is based on current demands of practice and needs to correspond to the ever constant changes in practice.

Before teaching can begin, the educator must take the time to first try to ascertain the level of readiness to learn. Readiness to learn can be determined by the learner's characteristics as follows: Physical readiness, Emotional readiness, Experiential readiness and Knowledge readiness.

These four types of readiness to learn may or may not prove to be obstacles to learning, but the few minutes the educator spends assessing learning readiness can help overcome these possible obstacles. The following factors must be taken into consideration:

Physical Readiness

There are several physical factors related to readiness that need to be considered by the educator because they may have an adverse impact on the degree to which learning will occur. There are five major components to physical readiness: measures of ability, complexity of task, environmental effects, health status, and gender.

Measures of Ability

If the task requires gross movements using the large muscles of the body, then there must be adequate strength, flexibility, and endurance. The style of movement ability is a good example of a psychomotor for which a student must have the physical ability to be ready to learn. If the educator is conducting an in-service workshop for staff on the subject to lifting and transfer activities of student, the educator must be cognizant of the endurance level required of the staff for them to be able to return demonstrate this skill. In addition, for information to be accurately processed, sense organs and receptors must be adequately functioning. For example, if a person has a visual deficit, are eyeglasses available to allow the students to see the lines or read the text. If not, the individual is not physically ready to learn. Measures involving visual and auditory acuity as well as the capacity to perform adequate movements affect the ability to learn. Creating a stimulating and accepting environment by using instructional tools to match learners' sensory abilities will help to raise and lift their interest in learning.

Complexity of Task

In learning to perform a skill, the educator must take into account the difficulty level of the subject or task to be mastered by the leaner. Variations in the complexity of the task affect the extent to which behavioral changes are necessary in the cognitive, affective, and psychomotor domains. Psychomotor skills, in particular, require different degrees of manual dexterity and physical energy output. Once acquired, however, they are usually retained better and longer than learning in the other domains. Once ingrained, psychomotor skills become habitual and may be difficult to alter. For example, if the learner has been performing a psychomotor skill over a long period of time and then the procedural steps of the tasks change, the learner will need to unlearn those steps and relearn a new way. This may increase the complexity of the task and put additional physical demands on the leaner as a result of lengthening the time needed to adjust to doing something in a new way. Older adults or those with low literacy skills will likely find the effort particularly difficult and time-consuming and may even refuse to make a change.

Environmental Effects

An environment conducive to learning will help to keep the learner's attention and stimulate interest in learning. For example, extremely high levels of noise can interfere with the accuracy and precision in performing manual dexterity tasks. Noise induces vibration of body parts and negatively affects concentration levels. Intermittent noise tends to have greater disruptive effects than the more rapidly habituated steady-state noise. Intermittent use of a jackhammer in the street outside the class room, for instance, is more disruptive to a student's ability to perform skills than a constant rear of traffic coming from the same street.

The senior students in particular, needs more time to react and respond to stimuli. The increased inability to receive and transmit information is a symptom of older age. Thus, tasks requiring large amounts of strength, endurance, speed or flexibility can be difficult for the older person. Complex motor tasks, with too much information given during demonstration by the educator, may result in the older learner becoming overwhelmed and can contribute to a tendency for an older person to focus on irrelevant information rather than on cues relevant to accomplishing the task at hand. When an activity is self-paced, the older learner will respond more favorably. Breaking down complex learning material into more simplified steps is helpful for all learners in improving their retention of information stimulating attention and increasing clarity and decreasing energy demands. As a result, we may increase physical readiness to learn.

Health Status

A sound mind is not possible with out a good health. Therefore, the assessment of the learner's health status is important to determine the amount of energy available as well as present comfort level because both of these factors impact heavily on readiness to learn. Energy-reducing demands caused by the body's response to illness require the learner to expend large amounts of physical and psychic energy, with little reserve left for actual learning. A person's health status, which can be classified as well, acutely ill, or chronically ill, must be taken into serious consideration when assessing for readiness.

Learners who are healthy have energy available for learning. Readiness to learn about health-promoting behaviors is based on their perception of self-responsibility. The extent to which can illness is perceived to potentially affect future well-being influences someone's desire to learn preventive and promotion measures. It is believed if learner feels a threat to their quality of life, more information will be sought in an attempt to control the negative impact of an illness.

Learners who are acutely ill focus their energies on the physiological and psychological demands of their illness. Learning is at a minimum because most of their energy is needed for the demands of the illness and gaining immediate relief. Any learning that may occur is related to treatments, tests, and minimizing pain or other discomforts. As these learners improve and the acute phase of illness diminishes, they can then focus on learning follow-up management and the avoidance of complications. The educator must assess an acutely ill person's readiness to learn by observing energy levels and comfort status. One observation that can signify increased energy and comfort levels is the ability to move more readily without becoming easily tired. Improvement in physical status usually results in more receptivity to learning. However medications that an induce side effects, such as giddiness, dizziness drowsiness, mental depression, stress, impaired depth perception, decreased ability to concentrate and learner fatigue, will also reduce task-handling capacity. Giving a learner a sedative prior to a learning experience will result in less apprehension, but cognitive and psychomotor abilities will be impaired, thus requiring a longer time, more physical output, and more frustration for the leaner to master a skill.

Chronic illness, on the other hand, has no time limits and is of long-term duration. A learner with a chronic condition, however, may experience acute episodes either as an exacerbation of the chronic disease or as a separate event, such as a motor vehicle accident. The physiological and psychological demands vary in chronic illness and are not always predictable. Students go through different stages in adjusting to their illness. If the leaner is in the avoidance stage, readiness to learn will be limited to simple explanations because the patient's energy is being spent on the stress involved in emotionally attempting to deny the illness. Energy levels become more stable when the student becomes aware of the realities of the situation or a situation is life-threatening or the level of anxiety will be high, and readiness to learn will be diminished. While teaching may be imperative, learning usually can take place only if instructions are repeated over and over again. In such circumstances, families and relatives should be educated instead. In later stages of adaptation, acceptance of illness will allow the individual to be more receptive to learning because anxiety levels will be less acute.

Some degree of anxiety is a motivator to learn but low or high anxiety will interfere with readiness to learn. On either end of the continuum, mild or severe anxiety leads to inaction on the part of the learner, whereas moderate anxiety will drive someone to take action. As the level of anxiety be gins to increase, emotional readiness goes to the maximum level and then begins to decrease. Discovering what stressful events or major life changes the learner is experiencing will give the educator idea as to that person's emotional readiness to learn.

Motivation

The motivation and interest on the part of the learner to achieve a task also lead to more meaningful teaching-learning experiences. Emotional readiness is strongly associated with motivation. Knowing the motivational level of the learner assists the educator in determining when someone is ready to learn. The learner must have intentions of improving performance. Otherwise, merely going through the action in a mechanical manner, disregarding important learning aspects and demonstrating unwanted activity will not result in task mastery. Assessment of emotional readiness involves ascertaining the level of motivation, not necessarily the reasons for the motivation. Readiness to learn will be indicted by the questions the student may ask.

Gender

Today, many Researchers are of the view that women overall are more receptive to education. This may be because women traditionally have been more responsible for activity they take therefore, are more open to learning-teaching. In addition, they have more frequent contacts with educators while getting knowledge and also for bearing and raising children. Men, on the other hand, tend to be less receptive and are more likely to be careless. Since a good deal of this behavior is thought to be socially induced, changes are beginning to be seen as increased attention is being paid to more prosperous lifestyles and this has occurred because of the blending of gender roles in the home institutions and workplaces.

Emotional Readiness

The learner must be emotionally ready to learn. As with physical readiness, emotional readiness also includes several factors that need to be assessed.

Anxiety Level

Anxiety is a factor that influences the ability to perform at a cognitive, affective, and psychomotor level. Depending on the level of anxiety, it may or may not be an obstacle to the learning of new skills. Fear is a major factor of anxiety and thus affects negatively on readiness to learn in any of the learning domains. The performance of a task in and of it self may be fear inducing to a learner, because of its very nature of meaning. There are many reasons why a learner may be motivated to learn. The level of motivation is related to what learners perceive as an expectation of themselves from others Interest in informal or formal educator-learner interactions is a cue to motivation. The learner who is ready to learn shows an interest in the subject educator is doing by demonstrating a willingness to participate or to ask questions.

Previous experiences, whether be past accomplishments or failures, will be reflected in the current level of motivation demonstrated by the learner for accomplishing the task at hand.

Risk Taking Behavior

Taking risks is intrinsic in the activities people perform daily. Many activities are done without thinking about the outcome. It has has been found that some students, by the very nature of their personality, will take more risks than others. They accept more challenge. The educator can help such students develop strategies to help reduce the risk of their choices by providing suitable measures.

Frame of Mind

Frame of mind or temperament involves concern about things here and now. If survival is of primary concern, then readiness to learn will be focused on meeting basic human needs. Physical needs such as food, warmth, comfort, and safety as well as psychosocial needs of feeling accepted and secure must be met before someone can focus on higher learning. People from lower socioeconomic levels tend to have an immediate orientation to present-day concerns because they are trying to satisfy everyday needs. Children and teenagers also regard life in the here and now because they are developmentally focused on what makes them happy and satisfied and are ore into concrete than abstract thought. Adults who have reached self-actualization and whose basic needs are met are more ready to learn health promotion tasks and are said to have a more futuristic orientation.

Experiential Readiness

Experiential readiness refers to the learner's past experiences with learning. Before the teacher starts teaching, he should assess whether previous learning experiences have been positive or negative in overcoming problems or accomplishing a new task. Someone who has had negative experiences with learning is not likely to be motivated or willing to take a risk in trying to change behavior or acquire new behaviors.

Level of Aspiration

The degree to which someone is motivated to achieve is related to the type of short and long-term goals fixed by the learner. Previous failures and past successes influence what goals learners set for themselves. Early successes are important motivators in learning subsequent skills. Satisfaction, once achieved, elevates the level of aspiration, and this in turn increases the probability of continued performance output in undertaking future efforts to modify behavior.

Cultural Background

Knowledge on the part of the educator about other cultures and being sensitive to behavioral differences between cultures are important to avoid teaching in opposition to cultural aspects etc. Things related to cultural influences allows the teacher to bridge the gap when necessary between the educational setup and the learners culture. Building on the learner's knowledge base or belief system rather than attempting to change it or claim it is wrong, will encourage rather than negatively affect readiness to learn. Language is also a part of culture and may prove to be a significant obstacle to learning if the educator and the learner do not fluently speak the same language. Assessing whether the learner understands English well enough is the first step. Often a relative, a friend, or a designated person within the educational system can be called on, if necessary. Enlisting the help of someone else to bridge cultural differences may at times, however, have a negative impact on learning, depending on the sensitivity of the topic and the need for privacy. There may be instances when the student does not want family members or associates to know about problems of education.

Remember, also, that some specific terms in and of itself may be a foreign language to many student whether or not the are from another culture. Besides, sometimes a native language does not have an equivalent word to describe the terms that are being used in the teaching situation. Differences in language compound the cultural barrier. Teaching should not be started unless you have determined that the learner understands you and that you have an understanding of the learner's cultural background.

Locus of Control

Whether readiness to learn comes from internal or external stimuli an be determined by ascertaining the learner's previous life patterns of responsibility and assertiveness. When learners are internally motivated to learn, they have what is known as an internal locus of control. They are ready when they feel a need to know about something. The drive to learn comes from within themselves. Usually this type of learner will indicate a need by asking questions. When someone asks a question, the time is prime for learning. If learners have an external locus of control, that is, they are externally motivated, then someone other than themselves has to encourage a feeling of wanting to know something. The responsibility often falls on the educator's shoulders to motivate them to have a positive feeling to learn.

Orientation

Students with a orientation tend to be most close-minded in their thinking and are more future oriented, as more open minded in their approach to situations, are more willing to learn new material and place. This type of orientation is more effective in the case of people have been raised in a small places of who come from protective family environments. People who are brought up in a cosmopolitan orientation most likely have a more worldly perspective on life due to broader experiences outside their immediate contacts and interaction. These individuals are more likely to be receptive to new ideas and to opportunities to learn new ways of doing things. One must be careful not to unfairly stereotype individuals, but learners usually possess representative characteristics of different types of orientation.

Knowledge Readiness

Knowledge readiness refers to the learner's present knowledge base, the level of learning capability, and the preferred style of learning. These components must be assessed to determine readiness to learn, and teaching should be planned accordingly.

Present Knowledge Base

How much someone already knows about a particular subject or how good they are at performance is an important factor to determine before designing and implementing teaching or instruction. If the educator makes the mistake of teaching subject material that has already been acquired then the educator is at the minimum risk. This could result in resistance to further learning. One should always find out what the students already know much before to teaching, and build on this knowledge base to stimulate readiness to learn.

Cognitive Ability

The extent to which information can be processed is indicative of the level at which the learner is able to carry out learning. The educator must match behavioral objectives to the cognitive ability of the learner. The learner who is capable of understanding, memorizing, recalling, or recognizing subject material is functioning at a lower level than the learner who demonstrates problem solving, concept formation, or application of information. For example the educator can assume that teaching staff or students who are able to answer questions related to a particular subject.

Individuals with cognitive impairment due to mental retardation present a special challenge to the educator and will require simple explanations and step-by-step coverage of course and course of instruction with frequent repetition. Be sure to make information meaningful to those with cognitive impairments by teaching at their level and communicating in ways that the leaner will be able to understand. Enlisting the help of members support system by teaching them requisite skills will allow them to positively contribute to the reinforcement of self learning.

Learning Disabilities

Other than those caused by mental retardation, learning disabilities and low-level reading skills are not necessarily indicative of an individual's intellectual abilities but will require special or *innovative approaches to instruction to maintain or boost the level of readiness to learn. It is easy for low-literacy and learning-disabled persons to become easily discouraged unless the teacher recognizes their special needs and seeks ways to help them accommodate or overcome their problems with processing information.

Learning Styles

There are various preferred styles of learning, and assessing how someone learns best will help the educator to vary teaching approaches accordingly. Knowing what teaching methods and materials a learner is most comfortable with or, conversely, does not tolerate well will help the educator to teaching to meet the needs of individuals with different styles of learning, thereby increasing their readiness to learn. The following learning style may enable us to develop more perception related to the present topic.

LEARNING STYLES

Learning styles refers to the way individuals receive and process information. Each learner is unique and complex, with a distinct learning style preference, which distinguishes one learner from another. The learning style models are based on the base that certain characteristics of style are biological in origin, whereas others are acquired as a result of environmental or institutional influences. Recognizing that people have different approaches to learning helps the educator to understand the various edcuational interests and needs of diverse populations. Accepting diversity of style can help educators create the atmosphere for learning that offers experiences that encourage each individual to reach his or her full potential. Understanding learning style also helps educators to make deliberate decisions about program development and instructional design.

No learning style is either better or worse than another. Given the same content, most learners can assimilate information with equal success, but how they go about mastering the content is determined by their individual style. The more flexible the educator is in using teaching methodologies related to individual learning styles, the greater the likelihood that leaning will occur. A learning style may prove to be more effective in a particular situation. The following are some of the principles of learning style as proposed by Friedman & Alley (1984)

1. Style, of learning and Teaching should be identified. Identification of different styles offers specific clues as to the way a person learns. By understanding one's own learning style, the educator can appreciate

why it may be easier to help one style of learner to master information while it may be more difficult to work with another learner who needs an entirely different approach to learning.

2. Teachers need to guard against over-teaching by their own preferred learning styles. Educators need to realize that just because they gravitate to learning a certain way does not mean that everyone else can or wants to learn this way. It is much easier for the educator to change the teaching approach than for the leaner to adapt to the teacher's style.
3. Teachers are most helpful when they assist students in identifying and learning through their own style preferences. Making learners aware of their individual style preferences will lead to an understanding of which teaching-learning approaches work best for them. Also, an awareness of their preference for a particular leaning style sensitizes learners to the fact that whatever style is most comfortable for them may not be the best approach for others.
4. Students should have the opportunity to learn through their preferred style. The educator can provide the means by which each learner can experience successful learning. Visual learners, for example, should be given movies, computer simulations, and videos from which to learn rather than insisting that they read. Concrete and abstract thinkers need to capitalize on their strengths; concrete thinkers need facts, and abstract thinkers need theories.
5. Students should be encouraged to diversify their style preferences. Today learners are constantly faced with learning situations were one approach to learning will not suffice if they are to reach their fullest competence and level. However, without encouragement, learners will automatically gravitate

to using their preferred style of leaning. The more frequently learners are exposed to different methods of learning, the less stressful those methods will be in future learning situations.

6. Teachers can develop specific learning activities that reinforce each modality or style. Educators must become aware of various methods and materials available to address and augment the different learning styles. To be effective, educational strategies should be geared to different learning styles because using only a limited number of approaches will selectively excluded many learners.

Three mechanisms to determine learning style are observation, interviews, and administration of learning style instruments. By observing the learner in action, the educator can determine how the learner problem solves. Learning style can also be determined by interview. The educator can ask the learner about preferred ways of learning as well as the environment most comfortable for learning.

All of these three techniques should be used to determine learning style. Once data are gathered through interview, observation, and instrument administration can be chosen to match the style of the learner. Educators can also use the learning style approach in directing students, or the staff towards ways they bet can learn. Implications for using the learning style approach to instruction are enormous and exciting. If learning style of the staff participating in the academic situations have been assessed and identified, then educational experiences to complement those styles can be designed. Adapting educational experiences to coincide with learning styles thus increases the likelihood that learning will take place. Understanding and recognizing various styles are useful when making decisions about planning, implementing, and evaluating educational programs.

4

Education and Pedagogy

EDUCATION

The word 'Education' has been derived from the Latin word 'Educare' which means to bring up or to raise child mentally and physically.

There is another Latin word 'Educere' which means to bring forth or to lead out. In other words, it means to lead out the best in the child or to guide him. Still others say that education is derived from Latin word 'educatum' which means the act to teaching or training.

As such a close study of the above meaning of education is the act of bringing up 'to raise', to lead out and the act of training. In the context the educationists have defined the education as under.

Definitions of Education

> 'Education means the bringing out the ideas of universal validity which are latent in the minds of every man'.
>
> \- *Socrates*

> 'Education is a process by which the child makes in internal external'.
>
> \- *Froebel*

> 'Education is the development of all those capacities

in the individual which enable him to control his environment and fulfill his possibilities.

- John Dewey

'Education is the manifestation of divine perfection already existing in man. We want that education by which character is formed, strength of mind increased, the intellect is expanded and by which one can stand on one's own feet'

- Vivekanand

'By education I mean an all round drawing out of the best in child and man-body, man and spirit'.

- Gandhi

Different Concepts of Education

1. Education is the development of Man

Education is a process of individual development. It carries on the individual's physical, intellectual, aesthetic, moral, economic, spiritual and social development so that the human being may get rid of animal instinct and become civilised.

2. Education is an act of Training

Education imparts learning to an individual so that he may have his own place in the society. Education makes its special contribution to train an individual to bring about change in his behaviour, develop innate capacities and lead towards process. An individual becomes a responsible man towards society on receiving such training. Such training is possible only through education. In the absence of such training an individual can not live in the society in a systematic way. In short one can say that education trains the individual's physique, brain and spirit.

3. Education is Direction

Education is not static but a dynamic process. It leads a person always towards progress. The education adopts changes according to the changing conditions of time, place and society and reconstructs the society. It gives directions towards the aim according to the capabilities, capacities, interests and powers of the children.

4. Education is a social Function

Education helps in bringing about a change in society. Economic, moral, cultural, social, scientific, spiritual and educational change is possible only through education. Education is a powerful instrument of social reconstruction.

5. Education is a demand of modern age

The modern age is scientific age. When we talk of national and international understanding, the need of education appears important in every field. This is why, these days we talk of adult education, social education, population education, formal education, informal education, and non-formal education.

6. Educational is a life long process

Education starts in the mother's womb and continues till death. Man learns one thing or the other at every moment. The sequence of learning through the medium of experiences continues uptill death.

7. Education is a Tri-polar process

John Dewey regarded education as tripolar process. According to him the process of education an not be talked about in the absence of social environment.

The different concepts of education give clear meaning that it has wider concepts and it touches the all aspect of human beings

Difference Between Education and Training

Education

1. Education goes on from birth to death.
2. The ultimate aim is personality development.
3. Education has three aspects: formal, informal and non-formal.
4. Education is imparted at home, in educational institutions, political groups, religious institutions, cultural and social centers.
5. The curriculum of education is broad and flexible.
6. The source of inspiration of a human being in education deserves social fame.

Training

1. The period of training is limited: some months, a year or some years.
2. The ultimate aim is skill development.
3. There is informality in training.
4. Training is mainly imparted in any college, hospital, office or training institution.
5. The curriculum of training is usually fixed.
6. Economic aspect is the source of inspiration.

Discrimination between Education and Instruction

Education

1. Education is a life long process.
2. Education is child centered and important.
3. The field of education is broad.
4. The places of education are home, educational institutions, social centres, cultural places, business are religious institutions.

5. There are formal, informal and non formal aspects in Education.

Schooling

1. Schooling is the process starting from child's entry (admission) to school and ending with his withdrawal (leaving it).
2. In schooling the teacher and curriculum get important place.
3. The field of education is narrow.
4. Formality alone is visible in schooling.
5. The place of schooling is limited to the school.

Discrimination Between Education and Indoctrination

Education

1. The scope of Education is very broad.
2. All the three types of education-formal, informal and non formal education are mixed up in education.
3. It continues from birth to death.
4. Various methods are used in education.
5. It is individual centred. The interest of the individual borne is mind.

Indoctrination

1. The scope of indoctrination is very narrow
2. There is formality in indoctrination.
3. The time of indoctrination is fixed.
4. Lecture method is emphasised in indoctrination.
5. Indoctrination is thought centred. In indoctrination the teacher's attention is towards the thoughts.

Types of Education: Basically there are three types:

1. *Formal Education*: It is that education in which there is a blending of formality. This type of Education is imparted in schools and colleges. Curriculum, methods of teaching and teacher are fixed beforehand. The teacher keeps in mind many rules and establishes relations with the students. It is deliberately planned to bring about specific influence in the educand. The teacher tries to bring about all round development of the child keeping in mind the needs of the individual and the society. The teacher influences the students by his experience and ability. Formality is found in co-curricular activities. School is thus a formal agency of education.
2. *Informal Education*: Psychologists very rightly says that child develops his most of the traits of personality during infancy. During the infancy child gets informal education. As education of this kind is obtained at such places as in the homes, temples, mosques, gurdwaras, social agencies, political parties, in the meetings etc. It is a deliberately planned education which modifies the behaviour with a particular view. Its influence is subtle and imperceptible but at the same moment very important and significant. It is said that informal education is exactly opposed to formal education.
3. *Non-Formal Education*: In the present age, it is felt that the formal and informal education is incompetent to fulfil certain shortcomings in the process of education. It is essential to bring into life the third agency i.e. non-formal education. The informal education is as elastic as formal education but the non-formal education is neither absolutely without bonds nor has rigidity in it. Non-formal education makes special contribution to continuing education. It is a strategy of teaching. It is a nice combination of

both the means: formal and informal.

AIMS OF EDUCATION IN MODERN INDIAN SOCIETY

After independence three main commissions were set up. All these commissions of education decided the aims of education and modern Indian society.

University Education Commission (1949)

The human life in a democratic country generally depends upon the vocational education and the education which meets day to day requirements of life. As such universities should work for the need of society. Development of intellects, consciousness about new concepts of knowledge, to know the meaning and purpose of life and organise vocational education.

Secondary Education Commission (1952)

The Secondary Education Commission formulated the following social aims of education keeping in view the needs of democratic India.

1. Development of Democratic Citizenship.
2. Improvement of vocational efficiency.
3. Development of personality.
4. Development of Qualities of Leadership.

Kothari Education Commission (1964)

In a democratic country like India man is to develop himself. The ultimate aim of education should give maximum opportunities to develop in all aspects of life. Kothari Education Commission suggests the following aims of education.

1. Vocational aims of Education.
2. Character building aims.
3. Citizenship aim.

4. Aim for the development of scientific attitude.
5. Education for social aim and national integration.
6. Education for international understanding.
7. Education for Modernisation.

1. *Vocational Aim of Education:* Gandhiji has very rightly said: 'If God were to incarnate in India it will have to assume the form of bread. If a person were asked to choose between bread and freedom, he will have to choose bread.'
2. *Character Building Aim*: Money is not needful, power is not needful, cleverness is not needful, even health is not the one thing needful but character alone and education must develop it.

   All out learning or recitation of the Vedas, correct knowledge of Sanskrit, Latin, Greek and what not will avail us nothing if they do not enable us to cultivate knowledge related to the building up of character.
3. *Citizenship Aim*: So long as citizenship is not developed, national progress cannot be conceived of. Education imparted should surely develop the following qualities.
   - *Clear thinking*. The success of democracy can be expected only when students think in a free and clear manner. If there is no clarity in thoughts, even proper action will never be performed. The students must have the knowledge of truth and untruth, right and wrong, good and bad etc.
   - Clarity in Speech and Writing. Fault speaking ad writing is dangerous for democracy. A such clarity in speech and writing is always needed.
   - Art of Living with Community. Man is a social creator. The development of qualities such as

tolerance, cooperation, respect and dignity of a person, moral qualities etc. should be developed by education.

- Development of the Sense of Patriotism: Patrotism means loyalty to our country. We should try to respect Indian culture. We should try to check the evils in the country and pledge to serve the country selflessly.

4. Development of Scientific Attitude: Modern age is a scientific and computer age. Technical experiments are based on science and technology.

5. Education for social and national integration: In reality, education is a powerful means to bringing social change.

   'Great changes which have taken place in the educational system must be maintained. Besides, it should be modified and revolutionised as per need and change of society.

   'India has to choose for herself a culture that derives inspiration from what is noble in our ancient culture and at the same time does not ignore the demands of the present age.' - Dr. Rajendra Prasad

6. Education for International Understanding: International understanding is very much necessitated for modern India for her social and economic development. When we are talking about national integration. We cannot ignore the role of international understanding.

7. Education for Modernisation: No reform is more urgent than to transform education to endevour, to relate to life needs and a spiration of the people and thereby make it a powerful instrument of social economic and cultural transformation necessary for

the realisation of national goals. Science and technology have enabled man in twentieth century to leave his foot prints on the moon. Owing to scientific progress, we have been able to make our relations with other countries.

- Education in India must create the spirit of democracy.

* * * * *

PHILOSOPHY OF EDUCATION

Definition of Philosopohy

> 'Whenever philosophy has been taken seriously it has been assumed that it signified achieving wisdom that would influence the conduct of life.'
>
> *- John Dewey*

Features of Philosophy

What is Education

Education is not a dead process. It is a lively, dynamic, bipolar process of transformation. According to this view, there must be two poles for its operation the one is the teacher and the other is the child as student. The teacher prossesses some beliefs, ideals and values and the child is influenced by these. In other words, we can say that the teacher is a philosopher who tries to develop the child according to his philosophy to attain a desirable type of individual.

Adams has rightly remarked. 'Education is the dynamic side of philosophy. It is the active aspect of philosophical belief.'

Relationship Between Philosopohy and Education

1. Philosophy determines the real destination towards

which education has to go. Education is a conscious and dynamic process which needs proper guidance and supervision. Without proper guidance and supervision, it can not achieve its goal. Philosophy determines the goal of life and also provides suitable and effective guidance and supervision for education to achieve that goal. Without the help of philosophy, education can not be a successful process of development and achievement. Spencer has rightly observed:

'True education is practicable only by a true philosophy.'

2. Philosophy determines the various aspects of Educations. Scholars believe that philosophy is concerned with abstract items and conceptions only while education deals with practical concrete things and processes.
3. Great Philosophers have been great Educationists Also. History bears eloquent testimony to the fact that great philosophers have been great educationists also of their times. Plato, Socrates, Locke, Rousseau, Froebel, Dewey, Gandhi, Tagore, Aurobindo and others who were great philosophers of their times have also talked about education. Their philosophical treatises have been important guide books for educational planning and dependent on education due to following reasons:
   (a) Education is the Dynamic side of Philosophy: Two things are essential for completing any task – 1. Thought or plan and 2. Application or practicability Philosophy is the thought or plan side and education is the application or practical side. Philosophy determines the aims of life and by analysis it lays down the principles to be

followed for achieving the set aims. Education translates these principles and ideas into practice. Thus, Adams has rightly said – 'Education is the dynamic side of philosophy'.

(b) Education is a mans to Achieve the Goal – It is philosophy which determines the aims of life. Through analysis and classification these are divided into goals to be achieved by the process of education. Herbart holds the same opinion.

Philosophy and Curriculum

By means of curriculum, desired behavioural changes are sought to be achieved to attain the goal of life determined by a particular philosophy. Thus, philosophy determines the aims of education so also it determines the curriculum. In other words the philosophy of a country at a particular time determines the curriculum in which such subjects, activities and experiences are included which are supposed to meet the emerging demands of the society at that time.

Philosophy and Methods of Teaching

Philosophy is also closely related to the methods of teaching. It is Philosophy that controls the teacher to change his methods of teaching accordingly. Method of teaching is conditioned by a philosophy of the individual and educational planning. In a sense philosophy is a way of thinking and a way of working. As such, these two factors determine the nature, style and actual operation of methods of teaching.

Philosophy and Discipline

Philosophy determines the nature and form of discipline. Whether school disciplines should be strict and rigid or flexible and free is also a philosophical problem. It may be noted that the social, economic and philosophical thinking of a particular country always determine the nature of discipline.

Philosophy and Text Books

To achieve the aims of life and education, text books are of great importance and value. As curriculum is powerfully influenced by the Philosophy of times, so the text books are affected by the prevailing philosophy of the day. Since text books contain matter which reflects the ideology ideals and values of society, the government should keep an eye on the production of desirable books for children.

Philosophy and Teacher

Philosophy has a great influence on the teacher both in the area of thinking and behaving. Really speaking, a teacher is not a teacher alone. He is basically a philosopher also. The teacher should know the needs of children and the demands of society and then plan his methods of teaching. He must keep in mind that his own beliefs, ideology and principles of behaviour have a powerful impact on the development of children. Hence he must possess a good understanding of all the philosophies of life and choose good and wholesome elements from them to from his own philosophy. Further, he must be a person full of high ideals and possess moral and spiritual values which go to form his character and shape his conduct. He must also be well conscious of national needs in all spheres and plan his teaching activities to fulfil those needs. Only such teachers imbused with high ideals, moral and spiritual values together with a sense of national responsibility for national prosperity. They can create patriotic, dynamic resourceful and enterprising citizens.

BRANCHES OF PHILOSOPHY

Meaning of Idealism

As a philosophical doctrine, idealism recognizes ideas. Feelings and ideals are more important than material object. At the same time, it emphasizes that human development should be according to moral, ethical and spiritual values so that he acquires knowledge of unity in diversity.

Idealism holds that spiritual world is more important than material world. The chief reason is that material world is destructible and mortal. It is untrue and myth. On the contrary, the spiritual world is a world of ideas, feelings and ideals the knowledge of which reveals the knowledge of the reality of mind and soul. In this way, according to Idealism only spiritual world is the essence of reality which is undying immortal and true. Nothing beyond the spiritual world of spiritual values is immortal and true. In this way, Idealism, recognizing human ideas, feelings and ideals more important than natural and scientific phenomena, emphasizes on the study of man and his mind.

Definition of Idealism

To make the meanings of Idealism more clear, the following definitions can be of help.

> "Idealistic Philosophy takes many and varied forms, but the postulates underlying all this is that mind or spirit is the essential world stuff, that the true reality is of a mental character."
>
> - *J.S. Roos*

> "Idealists point out that it is mind that is central in understanding the world."
>
> - *Brubacher*

Idealism and Aims of Education

The following are the aims of education according to the philosophy of Idealism:

1. Self-realization or 'Exhaltation of Personality: According to idealism, man is the most beautiful creation of God. The advocates of Idealism lay great stress on the exhaltation of human personality. By

exhaltation of human personality, they mean self-realization. Self-realization involves full knowledge of the self. The first aim of education according to Idealism, is to develop the 'Self' of the individual higher and higher till self realization is achieved.

"The aim of education specially associated with Idealism is the exhaltation of personality, or self-realization, the making actual or real the highest potentialities of the self."

- J.S. Ross

2. To Ensure Spiritual Development: Idealistis give greater importance to spiritual values in comparison with material attainments. Thus, according to them, the second aim of education is to develop the child mentally, morally and above all spiritually. Therefore the teacher should organize the relevance of education for the development of the child's spirituality.
3. To Cultivate Truth, Beauty and Goodness: Truth, Beauty and Goeness should be encouraged more and more in order to develop values. The more an individual realizes these ideals, the more spiritually developed he will become. Education should strive its utmost in developing the child morally the spiritually so that he achieves self realization.
4. Conservation, Promotion and Transmission of Cultural Heritage: Man is the only being edowed with a keen and penetrating intelligence and an enormous capacity of assimilating knowledge of the world. His mental and intellectual capacities develop cultural, social and artistic values in human life in all its aspects. Men's achievements in the areas of science, art and culture are of great intrinsic value. His creativity is dynamic and working since the very early times. Our cultural heritage is of immense value and worth.

5. Conservation of Inborn Nature into Spiritual Nature – Idealists hold the view that the inborn instincts and inherent tendencies of the child should be sublimated into spiritual qualities and values. This is real development of the individually. Only then it will be possible for the individual to attain fullest and highest development of personality. One of the aims of education according to Idealism is to sublime to the inborn raw instincts of the child into spiritual qualities.
6. Preparation for a Holy Life: Idealists uphold that education should create such condition and provide an environment which are conducive to the development of spiritual values in a child. A holy life full of piety and good ideals will lead naturally towards spiritual development and self-realization. Finally, the aim of education according to idealistic philosophy is to also prepare the child for a holy life.

Idealism and Curriculum

a. Physical, Social, Moral and Religious – In this the subjects especially included are culture, sociology, ethics and religion etc.
b. Literary subjects, Aesthetics, Geography, Science and Mathematics etc. Ross holds the view firmly that man can develop spiritually only when he is physically healthy. In short curriculum must include physical and spiritual subjects.

Idealism and Methods of Teaching

The aims of Idealism are concrete and definite. But there is no specific method for achieving them. Socrates used 'Question – Answer' method. Plato emphasized 'Discourse Method' and Aristotle advocated 'Inductive – Deductive' method. In the works of Hegel, Logical Measuring is evident.

Some advocates employed the device of Simple to complex. Pestalozzi laid stress on education of the physical organs and allied activities. Herbert advocated 'Instruction Method'. Froebel insisted upon 'play-way Method'. Not only these, other Idealists advocated many more methods namely Discussion, Lecture, Talk in groups. In this way, according to Idealists no specific method is to be adhered to. In their opinion, any and every method may be employed to realize the ideals set and determined before.

> 'Idealists consider themselves as creators and determiners of methods not devotees of some one method.'
>
> \- *Butler*

Idealism and Teacher

In the real of Idealism, the role of teacher is very important and glorious. Idealistic philosophy believes that this planned creation has two parts (a) The teacher and (b) The child as student. Both aims at one target only – The development of the individual child in a spiritual way. The realization of this great aim is possible only through education and the essential agent, the teacher. In reality, an idealist teacher is imbued fully with high degree of self knowledge, self dynamism and essential qualities of spiritualism. By his own model of life, he tries to shape the spiritualism and the individuality of the child to a life of purity, virtue and great achievements. He creates a wholesome conductive atmosphere by his own activities and planned experiences for the child. He guides the child with such genuine love, affection and sympathy that he attains his full mental and spiritual development.

REALISM

Realism as philosophy emerged out of a revolt against Idealism. Since Idealism was based on imagination and principles related to soul and abstract idea. It was found that

Realism focuses on only those things that exist and we can see and experience them.

Realism as a deliberate and complete philosophy did not emerge until nineteenth century. The rapid growth of scientific knowledge and materialism has led to its increased growth and its acceptance as a distinct philosophy.

Realism takes into consideration the basic fact of life. It postulates only one criterion that all knowledge is derived from experience. Experience is the outcome of what is real. Realism believes in the world of nature and reality. It is a philosophy that is much away from the world of ideas or imagination.

The realists believe that the physical universe is operated by natural laws. Therefore, realists try to discover truth with the help of scientific methods. "Seeing is believing", 'discovering is believing' are the key-words of realism. Some of the realists believe the religion is merely man-made and there is no God. However, the existence, of God should not be discussed by the realists or any other because it can't either be proved that there is God or not.

Going away from the discussion of relevance of 'Realism' as a philosophy, we may discuss its importance for Education. The summary is presented herewith. Accordingly to Realism, there are two aims of education:

(a) Equipping students with knowledge and skills needed to understand an environment.

(b) Enabling student to manage their own affairs. The vocational aims of education is given importance.

Regarding curriculum, it emphasizes the teaching of physical sciences. These subjects are to be followed later on by vocational studies as future career.

Realism advocates that there should be proper sequence of teaching-learning so that whatever is taught must be taught clearly, easily, thoroughly and pleasantly. The teaching method should involve concrete and scientific references in the process of teaching-learning. Understanding and perception are the top priority. Inductive method of teaching is always preferred by a Realist. Scientific evaluation is the most important contribution made by realism in education.

The realist does not attach special importance to the personality of the teacher. The following principles can be emphasised by the 'Realistic Philosophy'.

(i) Whatever is to be known must be taught,

(ii) Whatever is taught should be taught in a straight forward manner,

(iii) Whatever is taught should be taught for practical application in everyday life,

(iv) If anything is to be learnt its general principles must be explained followed by further details.

NATURALISM

The naturalists are considered as empiricists. They believe that knowledge is acquired through sense organs and with the help of the brain. They do not accept the rationalist's position that all knowledge is innate. They believed in the possibility of direct knowledge. The naturalists believe in living according to Nature as the best type of life. 'Follow Nature' is their slogan. Be natural is their ultimate aim.

Forms of Naturalism

The following three forms of naturalism are distinguished:-

1. *Naturalism of physical world:* The principle attempts to explain human actions, individual experiences, and

feelings on the basis of physical sciences. It explains the entire universe in the light of the principles of physical sciences. It points out that not only is science one form of knowledge, but that it is the only form of valid knowledge.

2. *Mechanical Position:* According to this principle, the entire universe is a machine of a self driving energy that ensures its functioning. This is in one way like materialism as it suggests that matter is the only reality, and anything that exists is a form of matter. The human being is thought of as nothing but an active machine which is activated by certain environmental influences. The impact of this kind of positivism led to the emergence of the behavioural school that explained all human behaviour in terms of stimulus and response. Behaviourism thus seeks to explain the entire range of human activity as mechanical process.

3. *Biological naturalism:* It is naturalism in this form, as biological naturalism, has elaborated the theory of the natural man, and has explained that the evolution of man and animal is a single process. It refuses to admit the spiritual nature of man and expounds that his nature is the heritage he has received from his ancestors. Biological naturalism contains that all the processes of Nature. The entire existence of the universe cannot be explained in terms of mechanical and physical processes, because in the biological world, evolution is a more important phenomenon. The principles underlying evolution stops at the material or physical level, but in the case of human beings it is also manifested in the mental, moral and spiritual levels.

Naturalism and Educational Aim

Regarding the aims of education, Naturalists adopts a biological and evolutionist attitude. Mechanical Naturalism suggests that education should aim at the efficiency and perfection of the human machine. But this concept does not represent completely the naturalist school. There should be complete training of the life of humans. It also includes the relevance of spiritual aspect of life of human beings. Bernard Shaw believed that education must aim not only at the individual's development but also at making he individual capable of stimulating and sustaining social development, for this will add to the social heritage of the succeeding generations. Naturalists believe that education should achieve a synthesis and adjustment between individual and society, and also between man and nature.

According to Rousseau, "Now of the three factors in education nature is wholly beyond our control; things are only partly in our power; the education of men is the only one controlled by us; and even here our power is largely illusory, for who a hope to direct every word and deed of all with whom the child has to do." "What is the goal?

Naturalism and Curriculum

1. *Scientific subjects:* As a system of philosophy, naturalism has been exceptionally susceptible to the development of Science, and by virtue of this influence, it has attached much importance to evolutionary theory, empirical teaching and scientific analysis, etc. Language and Mathematics, for the Naturalists, are tools for the learning of Science. But Physical and Social Sciences should be preferred on Humanities.
2. *Study of History:* Considering that the present is more important than the future, the naturalists have not made any mistake of ignoring the past, because the

past contains many valuable suggestions for the education. Therefore, Naturalists believe in the value of historical study. Studies like History will enable us to construct a new social structure and thus plan for the future.

3. *Development of emotional instincts:* Evolutionists believe that the man had developed or evolved, from the animal stage. They also believe that there is no gap or discontinuity in the transition from the animal to the human. Therefore they want education to be used as the means of developing the instincts and emotions.
4. *Different theories of Curriculum:* On the subject of curriculum, naturalists have proposed theories which differ from each other to some extent. Comenius wanted the educand to study every subject, without making any selection. Locke refuted this notion by demonstrating that every individual cannot be made to study the same subject, because of certain natural handicaps. Hence, much emphasis was laid upon modifying the curriculum to suit the needs of the individual. Herbert Spencer arranged the curriculum with Science as its nucleus, and tried to synthesize the other subjects to Science. The Arts were given a secondary place in his programme because he believed that one must first create the basic elements before this knowledge directly and that endeavours to prepare the way for reason by the proper exercise of the senses." Negative education consists in training of the child to use his sense organs and motor organs instead of filling his mind with bits and pieces of information. By using the various bodily powers at disposal, the child will generate much knowledge for himself.
5. *Playway method:* The playway method of education

is very popular with Naturalists because, during play, the child gets the opportunity to manifest his abilities and powers. He is often faced with situations which compel him to use these powers. The games provide an outlet for man's creative power. It is true not only of the child's games but also of games played in adult life.

6. *Extra-Curricular Activities:* Artificiality of any kind is another aspect which the Naturalists don't endorse. The atmosphere in the class and the school should be informal, and the time-table should not be rigorously adhered to. Apart from the subjects taught as part of the prescribed syllabus, the child must be encouraged to take active part in various extra-curricular programmes. If the educator wants to know what this method is, he should observe the child. Through such observation he can learn what the child wants which direction he is inclined to in what things he is interested in. Consequently, the teacher will be enabled to modify his own technique to suit the child.
7. *Role of Teacher:* Naturalists suggest that the educator should be a guide and a friend, and that in his behavior with the child, the educator should try to recollect his own childhood and infancy. The child is naturally inclined to laughter and happiness. Hence, the educator should be jolly and not grave. He should facilitate the child to grow in the nature-oriented environment of the Education-process where teaching-learning can automatically or naturally take place.

Contributions of Naturalism in Education (Summarised)

1. Child centered education is one of the contributions of Naturalism.

2. This thought gave incentive for the study of child psychology. Investigation in the filed of psychology was started for he fulfillment of the need for the knowledge of child psychology in order to teach him.
3. In the method of teaching, Naturalism emphasized experiences instead of words. Only words are not sufficient for education, experiences are also necessary.
4. Play was method in education is another contribution of this thought.
5. Return to Nature is the main principle. The Naturalists emphasized going back to the peaceful lap of nature away from the complexity of civilization. This tendency increased the love for nature.
6. Important place was given to empirical knowledge instead of bookish knowledge.

PRAGMATISM

Pragmatism believes that man creates his own values in the course of activity. According to Pragmatism, judgement is good which gives satisfactory results on the experimental basis. Truth is that which happens to a judgement. Belief is good as long as it works, otherwise it is not good. John Dewey contributed a lot in the field of Pragmatism. We must find out the nature of that truth we believe in. According to Pragmatism, nothing is true for ever because the world is changing. Needs change, therefore, with them the principles concerned, also change. The situations are always changing, therefore, those facts and principles are true which help us in adjusting ourselves to these changing situations. Therefore, environment is the most important factor for us. We have to understand the environment carefully. Philosophy of Pragmatism must be described in terms of the problems with which it deals. Pragmatism is the theory of practice. It lies behind the practice.

Education, according to Pragmatism, is not a search for eternal values but creation of new values by man himself. Pragmatism considers child as a potential creator of new values in the given environment. Thus, values are discovered. Like Naturalism, it gives a central place to the child in education, but it differs in modifying the child's development by providing desires and experiences. Education, according to Pragmatism is the direction of impulses, abilities towards the needs of the child.

Pragmatism postulates that the curricula and the aims of education should be related with the actual living. It does not care very much about the aims of education. Project method is the product of Pragmatism. According to it, education is life and school is society. Really pragmatism has influenced education very much. It is a praiseworthy theory but we cannot be blind toward its negative side. It does not pay attention to individual differences. It neglects cultural heritage. Mot important fact to be noticed is this that according to Pragmatism ,nothing is true for always, then how can pragmatism be true for all the time?

Pragmatism and Education

There are three aspects of pragmatism: (1) Humanistic pragmatism, (2) Experimental pragmatism, and (3) Biological pragmatism.

Humanistic pragmatism means that every act should be for the benefit of man. According to it only that is truth which may fulfill the needs of mankind. The second and third practical aspects of pragmatism believe in truth proved by experiment and change according to the environment. Dewey advocates that the progress of the universe is based on truth proved by experiment.

On the basis of the above interpretation, we can establish

general and specific relationship of this philosophy with education.

Like Naturalism, this philosophy also gives importance to the place of the child. Child is child, not a younger form of an adult. There is a difference between the needs, desires and interests of a child and those of an adult. It is improper to talk of the child's education for future by considering truth changeable. We are only concerned with the present, and how we can talk of the future. The Pragmatists do not lay emphasis on the aims of education.

They believe in 'education for the child' instead of 'education for education'. The importance and needs of education are the fulfillment of some desires of the child. Education has a role to play in enabling us to adjust to the environment. Thus, we see that Pragmatists are nearer to Naturalists.

Taking the mind of man as a unit the pragmatic theory of education comes near psychology and both affect each other. The effect of this philosophy on the modern age is quite obvious. The ideals of education cannot be similar in the changing world, Education should be interesting, should fulfill the needs. It should be society-centered and its power should be applied in the development of society. By means of such principles, the pragmatists have provided new life to education. Education has also been strengthened by this philosophy with its belief in Deductive Method, experimental theory and external values.

This philosophy has saved education from the clutches of old aims, and useless ideals like bookish knowledge by emphasizing change of subject according to the needs of society, change in aims, man's creative activities and regarding ideas inferior to activities.

* * * * *

MEANING AND DEFINITION OF SOCIAL CHANGE

The political, economic, religious, moral, cultural, social, educational and other changes are given the name of social change.

Social change is change in society. Society is a network of social relations. Thus social change is a change of social relations.

> "Social change may be defined as modification in the way of doing and thinking of the people."
>
> - M.D. Jenson

Different Aspects of Social Change

In present age, India is passing through many social changes. The social changes which are taking place can be seen as under:

1. *Economic Aspect*: In the economic aspect, the changes in the process of production causing poverty can be seen. The material viewpoint has developed in the people because of industry, business, agriculture etc. Lust, theft and corruption etc. have been encouraged due to economic considerations.
2. *Social Aspects*: It includes the social changes which are taking place and by adopting them the human society is trying to be secular, thinking for equality, equal justice and freedom to all classes of the society.
3. *Religious Aspect*: In the religious aspect those changes are included which are caused by religious institutions such as Gurdwara, temple, church etc. Their importance in the present age has decreased because of modernisation. It is also a kind of great change.
4. *Moral Aspect:* Moral changes are the changes in values and thoughts e.g. co-education is not regarded as

immoral in the modern age. It was not thought to be good in the ancient times.

5. *Political Aspect*: It includes political power and changes concerned with administration, e.g. adopting the values of secularism, equality, justice and freedom etc.

Factors Affecting Social Change in India

Physical Environment: The Geographical specialists have laid great stress on the effect of change in physical environment on the human society. Herrington has even gone to the extent of saying that climate is the only reason of rise/downfall of civilizations and cultures. Food, earthquake, famine, excessive rainfall, drought (lack of rainfall) and change of seasons etc. exercise considerable influence on social relations.

Every man lives in particular geographical conditions. The geographical conditions such as climate, earth, river, mountains , oceans etc. do affect the social life. These changes are a part of social change. Because these physical changes affect the society.

Biological Factors: The qualitative aspect of population related to heredity is included in Biological factors. Biological state in India can be seen in merits and demerits of population, shape, size, description, structure etc. Changes in the aspect of population cause may social changes.

1. The change is mutual relations of man and woman in the institution of marriage can be seen due to the change in the ratio of men and women in population.
2. The standard of health of the society falls down due to explosion of population.

   The effect of population çan be seen in India. In the area of poverty increased due to increase in population. The villagers started moving towards the cities. Slums, increased in big cities like Delhi and Bombay as a matter of migration. There was a shortage of food grains in the country also because of over population. single families emerged because of domestic quarrels and materialistic attitudes etc.

3. *Cultural factor* – Culture is a religion of values, styles and emotional attachments. These values, styles and thoughts also influence the social change. By the value is meant that goal in order to obtain which any person or institution is striving.

   Max Weber regards cultural factors as the main reason of social change. According to him, social changes take place along with cultural changes. In reality, it cannot be denied that the social relations are necessarily influenced by changes to material and non-material culture.

4. *Technological Factor*: Technological factors exercise considerable influence on social change.

   The following four factors mainly function in technology.

   1. Use of machines in industries.
   2. Development of means of communication.
   3. Development of means of transport.

4. *Development of new methods/processes of agriculture:* Urbanisation increased in India due to the influence of industries and the factory system. New classes emerged because industrialisation and new revolutions were seen. The position of women changed. The standard of morality fell. In this way too much influence of technology can be noticed.

5. *Economic Factor*: The changes in economic aspects necessarily influence social changes. Considerable difference in the extent of various kinds of social

changes can be seen in the agricultural and hunting societies.

The use of machines in production on a large scale in India started due to the influence of Western culture and in the beginning because of the spread of the Britishers. The difference in India before and after the coming of the English men can be well observed.

As a result of the construction of big factories of production, the labourers started moving towards cities. The joint families started breaking down. Competition between men and women increased. Marriage became a social compromise.

Role of Teacher or Education in Bringing Social Change

1. *Education as an Instrument for Social Change:* One come to know by looking at the history of education that it follows special change. Before the achievement of independence, Indians adopted western culture because of British rule as the education was drafted in such a way that Indians should be influenced by western culture. After independence, because of the coming of social change there was a change in education and democratic outlook was adopted in education as the established democratic rule. Such Education policy was made with which development of domocratic citizenship, professional efficiency and development of individuality could be possible. Education followed certain systems and norms and later lead social change.

2. *The Aims of Education:*
   1. Stress was laid on science education, work experience, vocationalisation and use of science in technology.
   2. Importance was given to ordinary schools,

national service progamme etc. for social and national integration.

3. Emphasis was laid on acceleration of the process of modernisation.
4. Importance was given to social and spiritual values.

3. *Stabilizing Democratic Values:* Democratic values such as equality, liberty, feeling of brotherhood and secularism etc. are stabilized through education in free India. Where the students indulge in negative changes like strike, burning buses and destruction of buildings, at this time, education should tell them that freedom does not mean that they should follow the wrong path.

'I call, therefore, complete and generous education, that which fits a man to perform justly, skillfully and magnanimously all the offices, both private and public, of peace and war.'

- *John Milton*

4. *Increasing Knowledge:* Every man is a philosopher. He is desirous of having and giving more and more knowledge. Research is carried out in various fields of study by the people through of education. Many doctors of Philosophy come out of the universities. The expansion of knowledge is the main cause of social change.
5. *Analysis of Social Change:* Social change are generally analysis through education. The knowledge of good or bad social change can be only formulated through education.
6. *Popularising Different Social Change:* The knowledge of Social change can be popularised to the society through the medium of education.

7. *Providing Leadership in Social Change:* Education gives birth to social engineers which provides good guides to the people in the society.

   From the above, we conclude education is the only source which can bring social change in a more organised manner and can remove evils from the society.

ROLE OF THE TEACHER

All the activities of education moves round the teacher. No doubt a conflict is going on between two opposite schools of thought regarding the time of future outline of the society. Some people want India to be exact copy of the west whereas the others are advocating the type of Education prevailed at the age of the Vedas and the Upanishadas.

A patient is easily cured by a specialist but all persons start giving their opinion. Some of them do the same in connection with the serious topic of social change. It is correct to some extent because only the people living, in a society have the knowledge of its defects just as a patient knows about his illness.

Teacher is the one who is instrumental in the process of social change. They are well acquainted with the outline of the society, its nature, its processes and the laws of its change etc. It is his task to guide in bringing about social changes easily. A teacher performs double role in presenting social change in Indian society. First, he gives constructive suggestions for change in every aspect. Second he makes arrangements to remove the obstacles in his way for implementing these suggestions.

There is necessarily a conflict in the immediate interests of the groups in every society and every group tries to bring maximum change on his side and sharply oppose the change in the interests of others. Persons with orthodox feelings oppose any form of change in social organisation. They want to stick to old customs and tradition and consider it their welfare as well as that of the society. In such a state of affairs, the teacher not only makes suggestions in the direction of reform but tries to see that there is no conflict between these opposing groups and parties. In this direction, the foremost task is to remove the superstitions spreading in the society and the ignorance regarding social change.

A teacher is like sun which gives light. He is like a gardener who devotes himself heart and soul to beautify the garden. He is a sailor who rows the boat carry the students safely to the shore.

In the present age, he should take interest in a dult education, social education, woman education and science education. He should participate in the programmes of social and national service and non-formal education and make his contribution towards social change. He should acquire the knowledge of the society by visiting the students houses if needed and participating in social programmes.

* * * * *

MEANING OF NATIONAL DEVELOPMENT

The term 'National Development' is an all round development of a 'Nation'. It includes in itself all aspects: economic, social, political, religious, cultural etc. National development is an individual as well as social, political, economic, cultural development. It is both urban and rural. It is also social and regional. No doubt it is difficult, because many forces act and react. If these aspects remains ignored the development will remain incomplete. It will finally have no relevance. It is not a synonym for economic development although economic development is an important organ of national development. In Kothari commission Report (1964), we come across the detail description of the problems related to national development e.g. self reliance, economic development national integration, social reconstruction, development of political values, establishment of religious and cultural values etc. These make clear that the commission has also taken its comprehensive meaning as total national development. In our view, it is the capacity of working on the part of all countrymen, making us of natural and human resources.

> "National development is the total effect of all citizen's forces and addition to the stock of physical, human resources, knowledge and skill."
>
> \- *John Vaizey*

ROLE OF PLANNING IN THE ECONOMIC DEVELOPMENT

The economic development of a nation means increase in national income. The increase should be there in national income.

> "Economic development means the proportion of national income in relation to he investment."
>
> "The economic development at any time is the name given to the capacity of working on the part of national labourers by means of natural resources of the country."
>
> \- *Prof. Marshall*

Planning can play its role in economic development in the following ways:

1. *Increasing production:* An addition to production is an important aim of planning. Through this medium,

knowledge, skill, utility etc. are used in increasing production. The productive capacity of traditional type of industries can be increased and new industries can be encouraged for working in undeveloped fields. Planning awakens that indigenous and foreign economic aid be sought to increase production. Provision is made for import and export of material produced.

Planning establishes blending of material and human resources for the sake of economic development so that economic development is possible in a proper way. Planned progamme can be adopted in the field of agriculture which would accelerate the rate of development. Thus, planning can be helpful in increasing productivity in agricultural as well as other fields.

2. *Spread of Education:* Education is the basis of economics. Planning in education increases the rate of economic progress. Those nations which make more investment on education become strong from economic point of view and those which do not do lag behind. New technique, knowledge and skills can only be obtained through the medium of education. By their means, we can proportionately increase our produce with limited means. The unrest, ignorance and poverty present in the society can also be removed by education.

Use of Planning for Accelerating the Economic Development

The economic development can be achieved speedily with the help of planning. Planning can help in minimizing the expenses with available resources. Such savings can further be invested for the country's economic development. Planning was adopted to accelerate the economic development so that democracy functions successfully in India. When India became free and independent, poverty, unemployment, famine, hunger, shortage of food started in her face. Indian Government introduced 'Five-year Plans' to plan and accelerate the national development. Country's physical and human resources could only be utilised for nation economic development effective through planning.

Importance of Planning in the Economic Development of the Country

"Planning means 'arrangements' and arrangements are cited before to solve the problems which may arise in the future. Problems, may drop up in any field of human life. When we talk about the country's economic development it means we are thinking for the uplift of the standard of citizens.

'Planning is an organization which is connected with production, distribution and consumption.' (Dickinson)

Role of Education in the Planned Economic Development in India

1. *Education as an Instrument for Economic Development:* Education is the concrete base for development. Mere investment does not contribute to economic development. The production will remain incomplete in the absence of educated persons. Money, time and energy will be misused. Education is the only source that impart knowledge and provide training to the people and play positive and constructive role towards national development.

2. *For Individual Prosperity:* Education confers great indirect benefits even on the ordinary work man. Thus education can prove to be a means of economic development. It may increase personal income because the person receives education and gets a job. His income is increased by production. With the increase

in income he becomes economically prosperous. Education provides an opportunity to the individual to think about future needs in addition to his immediate needs and develops his abilities to solve his problems. It also provides a basis to his material wealth. Skilled man makes more progress as he is engaged in economic activity thus makes money.

3. *Curriculum and Economic Development:* Curriculum as per the recommendations of Kothari Commission should be changed especially by including work experience. The object of science should be emphasised. Training of new technique should be obtained for increase in production. The curriculum should be related to the life of the students, prepare them for a living and become a means of national development. In the curriculum of the education pattern (10+2+3), importance is given to work experience. Science and productivity are being used in increasing productivity.
4. *Aims of Education and Economic Development:* Education will have to be reframed its objective to make it an effective means of the national economic development. It will change according to the needs and ambitions of a common man. This aim will develop the sense of dignity of labour. National income increases with the increase in production and the nation goes ahead towards economic development.
5. *Technical Methods and Economic Development:* The economist usually ask to produce skilled talent like engineers, doctors, scientists and teachers. The skills of the students can be developed through the medium of training and they can be made an internal and stole part of their personality so that they may become their permanent assets. In the school, there should

be teaching through experiment, project etc. The physical and mental skills can be developed through the medium of proper and scientific methods. They can play an important role in national construction.

Teacher and Economic Development

No doubt the teacher is the nation builder. He is an important means of economic development. He can implement educational programmes and make important contribution in this process in the ways given ahead:

- His point of view should be national.
- While teaching curriculum in the school, he should establish correlation of subject with national development so that the feeling of development may be inculcated in the students.

Education as Human Capital

The item which multiplies the incomes and production is called 'Capital'. Capital is of following nature:

a. Capital in the shape of goods: Capital goods are there which have direct relations with production.

b. Human Capital: Human capital is that capital which transforms man into manpower. (It can further develop other capital).

Capital plays an important role in economic development. Education as human capital like capital goods also contributes to economic development. Investments in Capital goods produce immediate and visible results whereas investments in human capital are long term investment. Considering machines to be capital, businessman invests in them with the hope that they will produce more goods. In the same way investment in education transforms a person into manpower by developing desirable skills and attitudes. These attitudes and skills are very helpful in increasing production. Education, therefore, is not consumption or investment or human capital. The development and expansion of human power depends on education because by themselves machines cannot increase production. Manpower alone can make use of them and increase prouction.

Human capital is defined as manpower. On the other hand, we can consider intellect as 'Human Capital'.

Thus, education is human capital which develops such traits and capacities in a person which as satisfy the material and non-material needs of a society. The development and expansion of human power develops only on education because the lifeless machines cannot increase production. Manpower alone can make out of them and increase production. Thus human power is the soul of national development. We can have national development in every filed by investing capital on education and by making available man power skilled and efficient. In this way education can bring qualitative improvement of human beings and make it an important and vital means of national development.

Education builds a society and satisfies means of development of human resource. Without it the object of economic development cannot be realised. Education also carries on manpower analysis. The selection of problems and use of available manpower can be done in it.

Education can become employment oriented and prepare skilled man power by which the base of national economic development is strengthened. Therefore, the expenses made on education is capital, not consumption. Therefore, education is human capital and the basis of national development.

> 'The most valuable to all capital is thus invested in human being.'
>
> \- *Smith and Marshall*

'Education is not consumption but capital which is an essential element of production on which depends the future productivity.'

- Edward F. Dawson

MEANING AND DEFINITION OF NATIONALISM AND NATIONAL INTEGRITY

Nationalism can roughly mean as loyalty for the Nation. "Nationality is evidenced by such other terms as race, language, history, culture and tradition." *(Brubacher)*

'Nationalism is that which depends on we-feeling towards the Nation'. *(Dr. Humayun)*

'National integration is a psychological and educational process involving the development of a feeling of unity, solidarity and cohesion in the hearts of people, a sense of common citizenship and a feeling of loyalty to the Nation.

- National Integration Conference Report, 1961

Role of Education and Teacher for Developing National Integration

1. Changes in the aims of education.
2. Modifications in National System of Education.
3. Reforms in the methods of teaching.
4. Re-orientation of text books.
5. Organising daily morning assembly programmes.
6. Celebration of National Festivals.
7. Celebration of the birth days of National Leaders.
8. Arrangements of different programmes at Inter-state levels.

9. Use of Radio and television.
10. Development of Hindi as national language.
11. Exchange of students at national level.
12. Exchange of teachers at national level.
13. Excursion.

MEANING OF INTERNATIONAL UNDERSTANDING

'Internationalism is a feeling that the individual is not only a member of his state but a member of the world.'

- *Oliver Goldsmith*

'International understanding is the ability to perceive, criticise and appraise the conduct of men every where, all nationalities cultures and races as equally important anywhere on this earth.

Educational Programmes in School for Developing Internationalism

Development of internationalism depends upon educational instructions. In school age the interests are cultivated with the development of child as whole. We have to create the atmosphere in the boundaries of schools and outside for internationalism. Schools can contribute to develop internationalism in the following ways:-

1. *Change in the Aims of Education*: The aims of education are required to be reevaluated for the development of internationalsim. The aim of education should broader. We should also develop the sense of world citizenship. Children will think about the world and goodness to be contributed after developing the world citizenship. They will have their own interests and their thinking will have broader surroundings. Our aims of education should prepare the students to

origin 'world peace.'

2. *Change in School Curriculum*: Students should be given right kind of knowledge pertaining to different countries of the world. This right type of knowledge means that facts in the text books should be described in their right setting. In the content of study, nothing should be included which should hold any countries to ridicule and hate. Neither by omission of significant facts should be there or insertion of subjective evaluation nor by misrepresentation of facts should there be an impression of social prejudice of international disharmony. It does not mean that the facts should be suppressed, nor does it mean that unwarranted dubious change should be given to such facts.

For example, in Literature the study of literature should be encouraged for the sake of international understanding. Literature emphasises human spirit. It is this feeling which binds humanity into a common fraternal relation. Literature expounds those universal values which are not limited by narrow bounds of particular countries. So, the study of literature is congenial to foster a cosmopolitan outlook among the young. Whatever Tagore, Kalidas or Shakeshpeare has written is for their country men alone but for the whole world at large.

Similarly in Art, there is a universal appeal and depiction. It expresses the noble and creative urges of the world. The language or medium of Art is international rather than national. It is not inhabited by distance or racial characteristics. So a lover of art always has a global outlook.

In the case of, it is found that it is the study of the past in order to understand the present and in the light of these experiences to make the future more successful and free from the mistakes committed in the past. In this way it can go a long way for promoting international understanding. The following points should be kept in mind for making the teaching of the History effective for international understanding. These principles are suggested solely for the purpose of making this subject broadbased.

(a) History should be taught with a social and cultural bias: While dealing with the history of other counties too much stress should not be laid on the political and military aspects. The aim should be to teach history of other countries explaining good aspects of societal and cultural norms and facts.

(b) History should also stress the impact of technological and scientific technique: Teaching of history in our schools should stress the impact of technological and scientific techniques on the lives of the people of the different countries of the world as now the world has steadily moved towards moral, social, economic and industrial unification.

Besides Geography and civics should also be taught properly to make proper use of these subjects for an international understanding. Civics is important from the international understanding point of view, because this subject teaches the students the value of adjustments and enables them to understand the complicated problems of human relationship more rationally and realistically. This will also imply art of living which teaches man how to live with ones own fellowmen with place and comfort in the world. But the corruption should not be taught theoretically or in its traditional from but through diverse practical opportunities which should be provided in the schools.

In the end, Science fosters scientific attitude of mind among the pupils. This subject also develops some other wholesome attitudes of mind which make the pupils curious and interested wishing to investigate, determined to find truth critically and scientifically. This will go a long way for developing proper dispositions towards international understanding among the students.

Co-curricual Activities

Inculcation of Democratic Values Among the Students: Aggression between the nations take place because some nations consider themselves to be inherently superior to others and to rule over them as them birth right. Therefore, right from the very beginning, our education should be such that it inculcates democratic values among our students. These democratic values are Equality, Fraternity, Sympathy, Freedom, Good Citizenship, Tolerance, Faith in Change etc.

Books and Libraries: Mental make up of a man depends upon a large extent the type of study material that can be made available to him. Therefore, the first step in this directions that libraries in all the schools and colleges should be strengthened. Students should be encouraged to visit these libraries and develop the habit of extra reading. Secondly, these libraries should be selected very honestly. There is a possibility that subject matter in certain books may encourage ill will between that nations. Such books should not be entered in the school libraries. Books which promote brotherhood of mankind should be encouraged.

Promotion of Sports and Cultural Delegation: Sports and cultural exchange should be encouraged between that nations. Such exchanges will generate a lot o goodwill among the nations. The relations between India and Pakistan in particular has been far from cordial. But whenever any hockey or cricket team visit India from Pakistan or Pakistan from India, it generates atleast a sportive feeling among the people of the two countries. It is because sportsmen are not politicians.

Unlike politicians they think and profess the same thing. Similarly exchange of cultural delegations can also lead to International Understanding.

Celebration of U.N.O. Days: There are certain days connected with U.N.O. and other agencies working for the peace and unity of mankind. U.N.O. day, Human Rights Day, World Peace Day etc. are its examples. These days should be celebrated with full enthusiasm so that the students may come to know the importance of these days.

Using International Scholars: If there is foreign scholar around he should be tapped and brought to school to address the pupils. He can provide a lot of knowledge about his country to the pupils. The possessions of such type of knowledge can go a long way in promoting international understanding.

Arranging Exhibition: Exhibition should be arranged between the countries to make the people of other countries to know their art, culture, music and life styles. The holding of trade fairs in Delhi every year able to provide an international plateform to learn foreign cultures etc. Not only the people come to know the progress made by different countries in different aspects of economy but also try to assess and evaluate the overall trend of change, and development made by some of the 'Nations' that provide.

* * * * *

IMPORTANCE OF TEACHING: SOCIO-PEDAGOGIC VIEWPOINT

Right from the emergence of human society, teaching has been regarded as the noblest activity. It is the teaching, however, the mode may differ, that shows us the way to live our lives in a better manner. Basically teaching is the process of interaction during which a more experienced person imparts knowledge to the less experienced individual. In this context, more experienced person is none other than the teacher. Sociologically, in the primitive age, teachers were placed on the top due to their respectable positions, Islamically, teachers and knowledge have been given a top priority. Knowledge, in particular has been mentioned in the holy Quraan as well as in other holy books, therefore, the function of a teacher becomes evident who subsequently acquires status of something that is highly honorable.

From the viewpoint of Pedagogy and Education, the position of a teacher keeps on changing from time to time. In the past, a teacher was like a father who was highly respectable. Children used to be quite afraid may be because of too much respect. Therefore, sons and daughters were not free and frank to discuss anything with their fathers. Teachers were also symbolic of fathers, consequently the students were bound to maintain a respectable distance. The teachers were not hesitant in giving punishment to the student if they were in the wrong. With the advancement of society, development of educational theories and psychological researches the teacher started enjoying the status of a friend. Therefore, they were not treated as a thing of fear rather the children started feeling easy and comfortable. Yet they maintain a respectable distance. The idea of the present change from father to a friend came in to practice for the simple reason that teaching is a 'Bipolar activity'. Unless learning takes place, there is no teaching. Some experts opine teaching as 'Tri-Polar activity' explaining that there are three poles or ends like: pole-1 (teacher); pole-2 (Students) and pole-3 (the activity or resource available). Moreover, there is no denying the fact that there are at least two ends or poles.

If we consider the two terms – Teaching and Learning

synonymous, the responsibility on the shoulder of a teacher becomes double because if the students do not learn, it is the teacher who is primarily responsible. The idea of accountability comes from the Behaviorist's view of Psychology that the teacher can train any student to any direction if the student possesses normal range of intelligence. However, the idea does not go against Cognitist's Psychology that advocates the theory that a child is born with certain inherent behaviour. By the time, a teacher starts training an individual child or student, usually at higher stage of education, he has developed a particular behaviour on the basis of his inborn quality. There is a little controversy over the issue of intelligence whether man is born with general intelligence or specific, yet there can be a consensus that intelligence (general) can be directed towards a particular or specific direction by training a student.

Sociologically, a child is a product of an environment. What he sees or listens he simply imitates with out knowing what is wrong or right. School is a miniature society. It is a collection of students belonging to different strata of society. Some boys are the product of bad environment and some may be good enough, therefore, it is responsibility of a teacher to have a close look on the student so that they should not do anything undesired and subsequently develop their behaviour and personality. The teacher, in the process of teaching at one time, functions as an instructor and the other time, he may work as a social guardian. Thus, the teaching is not merely like preaching or professing something to the students rather it is a balanced combination of knowing, understanding and analysing the students in order to develop their personality.

Teaching and gardening are treated synonymous to each other. The process of gardening involves thorough knowledge of farming or cultivating. The cultivation involves awareness and understanding of land, time of sowing seeds, watering, sprouting, growing of plants etc. Similarly, teaching involves many sub-processes. They are: knowing the level of students, designing courses, writing text books and more importantly evolving teaching methodology. Methodology includes motivation provided to the students who would achieve the targets of education laid down by the planners.

Another group of educational philosophers opine that teaching and pot-making is almost same. In both the process, the activities are highly delicate and skill-oriented.

Each society expects change and development in the future and the role and responsibility of a teacher in the entire process of change and development is evident.

Teaching is rightly said to be the process of reformation because it is the teacher who visualizes an ideal society. He tries to give shape to the students as he desires according to the need and requirement of the future.

Teaching depends basically on socio-moral philosophy. The teacher must process ethical values. He must be well read, knowledgeable and exposed to the world-situations. If the teacher is not highly equipped, skilled and intelligent, the students will not be benefited. As a result, they will not respect the teacher. Besides, the time devoted to teaching-learning will be a waste of time, money and efforts.

Teaching involves a clear cut vision, vivid apprehension of value system, thorough knowledge of purpose and aims of education and finally an effective methodology.

Importance of teaching need not be emphasised. Islam has given a particular place of knowledge and teaching. Teacher has been given a status higher than any body in the society except parents. Kabeer Das (a renowned Hindi poet) said that a teacher is more important than the god because it is the teacher who has let the student know about the god. Therefore, in the past, the teacher was considered as a highly respectable person and teaching was a very noble concept.

The concept of teacher, however, has got a little change. According to the new theories of Teaching-Learning, teaching is more like instructing. Instruction is a concept that is particularly limited to the classroom activities. By instructing less experienced lot (students), a more experienced person (instructor) brings out some desired changes.

People having philosophical blend of thoughts believe that the teaching involves guardianship. It may be of socio-moral type. Thus it becomes imperative on the part of the teachers to extend the traditional role of a guide and guardian to the students. They may perhaps be the role model of the students. It is usually found that the students have a disagreement on the account that their teachers have told such and such things so these words are final. In short, a teacher is expected to be right and ideal, therefore, an important responsibility may successfully be discharged by no other eminent personality than a teacher. Thus, they can not be treated as common people like others. A teacher is expected to develop his personality like one that suits a teacher. It is also important for the reason that he is a model and the students are going to copy him in totality or in part. A teacher must have a philosophy of life so that he can try to achieve the same through philosophy of teaching and education. He should know moral values which are important for human beings. He should have a clear cut vision of objectives of education/teaching. He should be knowledgeable in his field simultaneously with good amount of training. It is better if he is well equipped with application of audio-visual or technological aids. A teacher should be punctual and disciplined otherwise teaching will not be that effective as it is expected to be.

If the teacher possesses some of the prescribed qualities he is able to justify his noble position. It is then possible that teaching takes place in the right direction or the modern society has all rights to criticise and target the teaching-community for its failure.

The teacher's actual job is to build the character of the students. He is not only responsible for covering of the prescribed syllabus. He rather aims at long-term objectives which he has to attain. The objectives may be social, psychological, economic, political, moral or philosophical. It is perhaps the first and the foremost duty of a teacher to develop an allround development of the personality of the students. The teaching must inculcate socio-moral values among the target groups. In other words, it should endeavour to convert an ordinary man into a useful human being.

Techniques of Teaching

The following points should be kept in mind the concern teachers:

1. To select materials, aids and method that facilitate the learning process and stimulate the desire among the students for further learning.
2. To meet the needs, background and capacities of the children being taught.
3. To teach through variety of lectures, discussions, display and audio-oral presentation, experiments and community project etc.
4. To endeavour to obtain and maintain pupil's interest and attention.
5. To encourage them to develop critical faculty.
6. To develop desired work-study habits.
7. To analyse and evaluate pupil's participation and achievement in teaching-learning activity.

8. To maintain family and community relation,
9. To take active part in professional growth and ethics,
10. To ensure the development and proper utilization of human resource.

It has been rightly said:

"A poor teacher complains
An average teacher explains
A good teacher teaches
A great teacher inspires."

Dr. Radhakrishnan says 'The teacher's place in society is of vital importance. He acts as the pivot for the transmission of intellectual traditions and technical skills from generation to generation, and helps to keep the lamp of civilization burning. He not only guides the individual, but also, so to say, the destiny of nation. Teachers have therefore, to realise increasingly their special responsibility to the society."

Henry Adams states, "A parent gives life but as parent he gives no more. A murder takes life, but his deed stops there. A teacher affects eternity, he can never tell where his influence stops."

Dr. Zakir Hussain observed the role of a teacher in these words, "the teacher is not to dictate or dominate, his is to help and to serve, to understand and shape in faith, love and reverence – Yes, Reverence of the child". He further said, "It is the educator's business to ask whether his pupil has also been helped to become honest and truthful, socially cooperative and helpful if he can see any beauty in art and nature, if he can ever pursuade himself to subordinate is selfish ends to the good of the whole of which he is part... . He (educator) should seek to reshape the totality of his being... his hand, his mind and his heart."

On another occasion, he said, "... the teacher's function is to help the growing child is his hand to become what he is capable of becoming not what the teacher thinks he should be."

To what extend the teacher and teaching is important, has been made clear in the foregoing pages. The teacher being the agent of social reforms, character building, personality development and maker of future generation has to justify his position so that the noble idea like teaching can yield the desired socio-moral and political aims.

* * * * *

THE TEACHER

Teaching any subjects holds a greater responsibility as it is a bi-polar activity in which there must exist a process: input-activity-output. It is clearly said by pedagogues that unless learning takes place teaching is a failure.

When a target language or a subject is so important that without which the learning as a whole seems to be impossible, the teacher of the same must be indeed knowledgeable, well equipped, modern – innovative and dedicated for attainment of some pre-determined objectives. Such a teacher must possess certain qualities and characteristics so that the teaching – learning process becomes fruitful and result-oriented.

It is often said that a good teacher is always a good learner. That mans, a teacher welcomes any novel idea and he is ready to adapt to any new situation. Besides, he improves upon his knowledge and after all feels at home in learning even from his students in a particular teaching situation. Learning from a class does not mean that a teacher is not confident of his knowledge and simply accepts any information supplied by his students even if it is wrong.

Some people are 'born teachers'. They teach effectively in any circumstances. It is better if such people have some specialized teacher training so that they can further improve their inborn abilities. Some pertinent questions like who are the good teachers, what makes them good and what is effective teaching are attempted to be directly or indirectly answered in the following pages.

Teaching is a very important activity in the process of education. It is the teaching that makes the citizen of the country. It is the process of making future generation. Therefore, the teaching directly or indirectly is associated with the following issues:

1. Teaching guides the learner in academic, social and economic activities,
2. Helps them to decide about difficulties/problems,
3. Enables them to form opinion and ideas and later, develop their overall personality.

Teacher is said to be the process of enlightening the ignorant people, thus, the teacher is like a lamp that spreads light and removes darkness. The importance of a teacher can't be ignored.

The teacher is the hub in the entire system of Education. The success or failure of any method or procedure depends mainly on the effectiveness of the teacher. A teacher with specific qualification and expertise is needed for the successful teaching of such a subject which knowledge and scope is unlimited. Therefore, the teacher is required to deal with attitudes, skills and appreciations. He has to handle the raw human input and transform into the real human capital that is the actual investment of any government or nation. He is, thus the maker of future generation and shaper of human personality and behaviour.

Issue Related to a Teacher

The following are some of the important issues that a teacher has to face from time to time:

- Philosophical issue,
- Socio-linguistic issue,
- Psycho-linguistic issue,
- Pedagogic issue.

Philosophical issues are related to the policies, principles and planning related to the teaching-learning . The policies vary from situation to situation. Therefore, a teacher has to identify his role on the basis of his thinking, ideology or philosophy of teaching. The teacher should also have an idea about curriculum design, appropriateness of textbooks and teaching strategies to realize the goals for the ultimate development of the children group.

Socio-Linguistic Issue

The teacher has to keep in his mind some social factors and issues that may affect the learning process as a whole.. Such issues and factors may be found to be an advantage or disadvantage to the target group. For example, a particular group aspired to learn , may not be able to acquire the conceived level due to the following factors: family background, socio-economic status, social environment, locality, parental attitude etc.

A particular background of a particular community also affect the overall learning of any subject.

Ethnocentricity as a factor does not surprise an intelligent teacher that some studies may show negative effect on learning of some subjects in general and Humanities and Languages in particular.

Psycho-Linguistic Issues

Issues related to psychological factors that hamper educational attainments must be kept in mind while teaching a group of students. A particular child may not be suitably intelligent or not sufficiently motivated. He may have some family problem or he is economically backward. His personality type may also affect the learning of a subject.

Aptitude is commonly understood as very important as we hear people saying 'he has a flair for language', she has an interest in History and this has been proved in certain studies. Attitude is also very important in the case of Learning English or Second language or any other subject. It ensures the academic behaviour.

In terms of emotional responses to learning, a variable which has received much attention is anxiety. Bailey (1955) for example, links anxiety competitiveness and argues that if one can discover its various causes he will be in a better position to reduce it.

MacIntyre and Gardner (1991) looked in more detail at anxiety in the classroom. It was found that the greatest anxiety seems to relate to negative experiences in speaking activities.

Krashen (1985) has suggested the notion of the affective filter. This is a representation of the way in which affective factors such as attitude, anxiety, competitiveness and other emotional response can help or hinder language learning.

Individual difference can also be considered as an important factor responsible for the outcomes of teaching-learning. The difference may be due to intelligence, aptitude, attitude, motivation, and personality traits. Some learning theories may be considered to be employed to cope with the factor.

Motivation as mentioned above, is very important in the process of teaching-learning. Both the teachers and the students should be properly motivated towards attainment of educational/language aims. Any individual may be influenced by the variety of motivations which will affect such things as anxiety, attitude or willingness to try new learning strategies.

Pedagogic Issues

Among others, Pedagogic issues are the most important of all. The teacher while dealing with the actual classroom situations, is particularly concerned with such issues like errors, difficulties, methods evaluation and testing and overall performance. Besides, an in-depth analysis and understanding is important related to each subject.

The role of error is very significant and inevitable. There are conflicting views on the role of error correction in the classroom. The treatment of error that requires consideration of many issues. Whether or not to perform the role of the person who diagnose and corrects the errors is only the first issue. In order to correct the errors, the teacher has to diagnose the type of error committed by a group. The teacher will also attribute certain factors responsible for such errors.

Most discussions have focussed on the factors like personality characteristics, attitudes, emotional responses to the language learning process in general and English in particular. However, there exists a finding that an extrovert learner is more successful than an introvert learner.

Educational factors are of much relevance. Subjects like humanities, social studies etc. in bilingual countries are f greater importance. Some times there are problems encountered on the way to achieving the target. English as the language of communication and instruction play very important role in the entire process of achieving the target subjects. Unless one is at home in English, he is unable to get the target. We have to assess the textbooks, curriculum, methods and evaluation system. Among other educational factors like admissions, teaching and examination, teacher factor is the most important of all. A teacher, for example, is the authority to decide whether which method of teaching will be relevant in a particular circumstance.

In sum, a teacher has to play many roles in the entire system of education.

Profile of a Teacher: Summarised

The teacher should possess sound knowledge of Philosophy of Education so that he is aware of principles and theories needed and used in Educational process. The teacher should also be aware of Educational psychology. He should know about certain concepts of child psychology and its application. Besides, the teacher should be interested in gathering knowledge so that he can be well equipped. He should also be open to his surroundings. It is well known that a teacher is like a father, friend, philosopher and guide. This statement includes total concept of education: both formal and informal. It talks about a formal concept of instruction as well as preaching and instructing .

In addition, teachers can interpret the school to the community, the community to the school, the teachers to the parents and the parents to the teachers. He is in an ideal position to explain the past in terms of the present and the present in terms of the past. He can, bring together the past and the present, the new and the old. He can also visualise the perspectives in the near future.

Traits of a Teacher

Teaching is an art as well as a science. Without the proper development of teaching skills a teacher can not teach his classes. The teacher has to justify his position by showing different traits as under:

Scholarship and Qualification

Qualification and experience is the basic trait of a teacher, be English teacher or any other subject. Therefore, he should have:

- *A Sound knowledge of the subject*

  The teacher must possess mastery over his subject. He must have vision. He should be an expert in his filed of study so that he can yield the best possible results.

- *Should have knowledge of Educational Theory*

  The Teacher must be aware of the Educational aims that are desired ones for the development of personality and uplift of society.

- *Creativity*

  The teacher should be original and creative. He should innovate things and present novel ideas before the learners.

Professional Training

Professional background is very essential for a successful teacher. Professional training has the following dimensions:

A real teacher is one who choose and his job. He is totally dedicated to his profession. He is a teacher not by chance but by choice. The teacher should also know about foundations of Education: Psychology, Sociology and Philosophy of Education. Besides, the teacher should also know about Educational Technology.

Personality: Teachers personality should be impressive so that the teacher can act as a role model for students. The personality includes:

- *Good Personal Appearance:* It is better if a teacher should have a good personal appearance to produce good impression upon those who come in his contact.

- *Good Health:* Physical health brings smartness, enthusiasm, vigor, vitality, and activeness, so these are essential for an effective teacher. Good health will make the teacher cheerful and emotionally active. A sound mind can live only in a sound body. A sound body requires regularity and improvement of habits.
- *Modulated Voice:* The teacher should possess a clear and appealing voice. Regular practice and interest can make his voice more effective and impressive.
- *Dress Sense:* The teacher of should be smartly dressed. The clothes should always be neat and clean. He should use varied kind of dresses. Proper dress-sense is required for an effective teacher to prove himself to be an ideal in dressing as well.

Leadership: The teacher should possess the abilities of initiation, organisation, responsibility taking, self-confidence, commitment and leadership.

Human Relations: Human relation has become an integral part of Educational process. The teacher must build up and maintain the same with the students, teachers, guardians and the super-ordinates and everyone whomsoever he is associated with.

Moral Qualities: The moral and philosophical aspect of a teacher is very important. An effective teacher can also act as a philosopher, friend and a guide. Therefore, he should be sincere, honest and sympathetic.

The Qualities of an Effective Teacher: Summarised

An teacher's qualities may be summarised as under:

- He knows the objectives of teaching in general and English in particular,

- He knows his subject well,
- He uses psychological and sociological theories,
- Knows what has been learnt and what remains to be taught,
- Bothers about the performance of a learner,
- Communicates well,
- Reviews the previous knowledge and connects well to the new chapter or unit,
- Prepares well before starting a new lesson,
- Assesses the learning individually as well as among colleagues,
- Keeps good and update record of the students,
- Shares his personal and academic experience,
- Motivates students to learn the target,
- Knows about events, places, persons and history,
- Dedicates himself for the noble profession like teaching,
- Keeps himself in touch with the latest developments,
- Knows about use of technological aspects.

If we try to have a gist of overall qualities of an ideal teacher, the following correspond:

1. A good teacher must know why a subject is taught, what should be taught and finally how can the same be taught.
2. He has an access to different methods and strategies of teaching.
3. He is able to diagnose the weakness and strength of the students.

The teacher himself is solely accountable for attainment of aims and objectives of a particular subject. The teacher must know and try to fulfil those aims. He should be clear about the purpose of different activities meant for that subject.

Role of Teachers

Generally, a teacher plays many roles in a society. Sometimes, he is a guide therefore, he should be a well-informed person. He must afresh his knowledge and abilities by the use of technology and Mass Media. He should have critical faculty to arrive at some conclusions. The teacher can be proved to be a reformer of any society. He can transform an uneducated community into an enlightened one. A teacher can lead a 'Movement'. He is the instrument that should be aptly used for the change if the 'Nation' wants to bring forth.

In educational contexts, he plays different roles as well. These roles are highly specified and needs elaborations. The following is a modest attempt.

A teacher being very important in educational system plays different roles. The following are some of the main roles that a good teacher is expected to play.

a) The information provider

A teacher is expected to teach and the students believe that it is the responsibility of the teacher to pass on to the information, knowledge and understanding of a topic appropriate at the stage of their studies. This leads to the traditional role of the teacher as one of provider of information in the lecture context. The teacher is seen as an expert who is knowledgeable in his or her field, and who conveys that knowledge to students usually in the form of the words of mouth. In transmitting the knowledge, the teacher may also assist the student to interpret it using one of a varieties of educational strategies by which the teacher explains the subject matter to the students.

Despite the availability of other sources of information, both print and electronic including exciting interactive multimedia learning resource materials, the lecture remains as one of the most widely used instructional methods. It can be a cost-effective method of providing new information not found in standard texts, of relating the information to the local curriculum and context of Education. It has been found that although the teachers did not speak specifically of teaching as transmitting the content of their subject disciplinary knowledge was at the heart of their teaching approaches. The teachers used interactive ways, including the lecture to pass this knowledge on to the students.

There has been, however, a call for a reduction in the number of lectures scheduled in the curriculum, and a tendency for new schools to move away from their use as a learning tool. The exclusion of the lecture from the teachers' tool box, however, has been questioned and rightly so. A lecture in which the enthusiasm of an expert, who is also a good communicator, excites or motivates the students has much to commend it.

The importance attached to the role of the teacher as an information provider is partly cultural. It is found that Chinese students valued more than American students the professor's knowledge of the subject and their transmission of this to the students.

b) The practical teacher

The educational setting, whether in the institutions or in the community, is a powerful context for the transmission, by the practical teacher, of information directly relevant to the practice of medicine. The teacher selects, organises and delivers information. In the context of teaching, the most important factor related to student learning may be the quality of the teacher. Good teachers can share with the student their thoughts as a 'reflective informer', helping to illuminate, for the student, the process of teaching-learning.

In a study of distinguished practical teachers, it was concluded that a key element in teaching is the orgnaisation and presentation of knowledge "so that learners can comprehend it and use it to satisfy their learning objectives".

The teacher explains the basic skills in a simulated situations. Increasing use is being made of simulators to teach learning skills. This requires of the teacher additional skills not needed in more traditional context of teaching. One area of controversy in medical education is the extent to which learning skills should have specifically recruited and trained staff, whose role is to teach in the unit or whether teachers who teach in the context should also be expected to teach other skills.

The Role Model

a) The on-the-job role model

The importance of the teacher as a role model is well documented. Sociological research has demonstrated the extent to which an important component of learning derives from the example given in their own person by teachers, who significantly influence students such as in their choice of future career, their professional attitudes, and the importance they assign to different subjects.

The teacher should model or exemplify what should be learnt. Students learn by observation and imitation of the teachers they respect. Students learn not just from what their teachers say but from what they do in their learning activities and the knowledge, skills and attitudes they exhibit. Role modelling is one of the most powerful means of transmitting values, attitudes and patterns of thoughts and behaviour to students and in influencing students' career choice.

Indeed role modelling may have a greater impact on the student than other teaching methods. It was found role modelling to be educationally more effective than lecture/ discussion sessions in enhancing the students' ability.

b) The role model as a teacher

Teachers serve as role models not only when they teach students while they perform their duties as instructors, but also when they fulfill their role as teachers outside the classroom, whether it is in the lecture theatre or the small discussion or tutorial group or I the case of co-curricular activities. The good teacher can describe in a lecture to a class of students their approach to the educational problem being discussed in a way that captures the importance of the subject and the choices available. The teacher has a unique opportunity to share some of the magic of the subject with the students. They can kindle, in the students, a curiosity and quest for a better understanding of the topic by their own personal example that is difficult to reproduce in an instructional text or computer programme. One problem facing education today is that many teachers are not qualified. This may have implications for role modelling. One result is that students may have more difficulty understanding the relevance of what they are learning to their future career.

Reviewing the roles of teachers, it was noted "it is important to identify modelling as a distinct function and heading in order to draw attention to what is a pervasive but sometimes unconscious, and even denied process in education. Teachers may not see themselves as models and may even regret the very idea as pretentious and paternalistic, but it is difficult for learners not to be influenced by the living example set before them."

The Facilitator

a) The learning facilitator

The move to a more student-centred view of learning has required a fundamental shift in the role of the teacher. No longer is the teacher seen predominantly as a dispenser of information but rather as a facilitator or manager of the students' learning. The more responsibility and freedom given to the students, the greater the shift required in the teachers' role. Not all teachers adapt to this different role. Many teachers, suggested Jacques (1991), find the task of facilitator difficult to perform satisfactorily and fall back with some disappointment on their reserve position of authority, expert and prime talker.

The introduction of problem-based learning with a consequent fundamental change in the student-teacher relationship has highlighted the change in the role of the teacher from one of information provider to one of facilitator. The teacher's role is not to inform the students but to encourage and facilitate them to learn for themselves using the problems a focus for the leaning. This changing role of the teacher is also reflected in the constructivist approach to learning, in which knowledge is 'constructed' in the mind of the student and is constantly evolving. It is the role of the teacher to facilitate this process rather than to act simply as an information provider. Schmidt and Moust (1995) looked at the characteristics of an effective teacher in a problem-based curriculum. Teachers needed the ability to communicate with students in an informal way in the small groups sessions, and to encourage students learning by creating an atmosphere in which open exchange of ideas was facilitated. Teachers were able to function most effectively if, in addition to those skills, they also had subject-based knowledge.

The increasing availability and use of learning resource materials also brings with it the need for the teacher as a learning facilitator. No set of course materials, whether in print or electronic format, is perfect for all students. It is the responsibility of the teacher to facilitate the students use of the resources by overcoming any deficiencies in the materials and by integrating them with the curriculum.

The facilitative relationship between student and teachers is perceived by both as a key element in student learning and one that distinguishes good from poor teaching. This role of the teacher as a facilitator has been referred to as the 'supervisor' role, with the teacher providing the student with opportunities for working in the educational context, observing the student and giving feedback.

b) The mentor

There remains 'considerable semantic and conceptual variability about what mentoring is and does and what a mentor does'.

Megginson and Clutterbuck (1995) have defined mentoring as "off-line help by one person to another in making significant transition in knowledge, work or thinking." The mentor is usually not the member of staff who is responsible for the teaching or assessment of the student and is therefore "off-line" in terms of relationship with the students. Mentorship is less about reviewing the students' performance in a subject or an examination and more about a wider view of issues relating to the students. The mentor, suggests Megginson and Clutterbuck, has a role to help the learner grasp the wider significance of whatever is happening.

Mentoring can be viewed as a special relationship that develops between two persons with the mentor always there for support but not dependency (Ronan 1977). Lingham et al., .Gupta (1998) defined mentoring as a process by which one person acts towards another as a trusted counsellor or guide. It is not for educational supervision. It is about helping a person to learn within a supportive relationship. It may be a single event but is usually a longer relationship.

Easton and Van Laar (1995) showed that 97% of respondents in a survey of University lecturers reported having helped at least one student in distress during the previous year. Grayson et al. (1998) found that students both expect and want their lecturers to be a source of help. Professor John Radford, addressing a meeting of the British Psychological Society in 1996 on receipt of an award for the teaching of psychology suggested that in some respects academics resembled priests who had a caring, pastoral role.

Three emerging models for the teacher as mentor outlined by Morton-Cooper and Palmer (2000) are:

(1) The apprenticeship model and the mentor as skilled craftsperson. This role includes learning by observing. (Apprenticeship can be referred to as training period).
(2) The competence-based model and the mentor as trainer. This encompasses the role of the trainer as an instructor and coach who demonstrates and assists the student to achieve a set of competencies.
(3) The reflective practitioner model and mentor as critical friend and co-enquirer. This includes the promotion of collaboration and partnership in the learning process.

As can be seen, there are different concepts of what is a mentor. Some of the mentor roles described overlap with other identified roles.

The assessor

a) The student assessor

The assessment of the student's competence is one of the most important tasks facing the teacher. "Good teachers know how they must assess their students' learning" suggested Mapstone (1996) "and they want to do it well." Ian Lang, when Scottish Secretary and resisting pressure for parents to choose whether their children took part in national testing in primary schools, put in rather well: "I believe that teaching without testing is like cooking without tasting."

Assessment has emerged as a distinct area of activity for a teacher and one that may dominate the curriculum. It offers perhaps the greatest challenges facing education today. It is an area where the number of instruments available has increased dramatically but where their value may be difficult to determine in a field at risk of being dominated by the psychometrics.

Examining does represent a distinct and potentially separate role for the teacher. Thus it is possible for someone to be an 'expert teacher' but not an expert examiner. All institutions now need on their staff some teachers with a special knowledge and understanding of assessment issues. Such individuals act as test developers and provide guidance on the choice of instrument, marking procedures and standard setting. Examining however, must also be regarded as an integral part of the teacher's role and part of the occupation of teaching in higher education (Piper 1994). Most teachers have something to contribute to the assessment process. This may be in the form of contributing questions to a question bank, of acting as examiners faced with the key decision of who should pass and who should fail the examination. The assessment of students is an integral part of teaching, suggests Whitman et al. (1984), and requires the development of rapport and genuine interest in the student.

The assessor role of the teacher is often perceived as different from the other roles. While as information provider role model, facilitator and curriculum planner, the aim of the teacher is to assist the student in a variety of ways to achieve the course goals, as an assessor the teacher has the role of passing judgement on the student. This is particularly true in summative assessment, but is less so with formative assessment where the boundaries between assessment and teaching become increasingly blurred.

The teacher's role as an assessor is an important one. Murray et al (1996) suggested "Given the importance of assessment of student performance in university teaching and in students' lives and careers, instructors are responsible for taking adequate steps to ensure that assessment of students is valid, open, fair, and congruent with course objectives." Students can walk way from bad teaching, suggests Boud (1990), but they are unable to do so with regard to assessment.

b) The curriculum assessor

The teacher has a responsibility not only to plan and implement educational programmes and to assess the students' learning, but also to assess the course and curriculum delivered. Monitoring and evaluating the effectiveness of the teaching of courses and curricula is now recognised as an integral part of the educational process. The quality of the teaching and learning process needs to be assessed through student feedback, peer evaluation and assessment of the product of the educational progamme. Curriculum and teacher evaluation is a form of accountability which emphasises the obligation of those employed in the education system to be answerable to the public, to the profession, to those who fund the education and to the students themselves. In this sense, evaluation is an instrument of management and control (Nisbet 1990).

Evaluation can also be interpreted as an integral part of the professional role of teachers, recognising teachers' own responsibility for monitoring their own performance. Part of the expectation of the professional role of the teacher is as assessor of their own competence as a teacher. "Standards are the most effective when we set them ourselves" suggests Nisbet (1986). "Professionalism requires from us the capacity to apply the highest standards to ourselves even when there is no one but ourselves to judge. This is what we try to teach our students. They learn (or do not learn) from our example." Course evaluation is thus part of every teacher's responsibilities. Within the context of the curriculum, however some teachers may be expected to assume greater responsibility for overall assessment of the teaching and some may have this as a major personal responsibility.

Curriculum evaluation has been defined (Coles and Grant 1985) as "a deliberate act of enquiry which sets out with the intention of allowing people concerned with an educational event to make rigorous, informed judgements and decisions about it, so that appropriate development may be facilitated." The assessment of teaching and of the curriculum can be conducted at an institutional level with the teacher one of the stakeholders in the process. Just as important is the self-evaluation by the teacher of his or her teaching with the individual teachers reflecting on and analysing their own teaching.

Feedback from students and other teachers or 'critical friends' may be brought in to provide a further insight and to identify areas in teaching for the teacher's growth and development. The most widely used technique for obtaining feedback from students for the purpose of evaluating the teacher is the questionnaire. The use of focus groups, the nominal group technique, a Delphi technique, interviews with individual students and a study of diaries kept by students may give information which is perceived by the teacher as of more value.

The Planner

a) The curriculum planner

Most, schools and postgraduate bodies have education committees charged with the responsibility for planning and implementing the curriculum within their institution. Teachers employed by the school and members of the postgraduate institution may be expected to make a contribution to curriculum planning. Teachers can undertake few activities, suggests Diamond (1998), that will have greater impact on their students than their active involvement in the design of a curriculum or course they teach. Curriculum planning is an important role for the teacher. Different approaches to curriculum planning can be adopted (Harden 1986) and there are 10 issues that need to be addressed. The following should be specified:

§ The needs that the curriculum should meet,

- The expected learning outcomes,
- The content to be included in the curriculum,
- The organization of the content,
- The educational strategies,
- The teaching methods,
- The assessment procedure,
- Communication about the curriculum to staff and students,
- The educational environment,
- Procedures for managing the curriculum .

Curriculum planning presents a significant challenge for the teacher and both time and expertise is required if the job is to be undertaken properly.

b) The course planner

The best curriculum in the world will be ineffective if the courses which it comprises have little or no relationship to the curriculum that is in place. Once the principles which underpin the curriculum of the institution have been agreed, detailed planning is then required at the level of the individual course or phase of the curriculum. Traditionally much of the planning was discipline or subject-based. More recently there has been a move to inter-disciplinary or integrated teaching (Harden 2000). Such approaches need to be reflected in course design. Course planning, like planning the curriculum as a whole, requires dedicated time of individuals. The task is significantly more demanding in integrated progammes, but it is generally accepted that this is a small price to pay for the advantages of integrated teaching. Lack of attention to detail may lead to problems with the teaching programme.

Participation in course planning gives the teacher an opportunity to exert a significant influence on the educational process and to design courses which will achieve the learning outcomes specified by the institution. "Teachers in higher education" suggest Toohey (1999) "retain a very significant advantage over teachers in other branches of education their control of the curriculum. In much of primary, secondary, technical and vocational education, course design has been handed over to 'experts', to the impoverishment of the role of classroom teachers. Yet course design is an advantage of which many teaches in universities seem quite unaware. Much of the creativity and power in teaching lies in the design of the curriculum: the choice of texts and ideas which become the focus of study, the planning of experiences for students and the means by which achievement is assessed. These define the boundaries of the experience for students. Of course the way in which the curriculum is brought to life is equally important, but the power of good teacher-student interactions is multiplied many times by course design."

The Resource Developer

a) The resource material creator

An increased need for learning resource materials is implicit in many of the developments in education. With problem-based learning and other student-centred approaches, students are dependent on having appropriate resource material available for use either as individuals or in groups. Even in traditional curricula, students spend as much time with their workbooks as with their teachers.

The role of the teacher as resource creator offers exciting possibilities. Teachers will become, suggests Ravet and Layte (1997) "activity builders, creators of new learning environments." Indeed, the vision has been painted of the virtual university in which lecturers are replaced by instructional designers. The new technologies have greatly expanded the formats of learning materials to which the student may have access and make it much easier for the student to take more responsibility for their own education. As developers of resource materials, teachers must keep abreast with changes in technology. An investment in the further development of computer based learning material is needed. The use of computers in education is expanding and some schools make the purchase of computers by students compulsory. Computer-based learning however is often limited by the lack of good material for use by students.

Institute wide use of resource materials to support learning using traditional paper media or new technologies, however will occur only if at least some teachers possess the array of skills necessary to select, adapt or produce materials for use within the institution. The raising awareness and the training of staff in the role of resource developer is necessary for the appropriate development within an institution of technology supported learning.

b) The study guide producer

The trend from the teacher as an information provider to the teacher as a manager of students' learning has been discussed. While learning is facilitated by face-to-face contact with students, the amount of time available for this is restricted and can provide only to a limited extent the necessary guidance for students. Study guides suitably prepared in electronic or print form can be seen as the students' personal tutor available 24 hours a day and designed to assist the students with their learning. Study guides tell the student what they should learn – the expected learning outcomes for the course, how they might acquire the competences necessary - the learning opportunities available, and whether they have learned it – the students assessing their own competence.

The role of teachers as a producer of learning resource materials was highlighted in the previous section. It can be argued however that it is not cost-effective for the teacher to reinvent the wheel and produce instructional material and handouts on topics that are already covered in books or other resource materials.

What may be more valuable is for the teacher to identify the best resources available, direct the students to these and guide the students' use of them in study guides prepared by the teacher.

Study guides can facilitate learning in three ways:

- Assisting in the management of student learning,
- Providing a focus for student activities relating to the learning,
- Providing information on the subject or topic of study.

A 'study guide triangle' model can be used to represent these different functions, with one function at each point of the triangle. Guides can be placed at different points in the triangle reflecting the relative emphasis on these three functions.

* * * * *

LEARNING: THE CONCEPT

Learning is the lifelong, dynamic process by which individuals acquire new knowledge or skills and alter their thoughts, feelings, and behavior. Despite the significance of learning human development, disagreement exists over how learning occurs, what kinds of experiences facilitate or hinder the learning process, and what ensures that learning becomes relatively permanent.

There are many issues of debates over the concept and process of teaching and learning. Cognitists and Behaviorists always differed. The Nature-Nurture controversy has always been a matter of argument and a subject of debate. Moreover, there is an agreement over the issue that a man is born with certain inherent attributes or traits that can be used and polished to make a useful individual. The same may be useless if the qualities are not utilised properly.

The theories are explained and compared with regard to their procedures for changing behaviour, the assumptions made about the learner, the role of the educator in learning process, sources of motivation, and how learning is transferred to new situations and problems.

Learning theories are very important for teacher-trainees and educators as they supply prior knowledge of problems and factors that can attribute to the entire educational process. The importance of learning theories can be assessed by looking for answers to the following questions:

Is heredity more important than environment?

Is the learner found as passive or more active?

What is the educator's task in the learning process?

What motivates individuals to learn?

Is the transfer of learning more strongly influenced by the structure of the situation or by the learner's understanding and emotional learning?

The growing body of literature that has developed in educational psychology over the past century provides useful pedagogical tools to guide the teaching and learning process. Rather than offering a single or simple answer, educational psychology provides diverse theoretical perspectives on learning-alternative descriptions and explanations about how learning occurs and what motivates people to learn and develop their behaviour and personality.

Why do teachers, learners, trainers and educators need to know learning theories? Professional accountability and personal growth are two reasons. Increasingly, educators are required to demonstrate that they regularly employ sound methods and clear rationales in their educaiton and interaction, staff development and training, as well as community and continuing education. A solid grounding in learning theory is essential for effective educational practice. Beyond one's profession, however, knowledge of the learning process relates to nearly every aspect of daily life. Learning theories can be applied at the individual, group, and program levels to change unhealthy habits of small and young kids build constructive relationship among people develop effective behaviour, and become more adept at comprehending and teaching new material.

In the forth coming pages, the principal learning theories will be reviewed. In training and education, behaviourist, cognitive, and social learning theories are most frequently discussed and applied to teaching profession. Motivational concepts have also been studied as these are very pertinent to the teaching-learning context.

Behaviorist Learning Theory

The behaviorists view learning as the product of the stimulus conditions (S) and the responses (R) that is sometimes termed as the S-R model of learning. Whether dealing with animals or people, the learning process is similar and relatively simple. Generally ignoring what goes on inside the individual which, of course, is always difficult to ascertain. The behaviorists closely observe responses and then manipulate the environment to bring about the intended change. (Bigge & Shermis, 1992; Henton & Iverson, 1978).

To modify people's attitudes and responses, the behaviorists recommend either altering the stimulus conditions in the environment or changing what happens after a response occurs. Motivation is explained as the desire to reduce some drive hence, satisfied or complacent individuals have little motivation to learn and change. Getting behaviour to transfer from the initial learning situation to other settings is largely a matter of practice and a similarity in the stimuli and responses between the learning situation and future situations where the response is to be performed. Most of behaviorist learning theories are based on respondent conditioning and operant conditioning procedures.

Respondent conditioning (also termed classical or Pavlovian conditioning) emphasizes the importance of stimulus conditions and the associations formed in the learning process (Hilgard & Bower, 1966; Klein & Mowrer, 1989). According to this basic model of learning, a neutral stimulus (NS) — a stimulus that has no particular value or meaning to the learner is paired with a naturally occurring unconditioned or unlearned stimulus (UCS) and unconditioned response

(UCR). After a few such pairings, the neutral stimulus alone, without the unconditioned stimulus, elicits the same response. Often occurring without thought or awareness, learning takes place when the newly conditioned stimulus (CS) now becomes associated with the conditioned response (CR).

Respondent conditioning highlights the importance of the "atmosphere" and staff morale. Often without thinking or reflection, these are the associations that patients and visitors formulate as a result of their hospital experiences, providing the basis of long-lasting attitudes toward education, educational infrastructures and facilities, and the target groups.

Besides influencing the acquisition of new responses to environmental stimuli, principles of respondent conditioning may be used to extinguish a previously learned response. Responses are decreased if the presentation of the conditioned stimulus is not accompanied by the unconditioned stimulus over time.

Systematic desensitization is a technique based on respondent conditioning that is used by psychologists to reduce fear and anxiety in their clients (Wolpe, 1982). The assumption is that fear of a particular stimulus or situation is learned, and therefore, it can be "unlearned" or extinguished. Fearful individuals are first taught relaxation techniques, and while in a state of relaxation, the fear-producing stimulus is gradually introduced at a nonthreatening level so that anxiety and emotions are not aroused. After repeated pairings of the stimulus under relaxed, nonfrightening conditions, the individuals learns that no harm will come to him from the once fearful stimulus. Finally, he is able to confront the stimulus without being anxious and afraid. Taking the time to help patients relax and reduce their stress when applying some educational intervention, even a tough and challenging procedure lessens the likelihood that undivided will build up negative and anxious associations about the target that he intends to achieve.

Certain respondent conditioning concepts are directly useful in educational practice. Stimulus generalization is the tendency of initial learning experiences to be easily applied to other similar stimuli. With more and varied experiences, individuals learn to differentiate among similar stimuli, and discrimination learning occurs. Much of educational practice involves discrimination learning. Spontaneous recovery is another useful concept for teachers and educationists to know. Although a response may appear to be extinguished, it may "recover" and reappear at any time (even years later), especially when stimulus conditions are similar to the initial learning experience. Spontaneous recovery helps us understand why it is so difficult to truly eliminate unwanted habits, use of slangs and wrong pronunciation.

Operant conditioning, developed by B.F. Skinner (1974), focuses on the behavior of the organism and the reinforcement that occurs after the response. A reinforcer is a stimulus or even applied after a response that strengthens the probability that the response will be performed again. When specific responses are reinforced on the proper schedule, behaviors can be either increased or decreased. The responses may be increased or decreased by using the contingencies of operant conditioning. The two ways to increase the probability of a response are to apply positive reinforcement or negative reinforcement after a response occurs. According to Skinner (1974), 'using positive reinforcement or reward greatly enhances the likelihood that a response will be repeated in similar circumstances'. For example, if a student learns something and others should be motivated to do again. He should get some reward and appreciation. This is some sort of positive reinforcement. Negative reinforcement may also be employed if the learner make, some mistakes. But, the aims of both kinds of reinforcement remains the same – the development of the child. For example, if as a student is being instructed by her teacher, he says something humorous, and her instructor stops criticizing and starts laughing. Because the use of humor has allowed the student to escape an unpleasant situation, it is likely he will employ humor again to counter a stressful situation and an embarrassment.

In avoidance conditioning, the unpleasant stimulus is anticipated rather than being directly applied. Avoidance conditioning has been used to explain the tendency of some people to become ill in order to refrain from doing something they do not want to do. For example, a child fearing a teacher or test may tell his mother that she has a stomachache. If allowed to stay home, the child increasingly may complain of sickness to avoid an unpleasant situation. If a person becomes truly ill when fearful events are anticipated, sickness is the behavior that has been increased through negative reinforcement.

According to the operant conditioning principles, behaviors may be decreased through either nonreinforcmenet or punishment. Skinner (1974) maintained that the simplest way to extinguish a response is not to provide any kind of reinforcement for some action.

If nonreinforcement is ineffective, then punishment may be employed as a way to decrease responses, although there are risks in using punishment. Under punishment conditions, the individual cannot escape or avoid an unpleasant stimulus. Suppose, for example, the young students attempt at humor was met by the instructor's remark, "Right now, we are talking about the need for you to change your behavior, and if you continue to make the same mistake, the records will document your errors, and undoubtedly your grade will suffer." The problem with using punishment as a technique for teaching is that the learner may become highly emotional or deflect attention away from the behavior that needs to be changed. One of the cardinal rules of operant conditioning is to "punish the behavior, not the person".

If punishment is employed, it should be administered immediately after the response with no distractions or means of escape. Punishment must also be consistent and at the highest "reasonable" level. Moreover, punishment should not be prolonged (bringing up old grievances or complaining about a misbehavior at every opportunity), but there should be a "time-out" following punishment to make certain there is no opportunity for positive reinforcement. The purpose of punishment is not to do harm or to serve as a release for anger; the goal is to decrease a specific behavior and to instill self-discipline.

The use of reinforcement is central to the success of operant conditioning procedures. For operant conditioning to be effective, it is necessary to assess what kinds of reinforcement are likely to increase or decrease behaviors for each individual. Not every student, the teachers or instructors wants lots of attention or finds rewards. A second issue involves the timing of reinforcement. Through experimentation with animals and humans, it has been demonstrated that the success of operant conditioning procedures partially depends on the schedule of reinforcement (Hill, 1990). Initial learning requires a continuous schedule, reinforcing the behavior quickly every time it occurs. If the behavior is not emitted, then responses that approximate or resemble the desired behavior can be reinforced, gradually shaping behavior in the direction of the goal for learning. As an illustration, for students who appear lethargic and unresponsive, the teachers by rewarding small gestures then build on these friendly behaviors toward greater human and emotional association and connection with reality. Once a response is well established, however, it becomes ineffective and inefficient in the long run, reinforcement can be administered on a fixed (predictable).

Operant conditioning techniques provide relatively quick and effective ways to change behavior. Carefully planned programs using behavior modification procedures can be applied to educational practice.

The behaviorist theory is simple, easy to use, and encourages clear, objective analysis of observable environmental stimulus conditions and learner-responses. There are, however, some criticisms and cautions to consider. According to this model, learners are assumed to be relatively passive and early manipulated which raises the crucial issue of ethics. "Who" is to decide "what" the "desirable" behavior should be? Too often the desired response is conformity and cooperation to make someone's job easier or more profitable. In addition, the theory's emphasis on extrinsic rewards and external incentives reinforces and promotes materialism rather than self-initiative, love of learning, and intrinsic satisfaction. Another shortcoming of behavior modification programs is that individual's changed behavior may deteriorate over time, especially once they are back in their former environment-an environment with a system of rewards and punishments that might get them into trouble in the first place.

Cognitive Learning Theory

While behaviorists generally ignore the internal dynamics of learning, cognitive learning theorists stress the importance of what goes on "inside" the learner. The key to learning and changing is the individual's cognition (perception, thought, memory, and ways of processing and instructing information). According to this perspectives, in order to learn, individuals must change their cognitions. A highly active process largely directed by the individual, learning involves perceiving the information, interpreting the information based on what is already known, and then reorganizing information into new insights or understanding.

According to cognitive theorists, the individual's goals and expectations are the sources of motivation that create disequilibrium, imbalance, tension, and the desire to act. Educators and those trying to influence the learning process must recognize the variety of perceptions, ways of thinking about information, and diverse goals and expectations brought to any learning situation. To promote transfer, the learner must mediate or "act on" the learning in some way. Similar patterns in the initial learning situation and subsequent situations also facilitate transfer. From a cognitive perspective, however, rather than rote memory and drill, the key factor is understanding (including considerations of learner readiness, knowledge of one's learning style, and ability to reorganize information).

The Gestalt perspective of cognitive learning emphasizes the importance of perception in learning. Rather than focusing on discrete stimuli, Gestalt refers to the configuration or organization of a pattern of cognitive elements, reflecting the maxim that "the whole is greater than the sum of the parts". A basic Gestalt principle is that the structuring of perception is directed toward simplicity, equilibrium, and regularity. For example, look at the bewildered faces of some student listening to a detailed, evasive explanation about some rules and grammar they are learning. What they desire most is a simple, clear explanation that settles their uncertainty and relates directly to them with familiar experiences.

Another Gestalt principle is that perception is selective, which has several ramifications. First, since no one can attend to all the surrounding stimuli at any given time, individuals orient themselves to certain features of an experience while screening out or habituating to other features. Students may be tensed and worried about their results. Second, what individuals choose to attend to and ignore is influenced by a host of factors: past experiences, needs, personal motives and attitudes, reference groups, and the particular structure of the stimulus or situation. Assessing these internal and external dynamics has a direct bearing on how a teacher approaches any learning situation with an individual student or group. Moreover, because individuals vary widely with regard to these and other characteristics, they will perceive, interpret, and respond to the same event in different ways, perhaps distorting reality to fit their goals and expectations. This explains why an approach that is effective with one student may not work with another individual student or a group.

Some of the psychological tendencies used to organize the perceptual world that have been identified by Gestalt psychologists are of special interest to eduationists, pedagogues and teachers. For example, if one considers figure-ground relations, although the staff may think that the central need and requirement of a student receiving all the instructions, may view this requirement as unimportant.

Another perceptual tendency is to strive for closure. Closure involves the psychological desire to complete, end, or conclude a Gestalt situation that is unfinsihed. The more unclear or uncertain the perceived situation, the more people will (1) grasp at alternative patternings, (2) be influenced by external suggestions, and (3) be affected by their internal needs and motivations. For example, student felt unclear and uncertain while awaiting test and results and a examiners diagnosis are likely to be in a state of imbalance and tension. Some students may try to evaluate their own potential and performance and scenario based on deeper psychological desires and goals. Recognizing that some people have a greater need for closure than others, a minority of individuals may resort to extreme behaviors to reduce uncertainty.

Because individuals perceive, interpret, and respond to the same situaiton in different ways, it is no wonder that communication problems abound in the educational system. Experts of education and Pedagogy need to provide as much structure as possible, based on what is known about a students condition. If testing and evolution is unclear, it may be wiser to tell patients this information than to leave them wondering. A student with extreme needs for closure in an uncertain educational condition may benefit from counseling and guidance to help them accept what they view as a very difficult, anxiety-producing situation.

Cognitive and information-processing perspectives emphasize thinking processes: thought, reasoning, the way information is encountered and stored, and memory functioning. Taking issue with the behaviorists, to cognitive theorists, reward is not necessary for learning; more important are the learner's goals, expectations, and experiences. Experience, in fact, is the key to learning: by exploring and discovering the environment, individuals formulate their unique cognitive map about how the world operates. For example, some neo-learners about their aim, who have never been to a school have little idea are baffled and irritated by the way the teachers and administrators behave. Staff members, on the other hand, have highly developed, detailed cognitive maps about education and may view as routine what the patient perceives as bizarre, bewildering, frightening, or insulting. Also, cognitive theorists make an important distinction between learning and performance. Just because a behavior is not performed does not mean that leaning has not occurred; the learning may be demonstrated at a later time.

How information is processed, stored, and retrieved is useful for teachers to know. The first stage in the memory process involves attention to environmental stimuli. As an example, if a student is not attending to what a teacher is saying, perhaps because he is weary or distracted, it would be prudent to try the explanation at another time when the student is more receptive and attentive.

In the second stage, the information is attended to by sensory processing. Questions for teachers to ask themselves include (1) what is the student's preferred mode of sensory processing (visual, auditory, or motor manipulation), and (2) are there sensory deficits? In the third stage, the information is briefly encoded (transforming and incorporating information into memory in a particular form) into short-term memory, after which it is either disregarded and forgotten or stored in long-term memory. Long-term memory involves organizing the information by using a preferred strategy for storage (e.g. imagery, association, rehearsal, breaking the information into units). While long-term memories are enduring, a central problem is remembering and retrieving the stored information at a later time. The last stage involves the action or response that the individual makes on the basis of how information was processed and stored. An important implication for teaching is that if students are unable to remember or reproduce information accurately, teachers should examine closely how the student responds to, processes, and stores the information that is presented and then help the students "reprocess" what needs to be learnt.

Memory processing and the retrieval of information are enhanced by organizing information and making it meaningful. Forgetting or difficulty in retrieving information from long-term memory may occur because the information has faded from lack of use, other information interferes with retrieval (what comes before or after a learning session may well interfere with storage and retrieval), or individuals are motivated to forget for a variety of conscious and unconscious reasons. This material on memory processing and functioning is highly useful in educational practice-whether developing education brochures, engaging in one-to-one education, giving a staff development workshop, preparing lectures, or studying for one's courses and examinations.

Cognitive development is a third perspective that focuses on qualitative changes in perceiving, thinking, and reasoning as individuals grow and become mature. Cognitions are based on how external events are conceptualized, organized, and represented within each person's mental framework or schema-a framework that is partially dependent on the individual's stage of cognitive development. From infancy through adolescence, marked changes occur in the way youngsters perceive, reason, and represent the world around them, largely as a function of their growth, maturation and experience. Readiness to learn is an important consideration, which is based partially on the learner's stage of cognitive development.

How learning occurs and characteristic stages of cognitive development have been identified by theorists such as Jean Piaget and Jerome Bruner (1966). These theorists concur that learning is an active process that transpires as the child interacts with the environment. However, these are the basis of nature-Nurture controversy. Piaget's theory is perhaps the best known and explains that dual processes are involved in learning, as learners (1) assimilate information to make it fit their cognitive schema (e.g., a three-year-old child may think that the moon is following her around) and (2) accommodate information by changing their cognitive structures (e.g., although fearful of doctors because of a bad experience, several encounters with a friendly, nonthreatening individual conclude that not all teachers need to ascertain how students are interpreting and storing (assimilating or accommodating) their Pedagogic experiences in educational setup.

Through his observations of children's perception and thought processes at different ages, Piaget identified and described four stages of cognitive development (sensorimotor, preoperational, concrete operations, and formal operations) over the course of infancy, childhood, and adolescence. However, researchers have reported that while the cognitive stages develop sequentially, some adults never reach the formal operations stage. These adults may learn better from highly concrete approaches to education. Developmental psychologists have also proposed advanced stages of reasoning in adulthood beyond formal activities and processes. For example, it may not be until middle age that adults are able to deal with contradictions, synthesize information, and more effectively integrate what they have learned. Assessing each students' level of cognitive functioning is a first step in communicating effectively and accomplishing education.

The social cognition perspective within the cognitive theory highlights the influence of social factors on perception, thought, and motivation. A host of scattered explanations can be found within the boundary of social cognition. One of the most popular theories in education is the attribution theory which concerns the cause-effect relationships and explanations that individuals formulate to account for their own and others' behavior and how the world operates.

A significant contribution of the cognitive theory is its recognition and appreciation of the rich diversity in teaching and learning experiences. Consider, for example, the wide variation in the ways in which learners actively structure their perceptions, approach a learning situation, and encode-process-store-retrieve information. The challenge to educators is to foster insight, creativity, and problem solving. Difficulties lie in ascertaining exactly what is going on inside the mind of each individual and in designing learning activities that encourage people to restructure their perceptions, reorganize their thinking and behavior, and originate solutions.

Social Learning Theory

Most learning theories assume the individual must have direct experiences in order to learn. The social learning theory contends that much of learning occurs by observation-watching other people and seeing what happens to them. Learning is often a social process, and other individuals, especially "significant others", provide compelling examples or role models for how to think, feel, and act. While Miller and Dollard (1941) viewed social learning as a mixture of behaviorist and psychodynamic influences, Bandura (1977, 1986) is credited with outlining the behaviorist and cognitive dimensions of the theory as well as designing experiments to demonstrate the extraordinary power of the social learning theory.

Role modeling is a central concept of the theory. As an example, from educational context, a more experienced teacher who demonstrates desirable professional attitudes and behavior sometimes is used as a mentor for a less experienced one. Vicarious reinforcement is another concept from the social learning theory and involves viewing other people's emotions and determining whether role models rewarded or punished for their behavior. The behavior of a role model may be initiated, even when no reward is involved for either the role model or the learner. In many cases, however, whether the model is perceived by the observer to be rewarded or punished may have a direct influence on learning. This may be one reason why it is difficult to attract teachers to specialize in their field of interest.

While much of the social learning theory is based on

behaviorist principles, the self-regulation and the control that the individual exhibits in the learning process reflect cognitive principles. Bandura (1977) outlined a four-step, largely internal process that directs social learning. Research indicates that role models with high status and competence are more likely to be observed, although the learner's own characteristics (needs, self-esteem, competence) may be the more important determiner of attention. Second is the retention phase, which involves the storage and retrieval of what was observed. Third is the reproduction phase, where the learner copies the observed behavior. Mental rehearsal, immediate enactment, and corrective feedback strengthen the reproduction of behavior. Fourth is the motivational phase, involving whether the learner is motivated to perform a certain type of behavior or not. Reinforcement or punishment for a role model's behavior, the learning situation, and the appropriateness of subsequent situations where the behavior is to be displayed affect a learner's performance (Bandura, 1977; Gage & Berliner, 1988). Well suited to conducting education process and staff development programme, this organized approach to learning requires attention to the social environment, the behavior to be performed, and the individual learner.

The social learning theory extends the learning process beyond the educator-learner relationship and direct experiences to the larger social world. The theory helps explain the socialization process as well as the breakdown of behavior in society. Responsibility is place don the educator or leader to be an exemplary role model and to choose socially healthy experiences for individuals to observe and repeat (requiring the careful evaluation of learning materials for stereotypes, mixed or hidden messages, and negative impacts). However, simple exposure to competent role models correctly performing a behavior that is punished) does not ensure learning. Attention to the learner's individuality and the dynamics of self-regulation may help sort out the varying effects of the social learning experience.

Psychodynamic Learning Theory

Although not usually treated as a learning theory, some of the constructs from the psychodynamic theory (based on the work of Sigmund Freud and his followers) have significant implications for learning and changing behavior. Largely a theory of motivation stressing emotions rather than cognition and responses, the psychodynamic perspective emphasizes the importance of conscious and unconscious forces in guiding behavior, personality conflicts, and the enduring impact of childhood experiences.

A central principle of the theory is that behavior may be conscious or unconscious-that is, individuals may or may not be aware of their motivations and why they feel and act as they do. According to the psychodynamic view, the most primitive sources of motivation comes from the 'Id' and is based on libidinal energy (the basic instincts, impulses, and desires we are born with), which includes eros (the desire for pleasure and sex, sometimes called the "life force") and thanatos (aggressive and destructive impulses, or "death wish"). Students who succeeds or fails despite all expectations, to the contrary, provide illustrations of such primitive motivations. The 'Id' according to Freud, operates on the basis of the pleasure principle-to seek pleasure and avoid pain. Dry, dull education lectures given by teachers or lecturers who go through the motions of the presentation without much enthusiasm or emotion inspire few students to listen or to hear the instruction. This does not mean, however, that only pleasurable presentations will be acceptable.

The 'id' and 'superego' are medicated by the 'ego' which operates on the basis of the reality principle – rather than insisting on immediate gratification, people learn to take the long road to pleasure and weigh the choices or dilemmas in the conflict between the id and superego. Healthy ego (self) development, emphasized by Freud's followers, is an important consideration in the fields of Education and personality development as indicated by several examples. Students with 'ego' strength can cope with strenuous and tiring educational preparations because they recognize the long-term value of endearing discomfort and pain to achieve a positive outcome. Students with weak ego development, on the other hand, may miss their lectures and educational activities or may engage in short-term pleasurable activities that work against their development or improvement. Helping student develop ego strength and adjust realistically to a changed body image or lifestyle brought about by disease and educational interventions is a significant aspect of the learning process. Educationist themselves require personal ego strength to cope with the numerous predicaments in the everyday educational activity as they face conflicting values, ethics, and demands.

When the ego is threatened, defense mechanism may be employed to protect the 'self'. The short term use of defense mechanisms is a way of coming to grips with reality. The danger is the overuse of long-term reliance on defense mechanisms which allows individuals to avoid reality and may act as barriers to learning and transfer. Employing defense mechanisms is not limited to students or teaching staff. A common defense mechanism employed by educational staff is to intellectual level with the significance of education and development.

Another central assumption of the psychodynamic theory is that personality development occurs in stages, with much of adult behavior derived from earlier childhood experiences and conflicts. One of the most widely used models of personality development is Erikson's (1968) eight "crisis" to be resolved at each stage. Education, communication and development of people need to include considerations of the students stage of personality.

According to the psychodynamic view, personal difficulties arise and learning and perception are limited when individuals become fixated or stuck at an earlier stage or personality development. They then must work through the previously unresolved crisis to develop and mature emotionally. For example, some staff members and students feel an inordinate need to control the self, other people, and certain social situations. This behavior may have been rooted in their inability to resolve the crisis between "trust versus mistrust" at the earliest stage of life. It is essential in working with these individuals to build a trusting relationship and to encourage them gradually to relinquish some control.

Past conflicts, especially during childhood, may interfere with the ability to learn or to transfer learning. What people resist talking about or learning, termed resistance, is an indicator of underlying emotional problems, which must be dealt with for them to move ahead emotionally and behaviourally.

Serious problems in miscommunication can occur in educational set up. Although the teachers could do little as children to improve the situation, they may be compensating for their childhood feelings of helplessness and dependency as adults by devoting their careers to educational achievement. These motivations, however, may not serve them well as they attempt to cope, communicate, and educate some poor students.

Emotional conflicts are not always due to internal forces; society exerts pressures on individuals that promote emotional difficulties as well. The reluctance of educationists to be open and honest with a bad performer partially may be derived from other culture and environment. Staff may or may not be conscious of these pressures, but either way they are likely to feel guilty and "a failure" when dealing with such students.

The concept of transfer has special meaning to psychodynamic theorists. Transference occurs when individuals project their feelings, conflicts, and reactions-especially those developed during childhood with significant others such as parents-onto authority figures and other individuals in their lives. The danger is that the teacher-student relationship may be distorted and unrealistic because of the biases inherent in the transference reaction. For example, because a student is very poor, they may feel helpless and dependent and then regress to an earlier stage in life. Their childhood feelings and relationship with a parent for better or worse may be transferred to a teacher dealing them.

The psychodynamic approach reminds us to pay attention to emotions, unconscious motivations, and the psychological growth and development of all those involved in educational process and learning. One problem with this approach is that much of the analysis is speculative and subjective. Individual teacher's biases, emotional conflicts, and needs may distort their evaluation of other persons and situations. Another caution is that the psychodynamic theory may be used inappropriately; it is not the job of the instructor to probe into the private lives and feelings of students to uncover deep, unconscious conflicts. A third danger is that educationists teachers and counsellors may use the many psychodynamic principles as a way of explaining away rather than dealing with people as individuals who need emotional care.

Humanisitic Learning Theory

Underlying the humanistic perspective on learning is

the assumption that each individual is unique and that all individuals have a desire to grow in a positive way. One difficulty is that society's values and expectations and adults' mistreatment of their children and each other (e.g., inconsistent or harsh discipline, humiliation and belittling, abuse and neglect) may retard positive psychological growth. Spontaneity, the importance of emotions and feelings, the right of individuals to make their own choices, and human creativity are the corner-stones of a humanistic approach to learning (Gage & Berliner, 1992; Pine, 1977).

Motivation is derived from each person's needs, subjective feelings about the self, and the desire to grow. The transfer of learning is facilitated by curiosity, a positive self-concept, and open situations where people respect individuality and promote freedom of choice. Under such conditions, transfer is likely to be widespread, enhancing flexibility and creativity.

Like the psychodynamic theory, the humanistic perspective is largely a motivational theory. Maslow (1954),a major contributor to humanistic theory, is perhaps best known for identifying the hierarchy of needs plays such an important role in human motivation. At the bottom of the hierarchy are physiological needs (food, warmth, sleep); then come safety needs; next is the need for belonging and love, followed by self-esteem, cognitive, and aesthetic needs. At the top of the hierarchy are elf actualization needs (maximizing one's potential). An assumption is that basic level needs must be met before individuals can be concerned with learning and self-actualizing. Thus, students who are hungry, tired, and in mental tension will be motivated to get these biological needs met before being interested in learning rules, theories and other aspects of education.

Besides personal needs, the humanists contend that self-concept and self-esteem are necessary considerations in any learning situation. The therapist Carl Rogers (1961, 1994) argued that what people want is unconditional positive self-regard (the feeling of being loved without strings attached). Experiences that are threatening, coercive, and judgmental undermine the ability and enthusiasm of individuals to learn. It is essential that those in positions of authority convey a fundamental respect for the people with whom they work.

If a teacher is prejudiced against problems of the student, then little will be improving relationship with students until he/she is genuinely able to feel respect for the students as an individual. Rather than acting as an authority, according to the humanists, the role of any educator or leader is to be a facilitator (Buscaglia, 1982). Listening rather than talking is the skill needed. Since the uniqueness of the individual is fundamental to the humanistic perspective, much of the learning experience requires a direct relationship between the educator and the learner, with instruction tailored to the needs, self-esteem, and positive growth of each learner. Learners, not educators, choose what is to be learned, and within this framework educators, choose what is to be learned, and within this framework educators serve as resource persons whose job is to help guide learners to make wise choices. Mastering information and facts is not the point of learning. Fostering curiosity, enthusiasm, initiative, and responsibility are much more important and enduring and should be the primary goals of any educator.

Another humanistic principle is that feelings and emotions are the keys to learning, communication, and understanding. The humanists worry that in today's stressful society people easily lose touch with their feelings, which sets the stage for emotional problems and difficulties in learning (Rogers, 1961). "Tell me how you feel" is a much more important statement to the humanists than "tell me what you think", since thoughts and admonitions (the latter of which Rogers calls "the shoulds") may be at odds with true feelings.

The humanistic learning theory has modified the approach to education and changing behavior by giving primary focus to the subjective needs and feelings of the leaner and by redefining the role of the educator. The theory has its weaknesses as well. Research has not been able to substantiate some of the theory's strongest claims, and the theory has been criticized for promoting self-centered learners who cannot take criticism or compromise their deeply felt positions. Charged with being more of a philosophy or a cult than a science, the "touchy-feely" approach of the humanists makes some learners and educators feel truly uncomfortable. Moreover, information, facts memorization, drill, practice, and the tedious work sometimes required to master knowledge, which the humanists minimize and sometimes disdain, have been found to contribute to significant learning, knowledge building, and skill development (Gage & Berliner, 1992; Giaconia & Hedges, 1982).

Critical Estimate

A comparative summary of the five learning theories. discussed earlier is hereby presented. Generalizations can be made about the differences as well as the similarities in what the theories say about acquiring knowledge and changing feelings, attitudes, and behavior. Each one is relevant in a particular classroom situation.

Relative to the unique contributions of the learning theories, each theory gives focus to important considerations in any learning situation. For example, the behaviorists urge us to pay attention to and change stimulus conditions and provide reinforcement to alter behavior. While criticized for being reductionistic, the behaviourists emphasis on manipulating the environment and reinforcements is admittedly simpler and easier than trying to undertake an overview of an individual's internal dynamics (perceptions, cognition, feelings, and personality history and conflicts).

Moreover, getting someone first to behave in a more appropriate way, may not be as alarming to the learner as it would be to suggest the need for internal personality changes. Desired responses are modified and strengthened through practice; the new learned responses, in turn, may lead to more fundamental changes in attitudes and emotions. The social learning perspective is another relatively simple theory to use, stressing the importance of effective role models, demonstrate exactly what behavior is expected.

Cognitive, social learning, psychodynamic, and humanistic theories remind us to consider internal factors—perceptions, thoughts, ways of processing information, feelings, and emotions. These factors cannot be ignored because, ultimately, it is the learner who controls and regulates learning: how information is perceived, interpreted, and remembered and whether the new knowledge is expressed or performed. In practice, learning theories should not be considered mutually exclusive but operate together to change attitudes and behavior. Staff are highly respectful, and emotionally supportive of each student and create the time and opportunity to listen to them discuss some of their serious concerns (psychodynamic). Other factors facilitate the learners should also be kept in mind.

Another generalization from this discussion is that some learning theories are better suited to certain individuals than to others. While theoretical assumptions about the learner range from passive to highly active, passive individuals may learn more effectively from behaviorist techniques, whereas curious, highly active, and self-directed persons may do better with cognitive and humanistic approaches. One should also, keep in mind that some learners require external reinforcement and incentives, whereas other learners do not seem to need. Individuals who are well educated, verbal, and reflective may be better candidates for cognitive and psychodynamic approaches, whereas behaviorist approaches may be more suitable for persons who are uncomfortable dealing with problems. In addition, each individual's preferred modes of learning may help determine the choice of suitable theoretical principles and approaches. That is, why some individuals learn by acting and responding (behaviorist), the route to learning for others may be through perceptions and thoughts (cognitive) or through feelings and emotions (humanistic and psychodynamic). Most people appear to benefit from demonstration and example (social learning).

Common Principles of Learning

Taken together, the theories discussed above indicate that learning is a very complicated process. Besides, the distinct considerations for learning suggested by each theory, their similarities point to some core features of learning. The issues raised at the beginning of the chapter can be answered by synthesizing the learning theories and identifying their common principles. However, one theory in particular may be especially used for one aspect of English. For example, while teaching Poetry, Gestalt psychology can be proved to be of much relevance because it is holistic in approaches. Theory of insight in particular has to especial relevance for teaching of Literature, in general.

How Does Learning Occur

Learning takes place as individuals interact with their environment and incorporate new information or experiences with what they already know or have learnt. However, inborn qualities are the basis for any cognitive process, be learning, teaching or educating. Factors in the environment that affect learning include the structure or pattern of stimuli, the effectiveness of role models and reinforcements, feedback for correct and incorrect responses, and opportunities to process and apply learning to new situations. The individual exerts substantial effort for learning, often involving considerations of his or her developmental stage, past history (habits, cultural conditioning, socialization, childhood experiences and conflicts), cognitive style, dynamics of self-regulation, conscious and unconscious motivations, personality (stage, conflicts, self-concept), and emotions.

The learning theories reviewed here suggest that in order to learn, individuals must want to gain something which inturn creates in learner by arousing tension and the propensity to act or change behavior. The relative success or failure of the learner's performance may have an impact on subsequent learning experiences. In some cases, an inappropriate, maladaptive, or previously learned harmful behavior may need to be extinguished and then replaced with a more positive response.

Learning Facilitators

This is where the educator's selection of learning theories and structuring of the learning experience become important. To be effective, educators must have knowledge (of the material to be learnt, the learner, and educational psychology), and they must be competent (imaginative, flexible, able to employ teaching methods, exhibit solid communication skills, and possess the ability to motivate others). All the learning theories discussed in the foregoing pages indicate the need to recognize and relate the new information to the learner's past experiences (old habits, familiar patterns, childhood memories, feelings about the self, and what is valued, normative, and perceived as successful or rewarded in society).

Ignoring these considerations, of course, may hinder learning. Other impediments to learning may involve a lack of clarity and meaningfulness in what is to be learnt, neglect or harsh punishment, poor role models and rewards for unhealthy behavior, confusing reïnforcement, and inappropriate materials for the individual's ability, readiness to learn, or stage of life-cycle development. Moreover, learners with negative socialization experiences, deprived of stimulating environments, without goals and realistic expectations for themselves are unlikely to want to learn.

It is thus summed up that these are many dimensions of learning in general. Some aspects are equally important and feasible for the teaching of English. There is, of course, no single, best way to approach learning, although all the theories indicate the need to be sensitive to the unique characteristics and motivations of each learner. Educators cannot be expected to know everything about the learning process. More important, perhaps, is that they can determine what needs to be known, where to find the necessary information, and how to help others benefit directly from the learning experience.

It has been found that 'Motivation' as a whole is very important factor in the process of learning English.

* * * * *

MOTIVATION AND TEACHING

The term 'Motivation' is very important in the entire educational system. Its relevance was first felt and explored in the private sectors. However, these days, a lot of are busy exploring the relevance of 'Motivation' in the educational sector. It is equally pertinent and inevitable for administrators of education (Super-ordinates), teachers/lecturers (sub-ordinates) and the products (students/learners).

In this chapter, the first attempt has been made to define and explain the concept, its relevance for administrators and teachers, motivating factors, 'Motivation theories' etc. In the end, 'Motivation' and its relevance has been explored for the benefit of the learners. Some motivating factors and strategies have also been mentioned.

Motivation can be operationally defined as an 'internal force that influences an individual's behaviour'.

Because motivation comes from within the person, managers cannot directly motivate their sub-ordinates or the teachers can't do the same for their students. However, a good humanistic manager or a teacher can create suitable environment in which the followers may feel themselves to be motivated.

All human beings have needs that motivate them. Motivation may be of positive or negative type motivation in nature. The motivating techniques may include monetary or non-monetary incentives.

The term 'motivation' has been basically derived from the root 'motive' that is related to its simplest meaning 'to move'. Human motives are said to be internalised goals with in individuals. 'A motive is defused as an inner state that energises, activates, or moves and directs or channels behaviour towards goals'. Standford and Wrightman describe a motive as 'a restlessness, a lack, a yen, a force. Once in the grip of a motive, the organism does something. It most generally does something to reduce the restlessness, to remedy the lack, to alleviate yen, to mitigate force. Therefore, motivation has been defined as "the process of creating organizational conditions which will impel employees to strive to attain the goals of an enterprise". According to Dubin, 'Motivation is the complex of force starting and keeping a person at work in an organisation.'

The purpose of motivation is to create conditions in which people are willing to work with zeal, initiative, interest and enthusiasm, with a high personal and group moral satisfaction with a sense of loyalty, responsibility and discipline and with pride and confidence in a most cohesive manner so that the goals of an organisation are achieved effectively.

Motivation: Its Relevance in Institutions

Interest in the area of motivation has developed as sub-field in the recent past. Several factors appear to account for the prominence of this area as a focal point of interest. The following are the gist of it.

- Administrators and researchers cannot avoid a concern with the behavioural requirements of an organization or an institution. Every organization needs people (in addition to physical and financial resources) in order to function,
- Institutional effectiveness becomes to some degree a question of management's ability to motivate its employees, to direct at least a reasonable effort towards the goals of the organization,
- As technology increases in complexity, machines tend to become necessary, yet we find insufficient vehicles of effective and efficient operations. In other words, it becomes necessary for an organization to ensure that it has employees who are both capable of using the latest technology to achieve goals,
- The employees should be considered as future resources.

It has been felt that an individual can't achieve its goals within an organisation or institution unless there is a sufficient level of motivation. Similarly, a student can't achieve his target of education unless he is suitably motivated towards achievement of the same.

In other words, the two terms 'motivation' and 'achievement' are so closely interlinked that the former is the cause and the later is the effect. There may be some different aspects and kinds of motivating factor besides its various levels, however, it is agreed that an average human being possesses some kind of motivation which keeps him alive. And, if he is alive he has to work for achievement of some sub-goals of the ultimate goal-life.

There are two kinds of motivation-instrinsic and extrinsic motivation. Instrinsic motivation is directly related to the person's level of aspiration. Parents and person's values about what he or she wants to do and be. But, extrinsic motivation is enhanced by the job environment or external rewards. The reward occurs after the work has been completed. Both the kinds of motivation are very important for the development of an individual and his interest in doing some work for the achievement of some preconceived goals.

There are two important dimensions of motivation: material and non-material. It is believed that both play important roles in motivating people to achieve their goals, however, the situation may vary from place to place and individual to individual. It has been studied that material motivation (especially money) is the prominent factor towards motivation. It was an exact case in Indian Educational context in the recent past when the teachers were not suitably motivated as they were not suitably paid. As a result, the government revised the scale. But, later it was found that this motivation also did not last long and the motivation level took a U-turn and reached the same place. But, it is also a fact that good and dedicated teacher may surely perform better in any circumstance.

There are some well known means of effective motivation for the employees. Some of them are being mentioned here in order to arrive at the conclusion that if most of them are in practice, there is a likelihood of increase in the level of motivation among the employees consequently the organisation may be able to yield better results.

Means for effective motivation: The management can offer

several financial and non-financial as well as direct and indirect incentives to satisfy human needs in the organisations to realise goals. The Management can adopt the following means for effective employee motivation.

Fair Remuneration: Most of the basic and many of the secondary human needs can be satisfied by fairly remunerating the employees.

Job Satisfaction: The management should place its employees properly according to their merits, aptitudes, interests and capacities. The well placed employees take pride, interest and initiative in their work and enjoy job satisfaction.

Job Security: Job security is a great motivating factor. Security is a great psychological need of man and hence must be satisfied for boosting up his morale. An employee having possibility of being pushed out, cannot perform well. The employees must, therefore, be made permanent as early as possible.

Fair Promotion: The employees should get an opportunity to be given higher positions according to their skills, length of service and meritorious achievements. Not only the opportunity of promotion should exist in principle, but they should be made on certain predetermined, fair and honest rules and criteria and the conditions must be created where employees may prepare themselves for such promotions.

Congenial Working Environment: For satisfying the basic need for preservation of life and health, working conditions for employees must be made congenial. The adequate provision of light, canteen and cafeteria, gardening, medical aid offices, resources, equipment, and many of such other provisions may be very helpful in boosting the employee morale and satisfaction. They may feel good while working.

Honest and Competent Leadership: If the leaders and the managers are honest, impartial, sympathetic and capable of understanding employee, hopes and aspirations, emotions and sentiments, prospects and problems, motives and attitudes, they will be able to win the confidence of their employees. They should be competent to lead, excel, control, maintain discipline and motivate their employees for better and maximum results.

Efficient organisation, co-ordination and control: Efficient organisation may include adequate and efficient physical facilities and organisation of manpower. Proper delegation of authority and fixation of responsibilities avoid conflicts and being unity in action and purpose. Proper departmentation and grouping of activities lead to proper division of work and relationships. Efficient system of communication of command and suggestions, subordinate-superior relationships, clear assignment of managerial authority, all further the interest of motivation of employees by bringing a certainty, cohesion, confidence and competence. Similarly, efficient coordination of activities lead to harmonious relations and approach and the adequate system of control checks all splintering and cross-purpose activities. To a great extent, the feeling of security, certainty, fairness, confidence, interest and initiative is the direct result of an efficient organisation, coordination and control.

Freedom of Association, Mobility, Expression etc.: The need of association or of gregariousness is a great need of human beings. It is, therefore, the management which should satisfy this need by providing freedom to individuals to form their social and cultural associations in order that they can share their problems etc.

Participative Management Techniques: If the juniors are provided chance to take part in day to day activities they feel themselves as a part of the organisation. It satisfies the instinct of belonging to the organisation, gives them psychological satisfaction and foster the feeling of team-worker.

THEORIES OF MOTIVATION

There are many theories of motivation which need to be studied and analysed. The theory of motivation has undergone drastic change due to advance work of the behavioural scientists and educational experts. The following are the brief accounts of some of the theories propounded by a few well known scholars.

Maslow's Hierarchy of Needs Theory

Maslow has been regarded as the pioneer of the theory of motivation. He considered an individual's motivation as a predetermined order of needs each with its own order of priority. He has classified the need into five categories:

1. Physiological;
2. Safety, stability, and security;
3. Belongingness and love;
4. Self-esteem and the esteem of others; and
5. Self-actualisation, self-realisation, and self-accomplishment.

According to Maslow, "the concept of 'need hierarchy' the satisfaction of physiological needs, which are the most fundamental, results in the safety needs becoming more potent and felt by the individual concerned. Once these are fulfilled, the need for belonging becomes uppermost, and man's behaviour will be directed towards securing a respected place in his group consisting of both his superiors and his equals. Ultimately, the need for esteem and self-actualisation comes into play. It is said that a very few realise the fulfillment of these needs, thus, assuring the possibility of motivation in all human beings, wherever allowed in the management hierarchy."

In sum, Maslow's theory is built upon the idea that these needs are arranged in a natural hierarchy of urgency or priority. He emphasises that rising incomes have enabled many people to shoulder the financial burden of training for a new job. Thus, once basic lower-order needs are satisfied, individuals are able to move from jobs that are routine and boring to those who hold more potential for satisfying their higher-order needs. This theory, however, is not based on the uniqueness of the needs.

McGregor's Theory X and Theory Y

Douglas McGregor has proposed Theory X and Theory Y. These aimed at providing a framework for the proper management of people to achieve organisational goals. These theories suggest certain other aspects of the human nature. The basic assumptions of these theories have been given as under. The assumptions leads to corresponding administrative policies. But, these policies have not been illustrated here.

Assumptions of Theory X

1) The average human being has an inherent dislike for work and will avoid it if he can. He is passive,
2) Because of this characteristic most people must be coerced, controlled, directed, and threatened with punishment so that they will work towards the organisation's goals,
3) The average human being prefers to be directed, prefers security, and avoids responsibility. Therefore, they should be cooperated and directed.

Theory Y

1) Physical work and mental work are as natural as

play, if they are satisfying. Man has the potential to do something,

2) Man will exercise self-direction and self-control towards an organisation's goals if he is committed to them. (They need to be motivated),
3) Commitment is a function of rewards. The best rewards are satisfaction of ego and self-actualisation,
4) The average person can learn to accept and seek responsibility. Avoidance of it and emphasis on security are learned and are not inherent characteristics. (He should be trusted),
5) Creativity, ingenuity, and imagination are widespread among people and do not occur only in a select few. (Man should be encouraged).

The above assumptions guide management behaviour and thinking. There are administrators who follow the 'hard' or strict approach involving coercion and threat, and close supervision and control in dealing with their subordinates. Management can even be flexible (soft) attempting to direct by being permissive, relationship-oriented and satisfying people's immediate needs. Strict approach often leads to consequences like restriction of output, militant unionism, antagonism, etc. Flexible approach, on the other hand may lead to indifferent performance and abdication of management in favour of harmony. People may, at times, develop the habit of expecting more and giving less.

Herzberg's Motivation-Hygiene Theory

The *Two factor theory of motivation* developed by Frederick Herzberg is an interesting work in the field of Psychology. His model is based on research conducted among middle managers in engineering and accounting and presents the view that factors in the work environment that provide job satisfaction are not necessarily the same as those that cause dissatisfaction. Characteristics of the work environment that may lead to dissatisfaction are called hygiene factors and include the following:

1. Institutional personnel policies and management practices under which a job is performed,
2. Technical supervision received on the job,
3. Interpersonal relations with supervisors and peers,
4. Quality of working conditions,
5. Salary received for doing a job.

In the case of absence of these factors in work situation, employees' dissatisfaction is likely to occur. However, the presence of hygienic factors does not necessarily motivate employees. Instead, they help to prevent dissatisfaction and, in this sense, are similar to Preventive Practices recognised in medicine. The job content factors that produce satisfaction are called motivators and include the following:

1. Achievement on a job,
2. Recognition for job achievement,
3. Nature of the job and the work itself,
4. Responsibility for job advancement,
5. Advancement and growth in job capability.

Herzberg states that the absence of these motivational factors in the work situation does not bring about dissatisfaction on the job when these are presents they relate to a high level of motivation and job satisfaction. As such motivators relate on the intrinsic factors or actual content of jobs not just to extrinsic factors of the job environment. In this light, motivators are closely linked to the esteem and self-actualisation needs expressed by Maslow.

In sum, Herzberg reflected those factors of job satisfaction that relate to what the worker does while factors of dissatisfaction relate to the situation in which he works. Thus, the two factor theory reinforces the belief that motivators are the source of job satisfaction as well as effective role behaviour. Since hygiene factors are found to be responsible for job satisfaction, Management should not attempt to motivate people through these factors. Intrinsic factors need to be taken in account as they are positively related to job satisfaction. Management should therefore, attempt to make the job more meaningful and satisfying by providing necessary incentives and rewards.

Expectancy Theory of Motivation

The expectancy theories are based on expert-contributions of psychologists such as Victor H. Vroom, Layman W. Ponter and Edward E. Lawler. According to these expectancy theories, effort or motivation is primarily a function of three factors, their the importance to the person of a particular outcome or opportunity. The probability (expectation) he or she has of achieving that outcome, and the probability (expectation) the person has of being rewarded if the outcome is successfully attained. The expectancy theorists opine that there are no predetermined patterns of needs and a person's motivation is determined by forward-looking beliefs about what will happen. Moreover, it is not the extent of any reward that is important, but the degree to which the individual expects to be rewarded. Therefore, the managers consider the expectation model of the employees while trying to reward them effectively.

McClelland's Need Theory of Motivation

David McClelland of Harvard University and his co-workers have looked at certain peculiar motivating needs of the people in many cultures and many sections of the society. On the basis of their research, they have grouped the responses into three categories each representing an identifiable human motive or need. These are: need for power (n/PWR), need for affiliation (n/AFF), and need for achievement (n/ACH). Most people have some concern for each of these needs in their thoughts. However, all these needs do not strongly motivate most of the people. It has been found that as many as 90 per cent of people working in an organisation are not governed by these needs. Therefore, to motivate the majority of group, needs have to be identified.

Beyond Theory Y: A Contingency Model

Morse and Lorach suggested the contingency theory which puts stress of organising on a number of variables. The theory supports the idea that there is no one best way in which to organise. The design is conditional. The appropriate pattern of organisation-task-fit is contingent upon 'the nature of work to be done' and on the particular needs of the individual. There must not only be a fit between organisation and task, but also between the organisation and peoples as well as between task and people.

A new act of assumptions are proposed supporting the contingency approach:

1. Human beings have varying patterns of needs and motives into the organization but there exists one central need to achieve a sense of competence,
2. Competence motive exists in all human beings. Its fulfillment depends on how it interacts with the strengths of individual's other needs (for power, independence, achievement etc.),
3. Competence motivation is likely to be achieved when there is a fit between the task people and organisation,
4. Competence motivation is a continuous feelings: once a new goal is fulfilled, a new higher one is set.

The interrelationship between task-organisation-people fit can be complex but the best possibility for managerial action probably is in moulding the organisation to fit the task and people.

Maturity-Immaturity Theory

Chris Argyris has postulated a descriptive and multidimensional development process along which individuals in an organisation grow. Argyris examined industrial organisations to determine the effect of management practices on individual behaviour and their personal growth within work environment. He, in this process, has noticed seven basic changes that take place in the mature people over the years.

(i) Human beings have a tendency to develop from a state of being passive as an infant to a state of increasing activity as an adult,

(ii) Human beings have a tendency to develop from a state of dependence on others as an infant to a state of relative independence as an adult,

(iii) People have a tendency to develop from being capable of behaving in only a few ways as an infant to being capable of behaving in many different ways as an adult, erratic casual,

(iv) People have a tendency to develop from having a short time shalows, quickly dropped interest as an infact to a deepening of interest as an adult,

(v) Human beings have a tendency to develop from having a short time perspective as an infant to a much longer time perspective as a mature adult,

(vi) People in work organisations have a tendency to develop from being in a subordinate position in the family and society as an infant to an awareness and control over one's self as an adult.

People in working in orgnaisations, according to Chris Argyris, will have a tendency to grow from an infant to a matured state. The mature state is characterized by an endless series of challenges in which the reward comes from doing something for its own sake. The matured employee is characterized by full blow, wholeness, complexity and depth of knowledge and behaves like an adult.

Stacy Adams' Equity Theory

Adams' theory of Equity is one of the popular social exchange theories and is perhaps the most rigorously developed state of how individuals evaluate social exchange relationships. It is probably the clearest of the process theories. Basically the theory points out that people are motivated to maintain fair relationships with others and will try to rectify relationships by making them fair. This theory is based on two assumptions about human behaviour.

1. Individuals make contributions (inputs) for which they expect certain outcomes (rewards). Inputs include such things as the person's past training and experience, special knowledge, personal characteristics, outcomes include pay, recognition, promotion, prestige, benefits etc.
2. Individuals decide whether or not a particular exchange is satisfactory by comparing their inputs and outcomes to those of others in the form of a ratio. Equity exists when an individual concludes that his/her own outcome input ratio is equal to that of other people.

What motivates human behaviour is not a simple question. Psychologists have tried to explain the process and mechanism of motivation in a number of ways. We shall now discuss some of the viewpoints.

McDougall's Theory of Instinct

The oldest explanation for how and why we behave in a specific manner in a specific situation is given by the Theory of Instinct. Although it was William James who for the first time brought out the concept of instinct to explain behaviour. The credit for developing it into a full fledged theory must be given to Williams McDougall. According to this theory, our instincts are the springboards of our behaviour. These instincts are innate tendencies or inherited psychological dispositions or even the complex patterns of behaviour that lead to some purposive actions and they don't have to be learnt. Emphasising these views McDougall (1908) writes:

> 'The human mind has certain innate or inherited tendencies which are the essential springs or motive power of all thoughts and actions'.

Therefore, it may be pointed out that , all human behaviour can be explained on the basis of some instinct or the other. McDougall provided a list of 14 instincts and proposed that each instinct is accompanied by a specific emotional disposition (effective experience). The instinct of escapee, is accompanied by the emotion of fear, the instinct of combat (pugnacity) by anger, the instinct of repulsion by the emotion of disgust, and so on. He further claimed that all behavioral acts are essentially instinctive and this instinctive behaviour is found to have the following three aspects: (a) cognition (knowing), (b) affection (feeling or experiencing an emotion), and (c) condition (doing or striving). For example, when a child sees a bull coming towards him, he practices an instinctive behaviour by passing through the above-mentioned aspects or cycles. First, he sees the bull, second, he experiences an emotion of fear and third, he tries to run away. Thus, according to McDougall, what we do and how we do it can all be explained through our instinctive behaviour which is governed by our instincts accompanied by our emotional experience.

Hull's Drive Reduction Theory

In 1943, Clark Leonard Hull, a professor of Psychology at Yale University, developed a theory of motivation named the Drive Reduction Theory. He stressed that biological drives such as hunger, thirst, sex and escape from pain are mainly responsible for initiating and maintaining the primary responses. These drives produce internal tension, an undesirable state that the organism wants to change. In other words, all of his energy is concentrated on his efforts to reduce the heightened tension (drive). Thus, a hungry man activated by the need of reducing the tension created through the hunger drive may be compelled to engage in behaviour that would help him to reduce the hunger drive.

The drive reduction theory was supported by other psychologists and its sphere was broadened by including the psychological drives in it. For explaining the mechanism of drive reduction as a source of motivation, the term homeostasis was also coined. However, the failure of this theory to explain human behaviour especailly at the higher cognitive level has reduced its importance as a major motivational theory.

Freud's Psychoanalytic Theory of Motivation

Freud's psycho-analytic theory of motivation is centred around his concepts of instincts and the unconscious. Freud maintained that instincts are the root cause of all activities in a human being. He identified two basic instincts for this purpose. In his book (1953), he asserted willing to live (erotic instinct) and the death instinct or the desire to destroy even to the extent of destroying oneself are the ultimate bases of motivation. In fact, the life instinct, the urge for self-preservation dominates the earlier scenes of one's life. When the life instinct ceases to operate, the death instinct takes over. For example, the person who has failed in a love affair may think of committing suicide. However, what moves or energises the activities of the life instinct is the need for sexual gratification – a means to provide intense pleasure, satisfaction and meaning to one's life. Freud maintained that from birth onwards human beings experience sex gratification and the sex motives therefore is quite an important motive that activates human behaviour.

Beside the role played by one's life and death instincts and sexual urge, the unconscious also is a great determinant and activating force for the cause and operation of one's behaviour. The unconscious, which is $9/10^{th}$ of one's total mental content according to Freud, remains hidden and usually inaccessible. It consists of one's unfulfilled desires, wishes, ideas and feelings. It is like a great underworld with powerful unseen forces which is responsible, to a great extent, for all that we think, feel and do. Man, as Freud maintains, is but a puppet in the hands of the mighty unconscious and thus he has to behave in the way and manner in which the unconscious dictates. Therefore, the key to the why and how of behaviour lies in the choices made by one's unconscious which are usually the gratification of sex or the seeking of pleasure.

Behaviourists' Learning Theories of Motivation

According to the behaviourists' view, how and why we behave in a particular manner is fashioned by the experiences we receive through the acts of learning or training. Many times our behaviour is guided through a simple stimulus-response mechanism as emphasised by *Thorndike* or operated through the mechanism of classical or operant conditioning as advocated by Pavlov, Waston and B.F. Skinner. The role of reinforcement as a prime factor for the motivation of behaviour was properly emphasised in Skinner's Theory of Operand Conditioning. He asserted that an organism behaves in the way and manner in which its beahviour is shaped through a particular reinforcement schedule.

Moving in the footprints of Skinner, social theorists like Albert Bandura (1977) maintained that human motivation is mainly guided through social rewards like praise. Thus, a girl often praised for her skill in the kitchen will turn into a very effective cook and a good housewife.

According to him, the imitation of other's behaviour if it results in a reward, provides a valuable motivational source for most of us and that is why the concept of modelling is more commonly employed in the world of industry and advertisement.

Adler's Social Urges Theory

Disagreeing with the extreme views of Freud regarding sex as the basis of human motivation, Alfred Adler, a student of Freud, advocated that human beings are motivated primarily by social urges. For maintaining one's social self one requires a margin of safety besides simple security in terms of protection from danger. This margin of safety is achieved through domination and superiority, in order not to feel inferior or small, one strives or struggles for superiority. Therefore, the struggle for power, achievement and status or the will to dominate are really an outgrowth of the fundamental need for security. Thus, the motivation of human behaviour may be endorsed through a single basic drive known as the security drive or motive or in terms of a single need, the need for the security to maintain one's social self.

Goal-oriented Theory of Cognitivism

Unlike the mechanistic and instinctive approaches adopted by other psychologists, the cognitive school of psychology brings the role of cognitive factors in producing human motivation into the limelight. According to this views, human behaviour is purposeful and has a certain end or goal in view. An individual who aspires to reach a goal is helped by his cognitive abilities to develop a desirable drive or motive i.e., tendency to move towards that goal. The achievement of the goal satisfies the individual which in turn reinforces the maintained behaviour. The cognitive view of motivation was first propounded by the philosopher psychologist William James (1842-1910) who emphasised that the concepts of motivation was necessary to bring the psychomotor gap between ideas and actions. This view was further elaborated by psychologists like George Miller who advocated the construction of plans for bridging the psychomotor gap to meet certain ends. Another clue for the involvement of cognitive factors in bringing motivation comes from the theory of cognitive dissonance advocated by American psychologist Leon Festinger. Cognitive dissonance denotes an imbalance between what we believe (cognition) and what we do (contain). It may result in psychological discomfort to us. As a solution, we are motivated to set the imbalance right either by changing our beliefs or our behaviour. For example, information linking smoking with cancer and heart diseases creates dissonance in chain smokers. They cannot resist the temptation to smokes even though they are warned that cigarette smoking is injurious to their health. There is, in this situation an imbalance or dissonance involving the beliefs(cognition) and behaviour.

Theory Z

Ouchi (1981) was among the first researchers to present Japanese – style measured as an instinctive to contemporary U.S. Style management. He termed it as Theory Z (maybe as a expansion of McGregor's Theory X & Y). Components of Theory 'Z' includes decision making by consensus, fitting employees their job, an emphasis on a tendering towards job security, slower promotions, examinations of long-term consequences of management decision making, and a holistic concern to the workers.

Ouchi was able to find components of Japanese style of management in many successful US companies. The characteristics of theory Z include consensus in decision-making, quality circles, guarantee of life time employment, establishment of strong bond of responsibility between superiors and sub-ordinates etc.

Though the theory is based on some noble concepts and the suggested style of leadership is laissez faire, it has been fluctuating with its relevance. Sometimes, it is said to be quite fruitful, and the other time, it losses its charm. The reason might be very simple that the organisations have not been able to create a suitable atmosphere for the application of theory Z. In countries like USA and India, still people are not willing to work themselves unless they are not ordered or punished while this theory is based on willingliness because a follower of theory Z visualises an organisation as a family where each member is equally useful and responsible. He can't run away from his responsibility. The superordinate is the head of the family being the senior most member, more knowledgeable or more experienced. 'We feeling' is required in leadership style under theory 'Z'.

Motivation as a concept is equally important for the achievement of educational target – the betterment of students. Students, thus, are very important aspects of Motivation. It is because that all activities in an institution are carried out for the students because an administrator's motivation affect the performance of the teachers and their interest and motivation ultimately affect the students' motivation and performance.

The following summary of motivation theories and concepts would enable us to formulate certain important concepts and techniques of motivating.

It is nothing but the motivation that creates interest and willingliness to undergo learning process.

According to Kort (1987), it is the result of both internal and external factors and not the result of external manipulation alone. Implicit in motivation is movement in the direction of meeting a need or toward reaching a goal.

Lewin (1935), an early field theorist, conceptualized motivation in terms of positive or negative movement toward goals. Once an individual's equilibrium is disturbed, such as in the case of illness, forces of approach and avoidance may come into play. He noted that if avoidance endured in an approach-avoidance conflict, there would be negative movement away from a goal. His theory implies that there is a critical time factor relative to motivation. Ideally, the educator's role is to facilitate the learner's approach toward a desired goal and to prevent untimely delays. The time factor is usually not a critical consideration in motivational models of health behavior or motivational research. For example, teaching staff may request an in-service program about educational progress. The inservice educator may delay this request to the extent that the staff loses interest in the topic. Although untimely delays may be beyond the control of the educator, nevertheless, every effort should be made to capitalize on the staff's desire and readiness to learn.

The major premises of Maslow's motivation theory are integrated wholeness of the individual and a hierarchy of goals. Acknowledging the complexity of the concept of motivation, he notes that not all behavior is motivated and that behavior theories are not synonymous with motivation. There are many determinants of behavior other than motives as many as can be involved in one behaviour involving the principles of hierarchy of basic needs physiological, safety, love/belonging, self esteem and self-actualization. He notes the relatedness needs, which are organized by their level tendency. Some individuals are highly motivated while others are weakly motivated. When a need—is fairly well satisfied, then the next potent need emerging. An example of hierarchy of basic needs is patent need to satisfy hunger. This may be met by teacher who assists the students. The teacher-student relation may be one need out of love, belongingness and self-esteem.

There are relationships between motivation and learning, between motivation and behaviour and between motivation, learning, and behaviour. There are many ways to view motivation in the process of learning. Redman (1993) categorized theories of motivation that direct learning as behaviour reinforcers, need satisfaction, reduction of discomforting inconsistencies as a result of cognitist dissonance, allocating causal factors known as attributions, personality in which motivation expectancy theory encompassing value and chance of success, and humanistic interpretation of motivation that emphasize personal choice. Each theory attempts to address the complex somewhat elusive quality of motivation.

The main ideas of all the theories mentioned in the foregoing pages about motivation indicate that motivation is a key factor and responsible for the performance of a student. Learning of English as a second language is never possible unless the L2 learner is suitably concerned about the same as a result of positive motivation.

There can be many factors of motivation. The following is a gist of some of the factors that are responsible for motivation.

Motivational Factors

Factors that influence motivation can serve as motives or obstacles to achieve desired behaviour, creating incentives and decreasing obstacles to motivation pose a challenge for the teacher. The cognitive (thinking processes), affective for (emotions and feelings), social, and behavioural domains the learner can be influenced by the educationists can act as a motivational facilitator or blockes. Motivational incentives need to be considered in the context of the individual. What may be motivational incentive for one learner, a motivational obstacle to another. For example, a student who is assigned to work with an elderly woman may be motivated when the student see older persons in high regard. Another student may be motivationally blocked by the emotional domain because previous experiences with older women such as grandmother, were unrewarding.

Facilitating or blocking factors that shape motivation to learn can be classified into three major categories, which are not mutually exclusive: (1) personal attributes, which consist of physical, developmental, and psychological components of the individual learner; (2) environmental influence which include the physical and attitudinal climate; and (3) learner relationship systems, such as those of significant other, family, community, and teacher-learner influence on motivation.

Personal Attributes

Personal attributes of the learner such as developmental stage, age, gender, emotional readiness, values and beliefs, sensory functioning, cognitive ability, educational level, actual or perceived state of health, and chronicity of illness can shape an individual's motivation to learn. Functional ability to achieve behavioral outcomes is determined by physical, emotional, and cognitive dimensions. One's perception of disparity between current and expected states of education can be a motivating factor in institutional behaviour and can drive readiness to learn.

The learner's views about the complexity or extent of

changes that are needed can shape motivation values, beliefs, and natural curiosity can be firmly entrenched and enduring factors that can also shape desire to learn new behaviours. Other factors such as sensory input and processing of information and short-term and long-term memory also exert an impact on motivation to learn. Emerging interest about male-female behavioral and learning differences indicates the need for indepth research on gender-related characteristics affecting motivation to learn.

Environmental Influences

Physical characteristics of the learning environment accessibility and availability of human and natural resources, and different types of behavioral reward influence the motivational level of the individual. Environment can create, promote, or direct from a state of learning receptivity. Pleasant comfortable, and adaptable individualized surroundings can promote a state of readiness to learn. On the other hand, noise, confusion, interruptions, and lack of privacy can interfere with the capacity to concentrate and to learn.

The factors of accessibility and availability of resources include physical and psychological aspects. Can the student access an educational facility, and once there, will the educationists or Pedagogues available to the students. Psychological availability refers to the educational process and whether it is flexible and sensitive to students needs. This includes factors such as promptness of services, socio-cultural competence, emotional support, and communication skills. Attitude has always an impacts the engagement of the teacher with the students in an education system.

The manner in which the education system is perceived by the teachers' impacts on the learners' willingness to participate in education promoting activity. Behavioural rewards permeate the foundations of the learner's motivation.

Rewards can be extrinsic, such as praise or acknowledgement from the educator or the manager. Rewards can also be intrinsically based, such as feelings of a personal sense of fulfillment, gratification, or self-satisfaction.

Relationship Systems

Family cultural identity, work-environment, school and community roles, and teacher-learner interaction affect on an individual's motivation. The interactional aspects of motivation are perhaps the most salient because the learner exists in the context of interlocking relationship systems. Individuals are viewed in the context of family/ community / cultural systems that have lifelong impact on the choices that individuals make including education seeking and decision making. These significant—other systems may have even more of an impact on educational outcomes than commonly acknowledged, and the education promoting use of these systems needs to be taken into account by the teacher/ instructor as educator.

All of these factors interact to address the motivation of the learner. They are not meant to be construed as comprehensive theory constructs but as forces that impact on motivation, serving to facilitate or block desire to learn.

Mishel (1990) reconceptualized the concept of uncertainty of situation. She views uncertainty as a necessary and natural rhythm of life, rather than an aversive experience. Uncertainty in sufficient concentration exerts an impact on choices and decision making and can capitalize on receptivity or readiness for change. Premature uncertainty reduction can be counterproductive to the learner who has not sufficiently explored alternatives. For example, a teacher is uncertain about positions is presented with alternatives, then a thinking dialogue is carried out. If the decision to use a particular position is not premature, then uncertainty will promote exploration of alternative positions.

Assessment of Motivation

How does the teacher know when the learner is motivated. As a generic concept, assessment of motivation to learn has not been adequately addressed in the literature. Absence of adequate conceptually based measurement tools could be a factor. The view, on motivational assessment as a part of general educational assessment includes such areas as level of knowledge, students' skills, decision-making capacity of the individual, and screening of target populations for educational programs. Leddy and Pepper (1993) view assessment of motivation in relation to capacity to change. Rankin and Stallings (1990) list several questions for the educator to pose in terms of the learner such as previous attempts, curiosity, good setting, self-care ability, stress factors, survival issues and life situations.

Motivational assessment of the learner needs to be comprehensive, systematic, and conceptually biased. Cognitive, affective, physiological, experience-based environmental, and learning relationship variable need to be considered.

Variables of Assessment

The following is the outline of certain variables.

1. Cognitive Variables
    - Capacity to learn,
    - Readiness to learn,
        - Expressed self-determination,
        - Constructive attitude,
        - Expressed desire and curiosity,
        - Willingness to contract for behavioral outcomes.

2. Affective Variables
   - Expressions of constructive emotional state,
   - Mild to moderate level of anxiety,
3. Physiological Variables
   - Capacity to perform required behavior,
4. Experiential Variables
   - Previous successful experiences,
5. Environmental Variables
   - Appropriateness of physical environment,
   - Social support systems:
     - Family
     - Group
     - Work
     - Community resources.
6. Educator-Learner Relationship System
   - Predication of positive relationship.

These parameters incorporate Bandura's (1986) construction of incentive motivators, Ajzen and Fishbein's (1980) intent and attitude, Becker's (1974) and Pender's (1987) notion of likelihood of engaging in action, and Barofsky's (1978) focus on alliance in the learning situation. This proposed multidimensional guide allows assessment of the level of learner motivation. If responses to dimensions are positive, then the learner is likely to be motivated.

Assessment of learner motivation involves the judgment of the educator, since teaching-learning is a two-way process. Motivation can be assessed through subjective and objective means. A subjective means of assessing level of motivation is through dialogue. Through use of communication skills, the education can obtain verbal information from the students such as "I really want to learn English" or "I want to perform well." Both of these statements indicate an energized desire with direction of movement toward an expected learning outcome. A staff member or student may express a verbal desire to know more about a specific advanced technology. A nonverbal motivational cue could be expressed by the staff member of student carefully observing a senior student or educational expert performing an advanced technique in the field of education or educational technology.

Measurement of motivation is another aspect to be considered. Subjective self-reports indicate level of motivation from the learner's perspective. Self-report measurements could be developed for educational programs. Objective measurement of motivation, an indirect measurement, can be quantified through observation of expected behaviors, the consequence of motivation. These behaviors can be observed in increments as the learner moves toward present realistic educational or instructional goals.

Motivational Strategies

Incentives viewed as appeals or inducements to motivation can be either intrinsically or extrinsically generated. Incentives and motivation are both stimuli to action. Bandura (1986) associates motivation with incentives. He notes, however, that intrinsic motivation, although highly appealing, is elusive. Motivation rarely occurs without extrinsic influence. Green and Kreuter (1991) note that "strictly speaking we can appeal to people's motives, but we cannot motivate them". Extrinsic incentives are used for motivational strategizing in the educational situation.

Motivational strategies for the educator are extrinsically generated through the use of specific incentives or reward. The critical question for the teacher as educator to ask is,

"What is the specific behavior, under what circumstances, in what time frame desired by this learner".

Strategizing begins with a systematic assessment of learner motivation. When an applicable dimension is absent or reduced, then incentive strategizing is likely to move the individual away from the desired outcome. When considering strategies to improve learner motivation, Maslow's (1943) hierarchy of needs can also be taken into consideration. An appeal can be made to the innate need for the learner to succeed in his aim of education. This can be termed as achievement motivation (Atkinson, 1964).

In the educational situation, clear communication including clarification of directions and expectations is critical. Organization of material in a way that makes information meaningful to the learner, environmental manipulation, positive verbal feedback, and providing opportunities for success are motivational strategies proposed by Haggard (1989). Reducing or eliminating barrier to achieve goals is an important aspect of maintaining motivation.

One particular model developed by Keller (1987), the Attention, Relevance, Confidence, and Satisfaction (ARCS) Model, focuses on creating and maintaining motivational strategies used for instructional design. This model emphasizes strategies that the educator can use to effect changes in the learner by creating a motivating learning environment.

- Attention introduces opposing positions, case studies, and variable instructional presentations,
- Relevance capitalizes on the learners' experiences, usefulness, needs, and personal choices,
- Confidence deals with learning requirements, level of difficulty, expectations, attributions and sense of accomplishment,

Satisfaction pertains to timely use of a new skill, use of rewards, praise, and self-evaluation.

In motivational strategizing, it would also be beneficial to consider the students' education efforts as personal vulnerability, efficiency of proposed change, ability to effect the change etc.

Bibliography

Aggarwal, J.C., *Development and Planning of Modern Education with Special reference to India*, New Delhi, Vikas Pub. House, 1982.

Aggarwal, J.C., *Essentials of Educational Psychology*, Delhi, Vikas Pub. House, 1998.

Basu, B. & Rao, V.K., *The Concept of National Integration*, Hyderabad, NSR College of Education, 1979.

Bhatnagar, Suresh, *Indian Education – Today & Tomorrow*, Meerut: International Pub. House, 1990.

Delors, J., *Learning: Treasures Within*, Report to UNESCO of the International Commission on Education and 21st Century, Paris, Untied Nation, 1996.

Dev, R.B., *Introduction to Philosophy*, Sterling, New Delhi, 1989.

Dhiman, O.P., *Foundations of Education*, Delhi, Atma Ram Pub. 1987.

Dusk, R.R., *Doctrines of the Great Educators*, McMillan, 1974.

Halsey, A.H. et al., *Education, Culture, Economy & Society*, New York: OUP, 1997.

Interim Report – Committee set up by the Govt. of India, 1999.

Kenneth, O.D., *Evaluating Teaching*, Massachusetts, Lexignton, D.C.H. & Co., 1983.

Murthy, S.K., *Teacher and Education in Indian Society*, Ludhiana: Prakash Brothers, 1981.

National Policy on Educaiton. MHRD, Govt. of India, New Delhi, 1986.

Panday & Sharma, *Educational Philosophy of S. Radhakrishnan*, Ambala: Associate Pub., 1990.

Rao, V.K.R.V., *Education & Human Resource Development*, Bombay: Allied Publication, 1999.

Shankar Rao, *Sociology*, New Delhi, S. Chand, 1991.

Vidya R.T., *Education, Thought & Practice*, Delhi, Sterling, 1980.

Index

A

B

C